MEMPHIS RENT PARTY

MEMPHIS RENT PARTY

The Blues, Rock & Soul
in Music's Hometown

ROBERT GORDON

BLOOMSBURY PUBLISHING

NEW YORK • LONDON • OXFORD • NEW DELHI • SYDNEY

BLOOMSBURY PUBLISHING
Bloomsbury Publishing Inc.
1385 Broadway, New York, NY 10018, USA

BLOOMSBURY, BLOOMSBURY PUBLISHING, and the Diana logo are trademarks
of Bloomsbury Publishing Plc

First published in the United States in 2018

Bloomsbury Publishing Plc does not have any control over, or responsibility for, any third-party
websites referred to or in this book. All internet addresses given in this book were correct at the
time of going to press. The author and publisher regret any inconvenience caused if addresses have
changed or sites have ceased to exist, but can accept no responsibility for any such changes.

ISBN: HB: 978-1-63286-773-5; eBook: 978-1-63286-775-9

Library of Congress Cataloging-in-Publication Data is available

2 4 6 8 10 9 7 5 3 1

Typeset by Westchester Publishing Services
Printed and bound in the U.S.A. by Berryville Graphics Inc., Berryville, Virginia

To find out more about our authors and books visit www.bloomsbury.com
and sign up for our newsletters.

Bloomsbury books may be purchased for business or promotional use. For information
on bulk purchases please contact Macmillan Corporate and Premium Sales Department
at specialmarkets@macmillan.com.

For Knox Phillips and Jerry Phillips
Flame keepers

For Adam Miller
Flame starter

For Tara McAdams
Flame

At once: the humdrum and the miraculous,
the inelegant and the ineffable.
—Sally Mann, *Hold Still*

CONTENTS

Preface
Give Me Something Different   1

Sam Phillips
Sam on Dave   11

Jim Dickinson
On the Edge   20

Ernest Willis
Mississippi Reverie   36

Mose Vinson
No Pain Pill   44

The Fieldstones
Got to Move on Down the Line   47

Lead Belly
Nobody in This World   52

Robert Johnson
Hellhound on the Money Trail   61

Junior Kimbrough
Mississippi Juke Joint   78

Charlie Feathers
The Onliest   86

James Carr
Way Out on a Voyage   96

Otha Turner's Fife and Drum Picnic
Let Us Eat Goat   112

Mama Rose Newborn
Useless Are the Flowers   121

Townes Van Zandt
All the Federales Say   135

Jeff Buckley
Northern Light   140

Bobby "Blue" Bland
Love Throat   147

Tav Falco
Panther Burns Forever Lasting   153

Jerry Lee Lewis
Last Killer Standing   166
Cat Power
Kool Kween   186
Jerry McGill
Very Extremely Dangerous   200
Alex Chilton
No Chitterlings Today   206
Afterword
Stuck Inside the Memphis Blues Again   213

Acknowledgments   219
A Note on the Photographers   223
Digging Deeper for Different—Further Listening and Reading   225
Index   239

PREFACE:
GIVE ME SOMETHING DIFFERENT

A STORY: WELL INTO his career, my friend and mentor Jim Dickinson was feeling embittered, was complaining about some music business bullshit. His pal cut him off, saying, "You were fortunate enough to witness the end of something truly great"—referring to the gradual dissolution of the original Memphis blues giants in the 1960s—"and you were intelligent enough to understand some of it." Memphis has always been willfully ignorant of the transcendent artists walking its streets, willfully negligent of the African-American culture that produced them. Jim had experienced a fleeting treasure that too few appreciated, a treasure no one could gentrify. The assessment chastened Jim, and bolstered him. It reset the context of everything.

I came along in Dickinson's wake, when many of the greats had already passed away—but not all of them. Not all by a long shot. When I first began hanging out at bluesman Furry Lewis's dilapidated duplex, I wasn't yet old enough to drive and it was harder for me to get a ride to that part of town than it was to buy Furry's pint of Ten High bourbon.

I'd learned of Furry at an outdoor Rolling Stones concert, Memphis, July 4, 1975. Mick Jagger delayed the band's performance until the sun went down, mistakenly assuming night in Memphis would be cooler and his makeup wouldn't run. To assuage the young audience's simmering

"Furry Sings The Blues." That was the title of a song Joni Mitchell wrote after visiting the singer here at his duplex on Mosby. Paying Furry for his time was always understood, and I'd imagined she paid him like everyone else. He said she drove away in a limousine and made money off of him. I liked the song okay, but Furry resented it. (Courtesy of Axel Küstner)

restlessness, the Stones sent across town for a solo blues guitarist, about eighty years old, named Furry Lewis.

For this fourteen-year-old among fifty thousand rednecks on that hot football field, hearing Furry was life changing. The concert was an all-day 1970s spectacle, with three bands opening, plus the unscheduled bluesman. I'd enjoyed the warm-up acts; their big rock and roll sounds were just like their recordings, only livelier. But Furry's playing was unlike anything I could have anticipated; the still, small voice after the raging storms. His rhythms were slow, his songs full of space, his notes floated in the air. His music summoned us listeners instead of dazzling us with its size and force. His voice and laugh, the way the slide over his finger could elicit a moaning human voice from the guitar—there was an immediacy to his art that the Stones' big production could never match. The pageantry of the bands inspired awe while Furry's intimacy let me feel the wrinkles on the hands wrapped around the guitar neck, the texture of the strings; he let me hear the human being. The raw power of Furry's personality was so infused into his music and stories that his songs became his life, and he took me places I did not know, to times I couldn't have experienced. Transubstantiation.

I think I was familiar with the blues at the time—Memphis called itself "home of the blues." But I hadn't considered that the bluesmen might be alive.

Furry played so intimately to that crowd of 50,000 that he let us feel the wrinkles on the hands wrapped around the guitar neck, the texture of the strings. (Courtesy of Axel Küstner)

And still playing.

In my town.

Thereafter, I was a seeker.

Less than two years later, a group Dickinson played in named Mud Boy and the Neutrons took the stage at a civic blues festival on Beale Street. This was 1977, my first time seeing Jim perform. Mud Boy was a bunch of white bohemians who'd come up playing alongside elderly black bluesmen in 1960s coffeehouses, creating new friendships that defied long-standing rules of segregation. But they were rockers. Mud Boy sounded like what the Stones would have if the Brits learned the music at the feet of the players instead of from black vinyl platters. Rather than spectacle, Mud Boy honed personality, allowing space for the music to breathe. I could hear Furry at the core of Mud Boy's music even though their instrumentation and presentation, with dancing girls shaking their moneymakers in the bright light of day, was much nearer to the Stones. The festival promoters, however, were less enthused by Mud Boy's raucous, lascivious take on the blues. This was a *family* event. Backstage, a band ally, Danny Graflund, heard the developing kerfuffle and ran onstage to whisper this little power-packed poem into Dickinson's ear:

They don't like the rock 'n' roll.

They don't like the dancing girls.

They're gonna pull the plug.

Midsong, the massive speakers crackled to silence. Catcalls and boos erupted from the audience. The band, incensed, shouted from the stage ("Tear down Beale Street, the symbol of oppression!"), and they paced like animals newly caged. Violence in Memphis is always on a patrolled simmer—this was less than ten years after Martin Luther King had been assassinated five blocks away—and cops assembled down front. The crowd was unforgiving, and as the tension mounted, I felt the bonding of mob mentality, the sense that this mass of angry, slightly drunk people could erupt. There were negotiations onstage and off, then the band reassembled—without the dancers—and the crowd's fury never ignited. I remember thinking that behind the near riot, at the core of Mud Boy's sound, was the power of Furry's solo blues.

As I GOT deeper in, my interest in the mainstream and what was popular went out the door. I was hooked on the feeling of the blues, on having my soul rattled instead of my bones. Rock and roll is hormonal fireworks, a temporal shout at earthly limits (which is why parents rocking out is so funny to kids). But the blues is a more sustained illumination, against the humiliation, rage, and sadness of life, and in turn invests the artist with not eternal youth but a scarred mortality, blessed with poetry.

The blues felt like home, even though my actual residence was a four-bedroom, two-and-a-half-bathroom version of the American dream complete with private schools, summer camps, and professional parents. I responded to the power of the blues, though I did not experience that kind of want. My father was an attorney and my mother had her master's degree and worked as a speech therapist. (Rebellious, I've stuttered all my life.) We had income enough to live in lovely suburban homes in nice neighborhoods. My brother and I had our own bicycles and bedrooms. We had money, we didn't suffer need, we felt safe.

I began listening to the radio late in elementary school to get in with the cool kids. I was an outsider—in addition to my speech impediment, I was Jewish with uncontrollable curly hair. The barber rolled his eyes when I asked him to cut my hair like Johnny Cash. Rough as grade school was, the situation got more difficult among the preps at my private high school. I wasn't the football-playing, blue-eyed kid that sang in the church choir.

In Memphis, African-American music and culture was all around me. The city's population has long been split fairly evenly between black and white. The downtown streets were racially mixed, and by my teens, the most blatant displays of segregation—blacks stepping in the gutter so whites could pass on the sidewalk, or performing the crushed deference that racist whites expected from all African Americans—had largely retreated. But segregation's hold was still endemic, evidenced by the racial exclusivity of neighborhoods; the money was still in white hands. Which meant "race mixing" would persist because the whites would hire the blacks at low wages for menial domestic labor. Jim Dickinson used to say we—meaning the white kids—got it—meaning the blues—from either the yard man or the maid, because these were African Americans with whom white kids had daily contact in the familiar space of home.

The author, 1974 or so. I'd have beat my ass too. (Courtesy of Robert Gordon)

I got it from our housekeeper, Odessa Redmond. Odessa came to work for us in 1967. She'd quit her job in a high-end kitchen because her boss had cussed her, using the N-word. She answered our newspaper ad and worked for my parents for three decades. Odessa maintained the house, but her influence extended beyond the kitchen and laundry room. She didn't have the authority my parents had, but she was only once removed, and she could instruct and discipline me and my brother. Her husband was a city sewer worker, and the city regularly cheated him, making it difficult to collect full-time pay despite the full-time job. Odessa would occasionally share with us incidents of social humiliation—sometimes by friends of ours. As a child, I accepted this contradiction about the world: Racial prejudice was wrong, but it was universally accepted.

We learned from Odessa, and yet there was this: She picked up our dirty underwear from the floor, washed it, and put it back in our drawer, folded. She sometimes missed dinners with her family to serve Jewish holiday dinners at our house; sometimes her kids would help, which could mean we were served by our peers. That made me uncomfortable, but it was also a stark lesson in the haves and have-nots. Whatever the 1967 passing of the Civil Rights Act meant in Washington, D.C., in Memphis in the early 1970s, this was our normal. Skin color in the American South was still the first and ultimate signifier (even before gender) and pretty much everything was determined by that. That doesn't mean that love and kindness didn't exist, that relationships didn't thrive, that hearts didn't rebel against dehumanization. But by participating in the racial caste system, we validated it. We rejected its unfairness and its ugliness, but we were also a part of it. Reflecting, I marvel at the dignity and wholeheartedness of Odessa and her family, and I'm grateful we were able to love and be loved by her.

The hours we spent with Odessa affected not only how we kids saw the world but also how we heard it. When Odessa drove us to swim team practice, her car radio played black gospel. When she ironed clothes or cleaned the house, she hummed gospel melodies. (A gospel song without words sounds very much like a soul song.) When I got excited by the outlandishly funky Stax Records entertainer Rufus Thomas, both as a singer and as a local shill on TV commercials, she encouraged my interest. Over the years, I just kept getting in deeper, finding more folds beneath the surface, understanding through individual lives how racism had expressed itself, how it had metastasized and damaged the structure of society—and how society had done shoddy repairs that created ever more problems.

The defining moment of race in my Memphis childhood was the 1968 sanitation workers' strike and the assassination of Martin Luther King. I was seven years old. Six weeks in, garbage rotting in the spring heat, Dr. King arrived to lead a community march and the city's simmer boiled. The National Guard was called; I remember my mom aghast at seeing tanks on the main streets where cars usually traveled. To counter the violence and to reestablish the peaceful nature of his work, Dr. King called a follow-up march. I remember the massive April snow that postponed the second march, the snow that gave time for the assassin, James Earl Ray, to get to Memphis. I remember, days later, learning the word *curfew* when Dr. King was murdered, when martial law was established in this place that proclaimed itself the "City of Good Abode." At that young age, I felt race through three main channels: the riots outside, Odessa inside, and a music I would come to think of as the soundtrack of the two colliding.

WHEN I NEXT encountered Furry, he was performing during lunchtime at my high school to a crowd of about fifty. An upperclassman had brought him; he told me, I just called him, here's his number. Furry invited me to visit (he asked for that pint and also a raw Wendy's hamburger; I had them cook it a little bit). When I sat in Furry Lewis's duplex, I was keenly aware of the distance between his home and my comfortable suburban life, the ten miles stretched immeasurably if calculated by race, economics, age—so many differences. He'd worked for more than three decades as a street sweeper, and when he retired, a white boss looked at his wooden leg and said if he'd worked all that time as a gimp, he couldn't have done the job right—pension denied.

I visited Furry many times, my naïveté slowly ebbing. We would sip Ten High, and when he'd set his shot glass on the nightstand by his bed, he'd top it with a jelly jar lid. You see someone do this enough times, you've got to ask. He had a craggy voice, wore thick eyeglasses, and would often refer to himself in the third person. He answered, Furry's eyesight ain't too good and he don't want to get bit by a spider when he takes a sip. That was not a problem we had in my house, and it took a moment for me to digest all that it implied—that the spiders in his place were rampant enough to be a problem in his tableware, that he couldn't afford a pest control company or proper eyeglasses, that he'd probably been bitten on the lip or had a close call. All my other friends were middle class, and most of the old people I knew were related to me. Furry not only made me question my assumptions, he made me aware of the privilege that produced them.

I began to connect the art to the life, to understand how Furry's circumstances—his ramshackle dwelling and his history—were reflected in his songs. Furry's music was an extension of his life, defined by geography and temporality. He played what the rural Mississippi Delta land evoked. And demanded. His banter in the 1970s was direct from the medicine shows he'd worked in the 1920s, when he'd engage a crowd that—black and white, rich and poor, urban and rural—convened to buy medicinal hooch. Furry adapted to modern times—electric guitars, urban and suburban audiences—but what he played sprang from particular conditions in a particular place; not just the absence of wealth and comfort but the presence of distress and discomfort, the realities of poverty and the joys of transcending it, even if only for a moment. Blues is the mind's escape from the body's obligation. Blues amplifies the relief whenever and wherever relief can be found. The scarcity of that respite makes it ecstatic.

THE MORE I sought, the more there was to find. When I'd return after moving to the East Coast for college in 1979, the magic and the substance of what I'd tapped into at home was in high relief. I dug deeper into the marginal characters who were inspiring the contemporary culture—even as that same culture shunted them aside. Their shadow influence captivated me, and soon I was writing about them for magazines.

I'd thought I was going to be a fiction writer, but one day in the early 1980s—when I should have been making career moves and my parents were concerned about my foggy future (I was happy in my foggy present)—my father suggested I write about some of the unusual figures I'd come to know in Memphis such as Furry Lewis or barrelhouse piano banger Mose Vinson, whose face hung on his skull like three sheets to the wind.

In Philadelphia (Pennsylvania, not Philadelphia, Mississippi), after college, I began to write for a neighborhood weekly. I did one article, maybe two. A friend invited me to dinner and another guest was Ken Tucker, then the pop music critic at the *Philadelphia Inquirer*. We had fun telling Alex Chilton stories, and when the night was through I asked Ken if he ever hired freelance writers. He told me to bring him my clips.

I did. It was the right place and time, no talent or experience. The published material was not about music, and the one music piece was an unpublished interview transcript with the then up-and-coming indie band Camper Van Beethoven. The deal was, Ken was having kids and didn't want to cover late-night shows anymore. He asked me if I liked Sonic Youth and I told him I loved Sonic Youth. They were playing that weekend at a punk club, so he would cover Journey at the Spectrum and be home asleep before my show began. I left my meeting at the *Inquirer* and went to my punk rock roommate, Eddie "Hacksaw" Richard, and asked if he had any Sonic Youth records—I'd never heard of the group.

My first big lesson as a writer came with that review's publication. Untrained, I'd fashioned a piece that built to a climactic image—Sonic Youth leaving the stage, a boombox at the center playing Madonna's "Into the Groove." When the piece ran, the last line was lopped off to make space for a lingerie ad. I thought what was left made no sense and went to a friend's older brother at the paper to vent.

Don't worry, he told me, it's just words.

Even after all these years, I still find that advice liberating. For one thing, the power of the printed piece would overcome: Most people wouldn't notice that anything was missing, they'd just finish the article and go to the next page . . . after studying the lingerie ad. For another, all words are not created equal. Some can be cut without diminishing the piece, but others are worth fighting for. Since then, I've been easy to edit.

WHILE IN THE Northeast, I'd discerned something very basic about pitching stories to magazines: There was always a clamor for the cover story—in those days it seemed to rotate between Michael Jackson, Prince, and Madonna. When that maw was sated, I'd be the guy who'd approach the editor with an oddball idea to be stuck among the advertisements in the back—the article that lent the magazine a little credibility for its interest in what would later be called "roots music" or, later still, "Americana." And I just cycled through the magazines writing about characters I was interested in, black and white, who were unknown to the public at large. The roster of venues reads like a memorial plaque to an age of physical record store chains, to print journalism: *Music & Sound Output*, *Request*, *Pulse*, *Option*, *Creem*, *Spin*, *Details*, magazines that no longer exist for airlines that no longer exist, and fanzines whose remnants are dusty, crumbling pages in landfills hither and yon.

I was pitching the unusual, unaware that I was fulfilling the credo of Memphis's musical godhead Sam Phillips, who said to each of his artists in the 1950s: Give me something different. While the city buried African-American culture, Sam put it on the pedestal to exalt. He didn't talk down to the black musicians he recorded—including Howlin' Wolf, B. B. King, and Rufus Thomas—instead he elevated everybody: himself, the artist, and the audience. When he met other white musicians who, defying social norms, heard the world like he did, he encouraged them; Elvis Presley was the beacon. Carl Perkins followed, though first he went to Nashville and was told, before being sent away, I like what you're doing, young man, but I don't know *what* you're doing.

The roster of Sun Records is a testament to Sam's work as a producer, to his skill at drawing out the artist from the person. Elvis's jacked-up country blues wasn't something the young talent thought was a career; it was his impromptu effort to reinvigorate his sidemen when his recording session was flagging. Sam, in a different room, overheard it and asked what they were doing. When they said they didn't know, Sam replied, "Well, back up, try to find a place to start, and do it again," because Elvis's hijinks provided the doorway to the sound Sam wanted.

Memphis—my Memphis—*likes* the unquantifiable. Nashville, New York, and Los Angeles—they promise stardom. Had Elvis gone there, he might have enjoyed minor success as the lame-ass Perry Como imitator he thought he was supposed to be. Elvis needed Sam to identify and affirm his renegade spirit, to allow him to express what he felt rather than what he imagined others expected. Memphis wants something different.

These pieces were published because they were different. I was reporting from where others weren't, about something others were not heeding. But history was on my side—the music had lived on from generations before me. Now the magazines are gone, and so are most of these artists, but the art continues to thrive. None of us will be here to know, but I'd wager that this music, in a hundred years, will still be popularly unpopular—will still be hip. Its honesty abides.

Others left that Rolling Stones concert with their lives unchanged; another ticket stub for the collection. I left not realizing I'd been struck by lightning, that a fire within me was beginning to burn and the embers would be warm for my lifetime as I pursued an understanding of blues, of how music related to environment, of what made some people popular and others impoverished. My journey began with Furry at his 811 Mosby duplex and led to *It Came from Memphis* and a number of other books and films. More than two decades since that first book, more than four decades since that first personal encounter with Furry, it leads to this collection. I've chosen to run these pieces not in the chronological order of their publication but rather in something like the order of my immersion—who I met and when they influenced me. And now, watch this: In honor of Sam's credo, I break that rule immediately, entering the story on a spiritual plane with Sam Phillips.

Memphis can be slacker city, all ideas and no action—or, worse, all the wrong action. But if you listen to the past here, it propels you forward. There's truth in the spirit of our blues, rock and roll, and soul, and that's why they have each transcended their time. Each explosion remains vibrant and influential. Each was triggered by a defiance of society's norms, by benightedness and hubris, a striving for something new and different. Memphis is not for the moment, it's for the horizon. I learned from the generosity of Furry Lewis and Odessa Redmond, from artists and musicians, black and white, all living in the face of ignorance, sloth, and hate, what great art is possible in the shadows.

SAM PHILLIPS

MEMPHIS HAS BEEN mythologized, and so has Sam Phillips. The rough edges have been smoothed, the multitudinous stories have been blended into one, creating a macerated, noncontroversial, and all-American narrative. I think Sam hated that. If the conflicts were erased, if the controversies were diminished, the achievement could not be properly understood. The devil is in the details, and Sam welcomed the demons.

So I was fully gripped when I saw a VHS tape of Sam's 1986 appearance on *Late Night with David Letterman*. This was pre-Internet, when the mode of sharing was more arbitrary, when touring musicians were cultural pollinators, carrying tapes, tunes, and ideas from city to city. My friend Jim Spake was a busy bee. (Jim's Memphis sax has backed Mavis Staples, Rufus Thomas, Lucero, My Morning Jacket, and Screamin' Jay Hawkins.) After touring with rock and soul bands, he'd return to Memphis with new sounds and also VHS tapes—mostly freaky local cable shows from far-flung places. This was a time when cable was the domain of balloon artists, fetish talk shows, and rather unphotogenic hobbyists. In those analog days, someone who caught a great TV broadcast would duplicate it for a friend, the visual deterioration increasing exponentially with each copy. So if the image was really bad you'd know you'd tapped into a national cabal, were in on what was hip.

Sam Phillips: The man who sired rock and roll. (Courtesy of Ted Barron)

Jim's dub of Sam on Dave was worth fighting through the visual degradation. Letterman was just enjoying his stride, comfortably offbeat in the late-night world, cozily antiestablishment from his major network hub. Only four years on the air, Letterman's show was a late-night hipster paradise; showcasing the eccentrics and mocking their oddities, he augured reality TV. Irony was as comfy and unthreatening as the couch from which the viewer lounged and laughed. My guess is that Sam was unfamiliar with Letterman and had been warned about David's potential to ridicule. Sam was wary, and he was accustomed to being in charge. What we get is a battle of the producers—who's going to get what from whom. Because Sam was giving nothing, and certainly not going to help prepare a bland TV dinner version of his achievements—dismissive, simplistic, generic. This appearance is a beautiful window into how Sam Phillips worked, how he got that something different, those gleaming gems from musicians whom others would have paid no mind.

Sam on Dave

Oxford American, Spring 1997

More than thirty years after Sam Phillips first recorded Elvis Presley, he's tired of telling the tale. But it's 1986, and David Letterman has reinvigorated the talk show format with a rock and roll attitude. Letterman invites Sam Phillips to come on national television, figuring they'll spin the yarn one more time: How Sam was recording black blues artists when hardly anyone else paid them any mind or any money. How he thought a white kid playing that sound could make a marketing breakthrough. How he never suspected Elvis Aaron Presley would be that kid. And "That's All Right" and "Blue Moon of Kentucky," how they became beacons for Sam's label, bringing Johnny Cash and Carl Perkins and Jerry Lee Lewis. And Roy Orbison. And Charlie Feathers. *And Billy Lee Riley, remember how he got mad that night and poured whiskey on the console . . .*

But Sam must have figured otherwise, must have decided not to rehash the grand old tales. For his appearance looks like nothing less than a surprise emergence from retirement to produce David Letterman.

Samuel Cornelius Phillips, Florence, Alabama, born (1923), Memphis matured, had done it all by the time he was thirty-one, and when he sold his Sun Records label fifteen years later in 1969, he retired from the recording studio. However loud Led Zeppelin would play or however long Eric Clapton might solo, their contributions would not add to the sum of Sam's life experience thus far: He'd recorded Howlin' Wolf, dusty from the fields; Harmonica Frank Floyd imitating a barnyard with his instrument stuck longways in his mouth; B. B. King with a backing band that included jazz greats Calvin and Phineas Newborn. Before retiring from the studio to work in radio, Sam had even done his part for the British Invasion, recording the Yardbirds' primal "The Train Kept A-Rollin'."

"This man was inducted into the Rock and Roll Hall of Fame—you were there that night, Paul," says David Letterman to his band-leading sidekick, Paul Shaffer. "Folks," Dave continues, "it's a pleasure to have on our program tonight, Sam Phillips. Sam, come on out."

The video shows us the wall around which guests enter, and there's a good few beats where there should be Sam and there is none. A producer's best tricks are always the hardest to see.

When he appears, he looks remarkably good. His hair and beard are red and long, he's dressed casually, and goddamn, a record label with any sense would sign this man. Phillips spots the camera. He claps his hands together. He looks at Paul. He smiles wide, does a little twist, says something that, over the applause, only Paul can hear.

Letterman is up and across the set, his hand extended. "Hi Sam, how are ya?"

"Hello there, Mister David."

Sam has halted so Dave must invite him further onto the set, over there where the guests' chairs are, and his desk, and the microphones and the lights and all the equipment that makes these interviews possible. "Nice of you to be with us tonight," Dave tells Sam, who is walking with a distinct bounce to his step, a swing even. As he's seating himself, Dave asks once again, "How ya doin'?" and when he glances up he suddenly halts.

Sam has his back to the camera, his back to the national audience. Letterman's head tilts a bit sideways, like a dog that's heard an unusual sound.

"This is a beautiful set, David," says Sam's back, his arms spread wide.

Letterman leads his studio audience in some nervous giggling, and then Dave tries to move things along. "So how're things?"

We get our first close-up of Sam. "You know," Sam says, and he sort of licks his lips and cocks his head back, building a few seconds of his beloved silence into Letterman's preferred rapid and vapid patter, "you know everything is—uhh," he cocks his head the other way, thinks another second and then drawls, *"fihhne."*

While they've been situating themselves, the horses have begun moving. Now there are four hands on the reins, and though this is clearly not a hijacking, there's some confusion about who's in charge.

Before David can lead, Sam launches into a discussion about Robert Morton, the backstage staffer whose job is to pump the guests for stories so that on the show Dave can pull questions out of the air that, amazingly, draw fascinating responses. "Why don't you have him as a guest on your show?"

"We should do that, maybe. You know, from time to time we have staff members on and we talk . . ."

"You do?!" Sam responds, and the enthusiasm in his answer reveals that either Sam has never seen Letterman's show or that Sam perceives something about that concept as striking, and Letterman might want to pursue that line of discussion.

Alas: "We want to talk about you tonight, Sam."

"I see."

"Is that all right?"

WHAT IS A producer? It is a person who guides the recording process. But what does that mean, *guide*? The producer may be the person in the studio who knows the most recording tricks. But the producer can know few tricks and still manipulate the process—with psychology. If artists are trying too hard and have lost their natural feel, the producer can deflect their attention, loosing their innate artistry. A producer might also set an artist on edge, if that discomfort will create great art. Sam and Jerry Lee Lewis once carried on a heated argument: Could the devil's music save souls? Immediately after Sam withdrew from the room, Jerry Lee cut the master take of "Great Balls of Fire."

When Dave asks, "Is that all right?" it may be rhetorical—the host tricking the guest into thinking he's in charge. But Sam has, naturally if not consciously, designated Dave the artist, and he is extracting from him a nervousness and a deference that is very unlike the host's usual suave and cool performance. One man is at ease, slouched in his seat, an extension of the upholstery; the other man is upright and stiff, his movements sharp and jerky. Sam is producing Dave.

"David," answers Sam, and the camera moves in for a close-up as he jiggles his eyebrows up and down—for the cameras too are trying to get their footing—then he sits up and inhales, still unhurried and out of step with late-night banter. Sam leans over and, lampooning the southern peckerwood he knows Dave wants, he drawls like a minstrel, "David, we will try to talk about me just chere fo' a little while . . ." His statement ends with the high notes of a question, and there's silence while Dave awaits the answer. The camera leaves the close-up for a two-shot, revealing that Sam has more than leaned toward Dave, he's actually hypnotized him like a rooster, and during the dead air that follows, they are nose to nose, their eyes locked.

Dave breaks the spell, says, "Okay," and his hands automatically come up in defense. He turns away and tries to make a crack about his background scenery but Sam does not retreat, and he interrupts with, "Are you going to have your teeth fixed before long?" Letterman, who must be glad he doesn't hide a toupee, is getting a dose of his own; he is, after all, the one who changed talk show rules when he asked boxing promoter Don King, "What's the deal with your hair?"

Sam continues, "Now how did you, with buckteeth—" the audience's laughter halts—"make a million dollars? You know not a lot of people can do that."

Thunder cracks from the set's fake skyline as Dave gingerly reaches for the reins with, "Now, Sam," and Sam covers the hint of a smile with his hand and he looks away from the host, who is addressing him.

"Now tell me about the early days at Sun Records?"

Sam sits stone-faced.

"Now who, who—what kind of a sound were you trying to establish there?"

Sam Phillips stares at David Letterman. He is not incredulous, not shocked nor hurt. This is the question everyone asks, has asked for decades, and will continue to ask as long as Sam lives and, if Elvis is any indication, will ask long after Sam is resting in peace. If Sam Phillips's work at Sun was a question, the answer is the music and the national and international uproar that followed—or follows—in its wake.

"Let's see," says Sam. "Let me think about that." Now Dave is laughing and starting to relax, to settle in and roll with the punches. But only silence follows, and the audience is left to project their favorite rock and roll moment onto Sam's blank face.

"What kind of sound . . ." Sam mulls, as if he's considering it for the first time or, perhaps, for the first time seeking a different answer.

"Was there a specific—or would you just record anybody who came through?"

"Why certainly, David," says Sam in a solo shot, and from his movement, we know he's moving in to hypnotize Letterman again. But Letterman averts his eyes. Sam's behavior is erratic. If he's drunk, that's beside the point. He parks his head halfway across Letterman's desk and leaves it there, finally saying, "You gotta work for this a little while tonight, son."

Dave, needing to feel in control again, says to Paul, his lackey, "Yeah, I believe so, yeah, yeah."

"You know I don't give away all my secrets, because when this show goes under, you might want to start recording . . . If I give away all my secrets, what am I going to have to write about in a book and a movie, you know, you could copy me and you're so young, I might drop off dead."

Sam Phillips dials in David Letterman, preparing to hypnotize him like a rooster. (Courtesy of Trey Harrison)

"Well then," David says, the breakthrough of truth drawing great laughter, "let's just talk about anything you want to talk about, which I have a feeling we're gonna do anyway."

The new stagecoach driver leans back. "I'm old and retired—"

"Hey, Sam—" Shouldna leaned back, dude! Dave grabs the reins because he's got a show to run and no one wants the road of the old man's ailments. "Look at this, we've got some photos." When in doubt, pull out the props. "Take a look at some of these pictures, Sam. You just tell 'em your first impression and we'll talk about those for a little bit."

We see a shot of a young Sam sharing a guitar with a young Elvis Presley, a sort of student-mentor shot. "Here we have a picture of, that's Elvis Presley and, is that you there in the checkered jacket?"

Duh.

"What year was that, do you suppose?"

Sam will have none of this drivel, and he simply ignores Letterman. "Well I missed my calling. You know, Gregory Peck hadn't got a damn thing on me in that photo, has he?"

"No," Dave says, sounding dejected. "And he still doesn't and . . ." Dave trails off and then tosses that photo aside to reveal another one.

Sam's attention is now over the audience's heads—on the back wall— and he murmurs, "Well, thank you David."

"Now let's see who we have here." But Sam looks further from the photos. Dave continues, "Who's next in the big gala photo book of . . . that's you and—" Dave verbalizes a blank for Sam to fill in, their conversation as stimulating as a standardized test.

"Jerruh," says Sam, entertaining himself with sounds.

"Jerry Lee Lewis," translates Dave in the tone teachers use to lead students through hoops.

"The Killuh," says Sam, making it rhyme with "Jerruh."

"Now this guy," Dave begins enthusiastically before quickly petering out, "was one of the most talented musicians ever to uh, put anything on record, wasn't he?"

"No question about that," says Sam. "I think Mr. Paul will tell us all that." *You don't need me here to talk about what we already know.*

"Paul, you want to come over and get in on this?" The audience applauds as the ride loses more control. Sam is gleeful. As Paul leaves his banks of keyboards, Sam brays to the ceiling, "Mr. Paul-al." Then he says, "This is my baby," and Sam stands and hugs Paul Shaffer, who looks like a small turnip.

"Okay now," says Letterman, "We have other photos here. Paul, tell us what you know about these pictures."

And Paul Shaffer reaches across Sam Phillips—as if he weren't there, as Sam wants it—and points to a piece of cardboard that we can't see and says, "This would be Jerry Lee Lewis here. Probably Carl Perkins here. This would be, who would that be? Johnny Cash?"

"J. C." says Sam off camera, and it could be an answer or an exclamation.

The photo is of the Million Dollar Quartet. "And Elvis on piano," says Paul.

It's as if a tuxedoed stage manager has strolled out and announced, "The role of the legendary Sam Phillips is being played tonight by Paul Shaffer and David Letterman." Sam the Man is busy producing, drawing out the best, the most unsettled performance, which for Dave and Paul means hosting a vacant center. "The guests on talk shows don't matter," they seem to say, "their role is to fill the time between commercials." Sam's work is about people, while Letterman—and television, and the wretched pop music made in the name of Sam Phillips: Their work is about selling soap.

"And what were you recording there?" Dave asks Sam, "Was that an actual recording session?"

"Well Carl Perkins was doing a session," Sam begins with earnest interest, but then he too peters out. "And it just so happened . . . that all of a sudden there at 706 Union—" Sam pauses, opens his arms and drops his voice, "—our great big studio, it's almost as pretty as this studio, good God this . . ." and while Sam mutters something and makes a funny face with his eyes and eyebrows, Dave abandons the photograph idea and puts them all away. Paul has been listening somewhat intently, but now he begins to fidget and plays his discomfort for laughs. Sam leans forward into the hypnotizing position and says, "But they all dropped by, and it just so happened that they all dropped by, and they all dropped by. And so we got together. We all got—well . . ."

Dave drums his desk with his palms, and he says, "Yeah." Then he reaches for some index cards and says, "Well, you're certainly, you're certainly ["an interesting guest," interjects Sam] you're certainly a legend." Compliment though it may be, "legend" hearkens to the mythic and the dead. "You're responsible for the very formation of rock and roll." *The rock and roll that caused riots? The one that sells sneakers?* "Don't you think you had a hand in helping the sound of rock and roll evolve from bits and pieces of other influences?"

Sam's had enough. "David, you're getting awful serious for this show. What're you setting me up for?" Sam's work here is done.

Dave's had enough too. "I'm just trying to think of a real nice way to say good-bye, Sam."

Paul Shaffer laughs into his hand. Lightning cracks across the fake skyline. They'll cut to a commercial, and when they return, Sam will be gone and Dave will resume. Five minutes is too long for a pop song anyway.

Sam and Dave shake hands, laughing. Letterman, somewhat bewildered and clearly relieved, sums it up for a TV finish: "The legendary Sam Phillips."

JIM DICKINSON

"I have something Mick Jagger can't afford."

—Jim Dickinson

PETER GURALNICK'S *Sweet Soul Music* came out while I was living in Philadelphia, 1986. Cocky-ass me had dismissed Peter's previous books: What can this guy teach me about my hometown? But I bought *Sweet Soul Music*, and the answer came quick: a whole damn lot. (I later went back to find *Lost Highway* and its predecessor *Feel Like Going Home*.) The book's immediate impact, since I was just making my initial foray as a writer, was the resolve to interview Jim Dickinson on my next Memphis trip.

I'd known Jim Dickinson as a public figure when I was growing up—he played piano, guitar, and was a producer. Often quoted in the newspaper, he was hilarious, outlandish, insightful: "There's a lot of people that can play better than me. But they can't play with the Stones better than me." (He'd played on "Wild Horses," so he wasn't just hyperbolizing.) Another newspaper quote: "A record is supposed to be unique. If you can do the same thing over and over again, what's the use of making a record of it?" And: "*Ethnic* has become a bad word in the contemporary music business. There is this idea of generic music—raceless, sexless, androgy-nous. Prince, Michael Jackson . . . one size fits all. It's to tremendous advantage of the record industry to try to sell three million units, but . . . the regional aspect of the record business has been swallowed up . . . All regional culture is in trouble in the United States right now." And finally: "If they want us [Memphis musicians] to look like Nashville, we're not gonna. If they want us to look like Lawrence Welk's band, we're not gonna. We're a bunch of rednecks and field hands playing unpopular music." Sam Phillips had retreated from music production and from the public; Jim was assuming his mantle, and he had my attention.

With my Sonic Youth review from the *Philadelphia Inquirer* to parlay and a visit to Memphis imminent, I pitched a Jim Dickinson feature to *Option*, a magazine that focused on indie releases and embraced the edge. (Jim later liked to quote wrestler Randy "Macho Man" Savage: "If you're not on the edge, you're taking up too much space.")

Jim happily obliged my request. This would be my first assignment that wasn't just work; it was my passion. Home for the winter holidays, I drove down to Eudora, Mississippi, crossed a levee road with lakes on either side (a symbolic baptism), and pulled up in the daylight to a place that was kind of isolated behind some trees and vines. Mary Lindsay Dickinson, Jim's wife, led me to their back room; its three large windows overlooking the water made it feel like a porch. We sat on old, comfort-able sofas. A couple days after Christmas, a large fir was in the corner.

I told Jim I'd been at the blues festival a decade earlier when his band Mud Boy and the Neutrons unleashed the rock and roll and got their plug pulled. I told him I'd been bringing whiskey to Furry Lewis's duplex, had been to the cotton warehouse beer busts where punkabilly was being cre-ated by Tav Falco's Unapproachable Panther Burns, featuring Alex Chil-ton. I told him I liked that Memphis artists were working outside the mainstream and making an international impact. I liked the rawness, and that they became popular by flouting trends, not following them. I thought Mud Boy and the Neutrons should have been bigger than the Rolling Stones. They rocked harder, their interplay of voices and instruments was better, they were stranger and more singular. I wasn't indignant about their obscurity, but it did frustrate me.

Not Jim. In fact, he embraced the marginalization. There were no expec-tations to meet, no worries about losing popularity. Jim used to say, "I have something Mick Jagger can't afford," and with that he'd grab his belly's not inconsiderable heft. Mick couldn't afford to not look like a model; Jim could eat all the barbecue he could afford, could look like he needed to shower, could say what he wanted without worry about backlash. Dancing on the edge required a commitment to one's own beliefs and a willingness to go to strange places; to adhere to one's own muse; to make illogical, unprofitable, deeply personal decisions, like Jim cites Alex Chilton doing during the *Like Flies on Sherbert* sessions—intentionally flushing hits down the toilet.

Jim helped me understand the Memphis aesthetic as the inverse of a hit factory like Nashville. Oddballs and individuals thrive here, not homogeny, hegemony, or harmony. That doesn't mean Memphis doesn't want hits. It means Memphis insists on dictating its own terms, delivered via take it or leave it. Life may be short, buster, but art is long.

"The art form of the twentieth century is undeniably music," Jim told me in the mid-1980s. "And the most important thing that has happened to music happened in Memphis. It's like being in Paris at the start of the twentieth century. Culture has changed as much in the last twenty years as it did then, and the reason has been music."

Mud Boy and the Neutrons was four people—Jim, Sid Selvidge, Lee Baker, and Jimmy Crosthwait. Early in their careers, Jim and Sid had gained some experience in the commercial music business: Jim as a session man for Atlantic, Sid as an artist for Stax. "The evil underbelly," Jim called it: the experience of searching your soul to make art, struggling to express that art, and then seeing your hard work and your personal creation treated as if it were a washing machine or a hamburger. The intersection of art and commerce: Some are more suited to it than others.

The other two in Mud Boy, Jimmy and Lee—initially the music biz attracted them. They wanted to taste stardom. There were, however, practical hindrances. Lee had a felony conviction for pot sales and Jimmy's affection for alcoholic beverages had gotten him banned from airline travel. So constrained, Mud Boy settled into doing their thing, from home, infrequently, for themselves. Thirteen years after they began performing together, nine years after I experienced that near-riotous festival gig, they released their first album. I used it as the peg for my first magazine assignment. What follows is the transcript, edited, that the March 1987 *Option* article drew from.

In Eudora, hours passed and still we sat and talked. Jim stitched together a scene that I knew existed but was only beginning to understand. Daylight faded, talk intensified, and when Jim's wife, Mary Lindsay, flipped on the Christmas tree lights, bathing the space in a glowing warmth, I knew I'd made new friends.

Mary Lindsay sat with us for parts of the interview. Jim was, at the time, working with the Replacements on what would become *Pleased to Meet Me*.

I began by mentioning a recent article about one of Jim's collaborators, Ry Cooder, that had also run in *Option*. Jim had worked with Ry on several soundtracks, including the Wim Wenders film *Paris, Texas*, then already a couple years old but still impactful—capacious, evocative, and mesmerizing.

On the Edge
Previously unpublished, December 27, 1986

ROBERT GORDON: I think that *Paris, Texas* stuff is great.

JAMES LUTHER DICKINSON: Oh I'm real proud of that. That exceeds something like the *Streets of Fire* soundtrack, which took five or six weeks to create. *Paris, Texas* we did in three days. And we did it in sequence, from the beginning of the movie to the end, and all of the emotionality is there without being calculated. We watch the screen and we accompany it—it's so easy to do. My two favorite Ry Cooder movies are *Paris, Texas* and *Southern Comfort*, and they were both done that same way—very organically and without as many musicians.

On *Paris, Texas* I was playing an electric Kawai keyboard. I used reels of duct tape, rolling them across the keys. I rolled one of them down the black keys and the other one up the white keys, and the random harmonics were really nice—it's the sound in *Paris, Texas* that's like bicycle spokes.

RG: I saw you perform with Mud Boy and the Neutrons. Like Cooder, that seems like an ongoing collaboration.

JLD: It's hard to say what Mud Boy is. The Mud Boy sound is like a spirit we try to summon, like the Pygmies in the rain forest summon the shaman. And the most successful that we can get is that sometimes [Mississippi hill country harmonica player] Johnny Woods appears. We can't play too much because it becomes too familiar. When we started, we rehearsed for three months, and it took us seriously another three years to get over the three months' rehearsal. We're about the moments where the shit comes together, and Mud Boy tries to extend those moments.

I hear things between me and [Mud Boy guitarist Lee] Baker that if we stopped doing it, nobody on earth would be doing what we do, because of the peculiarity of our environment, because we both played with old blues players. Furry Lewis made a big difference in the way Lee plays. But it took away whatever little commercial value he might have had.

Lee plays on a lot of Alex Chilton's *Like Flies on Sherbert*. Alex told me that he had gotten too good to play the kind of music that he was interested

Johnny Woods with Jim Dickinson, left. (Courtesy of Tav Falco)

Furry Lewis, right, with Sid Selvidge, left, and Lee Baker, center. Ritz Theater, circa 1978. (Courtesy of Pat Rainer)

in. And I know just what he means, because I've preserved the way I played when I was fifteen or sixteen. I play just as bad now, and Alex, that's what he wanted, somebody to play like he was fifteen or sixteen, but controlled. Alex is playing almost all of the piano on *Flies*. I'm playing the guitar almost all the time. Lesa [Aldridge] is playing piano on "Lorena."

RG: That "No More the Moon Shines on Lorena" piano solo is so beautiful! It sounds like the fewest notes possible to create a melody. Was *Flies* banged out in a couple of hours like it sounds?
JLD: Oh Lord no, it was agonized ad nauseam. The actual playing was brief but the psychodynamics were pretty heavy. I've always lost control of Alex at the end. There's one song on that record, the title song—if I could have mixed that with Joe Hardy at Ardent, we'd have been on the radio with it. And Alex knew it, so he flushed it instead.

RG: He didn't want to get back on the radio? His recent "comeback" stuff on the New Rose label is so clean, he seems to aspire to radio now.
JLD: When I first met Alex he was living in his mama's house and he had the gold record for "Cry Like a Baby" on the wall, and it was sealed in a glass box, and the label had peeled off the record and fallen inside. I think that sums up Alex. I played with Arlo Guthrie on "City of New Orleans," and Arlo taught me the same thing: He was totally exploited and didn't get any of the money. And they both believe that if somebody is going to fuck it up, it's going to be them.
MARY LINDSAY DICKINSON: At one time, Alex was having four records released in the same month and we saw his mom taking him to a department store to buy a suit of clothes.
JLD: Alex never received the royalties for anything until *Flies on Sherbert*, and you can imagine how much he made on that. The exploitation factor, which is critical in any recording situation, just gets too ugly for some people and they want to control it themselves. On *Big Star 3rd*, I watched Alex sabotage every song that had real commercial potential. Paul Westerberg [from the Replacements] does the same thing with the comedy material. I think that's an interesting thing in common.

RG: But Paul doesn't have the same exploitation factor—he's not had the big hit.
JLD: No, but he's just as afraid of being incorrectly perceived. Alex doesn't want anybody to think he's serious. It means a lot to him for people to not think that.

RG: I really love "Kanga Roo" from *3rd*.

JLD: "Kanga Roo" was the time where I truly had control. Alex put it down with his voice and the twelve-string acoustic guitar on the same track, just to make it harder to mix. If they're on the same track, those levels are predetermined. He and Lesa did it in the middle of the night. He said, "You want to overdub on something, overdub on this." Defiantly. So I started stacking shit up on it. I did the strings first for the melodrama. Then I started playing guitars. Pretty soon Alex was out there with me. "Kanga Roo" is good, but it's just a prelude to "Dream Lover," which wasn't on the record and should have been. It's the single that was left off of *Big Star 3rd*, and, in a way, it's the whole point of the record. Alex is playing piano, and he wouldn't tell anybody even what key he was in. He said, "I've played the song twice. I played it when I wrote it, and I played it for Lesa, and I shouldn't have done that." He said, "If I play it one more time, I'm going to be bored with it." That's the kind of thing I'm sympathetic to, so I said, "Sing a little bit, then we'll do it." After the first bridge, I don't know if he forgot lyrics or what, but he says, "Play it for me, guitarist," and Baker starts into one of his funk solos and we overdubbed the Memphis Symphony on it—it's really pretty good.

Those sessions, we had an upright bass, a jazz player who did all the bowed stuff, and he thought we were completely insane. He would laugh openly while he was playing. As far as I was concerned, we just gotta get it while he's still laughing.

RG: *3rd* seemed to barely get released. Does that frustrate you?

JLD: I did a European tour in '83 where I first started realizing what *Big Star 3rd* had done, because where people knew enough to talk to me about anything, they knew enough to talk to me about Alex. I didn't think that stuff got around the corner. In America, it didn't. People have come to me and said, It changed my life. The first time I thought, Yeah, sure. But it's happened over and over. There was a generation of twelve-year-old boys that were devastated by *Big Star 3rd*; that's the only conclusion I can reach. They used to say that about the Velvet Underground's first record: Everybody that bought the record formed a band. Certainly that must be true of Alex now.

I'm real proud of that stuff. It's interesting to see it come back around. Like on this Replacements thing, the three people at Warner Brothers who recommended me for the project, all three of them turned down *Big Star 3rd*. And that album is the only reason I'm on the Replacements project. Nobody wanted to hear *3rd* when we were selling it. [The head of Atlantic Records] Jerry Wexler said, "Baby, that record you sent me makes me feel very uncomfortable." I went back and listened to it myself before the Replacements to see if I could figure out what was so appealing to certain people, and what I think it is, the record is so romantic. A lot of it is dark romance, yet it is still very very romantic.

As a producer, I am not for everybody. I shouldn't say this because I don't work enough as it is, but I don't make hit records. Why should everything have to be a hit? What a sick idea. All I do is make things sound better. And in terms of southern production, there's not too many people around doing what I do anymore. There's not anybody left who does it any better.

RG: Southern production—you're quoted in *Sweet Soul Music* talking about producer Quinton Claunch rattling the change in his pocket to affect the way someone plays. He doesn't say anything, he just stands there and rattles his pocket.

JLD: Southern production is a different approach, a little less confrontational. When I was a session player, I would work with southern producers and I thought they were nothing. I thought, Boy, if I could get to Hollywood and work with real producers this would all be different. And of course I completely misunderstood. It took me years to figure out what southern producers were really doing, because they didn't appear to be doing anything. Quinton rattling the change, I saw that work every time. If something's not working, the producer just has to change it until it does work. You don't have to be Phil Spector making huge orchestrations and dictating notes. For example, walking in or out of a room is very effective.

Jim Dickinson, Ace Studio in Jackson, Mississippi, 1978. (Courtesy of Pat Rainer)

It all comes down to contrasts, and what could be a bigger contrast to being in the room than not being in the room?

Think about silence. Silence is a thing in space, and when you break silence, you create rhythm. You divide the nothing with something. I think that as a producer, my part of the production is the space between the notes. It's what enables me to do different kinds of music. I think the artist brings the identity to the record, but what I bring is a series of flavors. I've said before that production was the barbecue sauce.

Straight people are afraid of artists, and I am an artist, and a lot of producers aren't. And that scares record company people, the idea of, This guy thinks it's art not business. The desire to make records, you've got to take it back to the primal urge. It is literally the fear of extinction; it's the wish to record the unretainable nature of the moment. Time is going away from us and the art wish is that desire to retain the moment. By recording and playing back, you have made time into space; you have captured the moment. It goes back to the cave paintings, the handprint on the wall in the back of the cave. The idea that by drawing on the wall, you affect reality, that you can in fact alter the moment and re-create it. And that's what, as a producer, I try to do. The event has a soul: It is the essence of the event that you record, and the whole idea of immortality is right there!

I know it's easy not to take it to that level, but if you do it over and over again, all day and every day, it's hard not to think about it.

RG: Have you produced yourself?
JLD: You have to be on two sides of the glass, so there's no way you can produce from inside. There has to be somebody listening. I'm a big foe of self-production. And almost everybody that I work with ends up thinking that they can produce themselves because they can't see what I'm doing. What I do is real small and almost never observed.

RG: I recall you describing the way you initially learned piano—
JLD: Three up and four down, just like poker. You take any note on the piano and you go three notes up and four down, you have a major triad. The Phantom showed me that.

RG: Who is he?
JLD: He was this black guy that my father's yardman brought over to the house. My father's yardman, Alex Teal, taught me everything he thought was important to teach a nine-year-old white boy: how to shoot craps, how to throw a knife underhanded—the important life lessons. He sang as he

worked, and when he realized I was interested in the music, he brought these two piano players over. One was Butterfly Washington and the other, I never knew his name—the Phantom. He said all music is made up out of codes, and I thought he meant a secret code like [in] *Captain Midnight*, a comic book which I was way off into. But of course he meant chords! And when he showed me that, I thought, All right, this is a system. I can do that.

RG: How did you get started as a producer?

JLD: I'd gotten some publicity locally as a folksinger. Bill Justis, who'd been at Sun with Sam Phillips, he was making party records for the Mercury label, instrumental covers of hits. This musician I'd known from high school was working for him in Nashville, and I guess my friend's mother sent him some publicity about this folk festival that I put on at the Overton Park Shell, but I get this call from Justis to come be on a record he's making called *Dixieland Folkstyle*. The session was all Nashville heavies: Bill Pursell, Bob Moore, Buddy Harman, Grady Martin, Boots Randolph, the Jordanaires, and the Anita Kerr Singers. And me. It was real tight union sessions, and in the middle of the second or third day these side doors to the studio, which had never opened, these doors *swing* open and here comes this big fat redneck all dressed in black with sunglasses, big greasy ducktail, and little Sherman cheroots [mini-cigars] with his name on the side that he handed out to everybody. He was talking and cussing real loud. I thought, Boy, they're gonna throw this son of a bitch out, he is history. But instead of throwing him out, the session stopped cold and everybody goes out to the parking lot to see this guy's matched set of midnight-blue Jaguar XKEs. I said to my buddy who'd gotten me the job, "Who *is* this guy? What is the deal?" And he says, "Oh that's Shelby Singleton. He's the producer." I said, "I thought Justis was the producer," and he says, "No Justis is the artist." I said, "Well what are you?" And he said, "I'm the arranger." And it was like lightning struck! I thought, Somewhere in here there's a job for me. Finally.

RG: You're producing the Replacements now. How's that going?

JLD: Westerberg is way way better than anybody gives him credit for. It may be the best stuff I've ever done. The Replacements even have a song called "Alex Chilton." "Children by the million sing for Alex Chilton." We have about twenty-one tracks cut.

RG: You making a double album?

JLD: I'm always the one who says, If you've got enough material for two records, you can make a much better single unit. With the exception of

Captain Beefheart's *Trout Mask Replica*, I can't think of a double album that couldn't be a better single album.

RG: *Exile on Main Street* included?
JLD: Although it's heresy, I couldn't think of a better example. There's a record ruined by cocaine. The idea of cocaine is what made it into a double record. I think *Exile* could be a motherfucker as a Stones single record. Keeping the slop, that's what I'd keep.

I'm going to try to retain two Replacements songs. We've got a cut of Chris Mars, the drummer, singing "Cool Water" that personally breaks my heart. I'm going to have to sacrifice that, so other sacrifices will have to be made. I see production as a series of compromises. You can compromise, I can compromise, we can compromise right on into corporeality.

RG: You seem to have been really busy lately.
JLD: Yeah, I actually made a living at it this year in Memphis, which I hadn't done since 1969. Memphis is a great place to be from. I did real well for a lot of years just shuffling my feet, wearing my hat and saying, I ain't got no nothing, and playing real dumb. That kind of petered out in the late seventies, but fortunately the movie deal came along.

MLD: You came out of retirement to produce *Big Star 3rd*.
JLD: That was for revenge—on Dan Penn.

RG: Well, explain that.
JLD: Yeah. In '73 my oldest boy was born and my best friend and guitar player died in the same month—Charlie Freeman, from the Dixie Flyers. And I kind of stopped, did nothing for a bit. I did a skin flick here in Memphis. I'm an accompanist, and to accompany a visual image is the ultimate form of accompaniment. I used to sit with the TV sound off and play. Before that, I'd been producing Ry Cooder, and I quit him to produce Dan Penn, who was the guy who produced the Box Tops. We got pretty far along the line, about eight or nine tracks, but we had a disagreement over money and I quit. So I produced *Big Star 3rd* for revenge, because Penn really wanted to produce Alex again. He had made hit records on him before, and he could do it again.

I think revenge is the noblest human motive.

RG: What became of your Penn project?
JLD: Never came out. *Emmet the Singing Ranger Live in the Woods* was the album title. The best thing I did on that session was a song called "Tiny

Hineys and Hogs" about Harley riders. I had two Harleys in the studio, one of them playing rhythm—it was held open—the other one was playing on the beat. The guy was retarding the spark to get it on the beat and then giving it gas to keep it from dying. It was shooting four feet of blue flame. It was unbelievable. The whole studio filled with carbon monoxide.

Knox Phillips, he's Sam's son and also a producer, his friend was visiting—Mike Post, who does TV theme songs. I was wearing this hat with a feather that hung down into my beard. Mike Post was afraid of my hat, and when he saw the motorcycles, he was terrified, thought he was in the presence of some kind of insanity. The fucking motorcycle takes a solo; it sounds like a saxophone at one point. It is unbelievable. Everybody is saying, "The motorcycle is right on the beat!" Of course, everybody is playing with the motorcycle, that's what's really happening. Real good sessions.

RG: Are you going to put any of this stuff out, these reels you've got?
JLD: Yeah, like the bank robber is a missing part of this. I've got some stuff on him that I'd like to put out.

RG: Who was the bank robber?
JLD: His name is Jerry McGill, and he was the youngest artist on the real Sun Records in the fifties. He had a record called "I Wanna Make Sweet Love." When I had my band in high school, he had the only other non-professional rock and roll band in Memphis. We've known each other off and on.

RG: He's still around?
JLD: Well, he's a fugitive. He comes and goes. But I did some really good stuff on him. In fact, Alex is singing background on some.

The title of the Mud Boy record *Known Felons in Drag* is from Jerry McGill. Mud Boy was opening for Waylon Jennings, and Jerry used to be Waylon's road manager. There is both good blood and bad blood between them, to the point where the cops knew that Jerry would show up to this gig. So they were all over backstage, waiting to get this fugitive. And Sid Selvidge [Mud Boy cohort] was outside, saw someone and thought, Yeah, that's got to be McGill or that's the ugliest woman I ever saw. And he walked up to McGill, who was dressed up as a woman, and that was the only thing McGill said to Selvidge: Known felons in drag.

RG: I missed the Tennessee Waltz, Mud Boy's farewell performance in 1978. You've got videotape of that right?

JLD: Oh yeah, there were more video cameras on stage than there were musicians. Bill Eggleston and his son were shooting. Bill has this video movie, *Stranded in Canton*, which I don't think the world is ready for yet. They showed it at Yale and MIT a couple of times. The classes say, No that's all put on, no one acts like that. People do not act like that.

RG: What is it, this footage?
JLD: Oh it's just Eggleston following us and a few other people around. The star of the film is the bank robber [Jerry McGill], and Campbell Kensinger, the guy who did the motorcycles. There's a chicken-head geek down in New Orleans and a couple of pretty good transvestites. It's amazing. Alex is in it.

RG: Wow, I've got to see this.
JLD: It's all black-and-white, shot in low light. He would go around with this infrared camera, and everybody figured it was just Eggleston drunk, that he didn't have any film or whatever. It started out they were filming this old drag queen down in New Orleans named Russell who is, if Mick Jagger ever saw this guy's act, he would go home and get in bed, he wouldn't bother to try anymore. And it kind of spread from there.

RG: What's the story with Tav Falco at the Tennessee Waltz?
JLD: At the Tennessee Waltz, Gus—Gustavo has always been Gus—I never knew Gus sang. The day of the event he said, "Would it be all right if I sang a song, Jim?" He had the fingers cut out of his gloves and he played "Bourgeois Blues," and for the solo he took a buzz saw and cut through his guitar. Alex was in the audience, and Alex just loved it. He came backstage and said to Gus, "Me and you, we're a band." And that was the birth of Panther Burns.

Gus was always a performance artist. He and Randall [Lyon] and some others had a performance group, the Big Dixie Brick Company. Gus would join us on stage as the three-legged man. He had a little fez on and some sunglasses and a tuxedo, with an artificial leg coming out of the fly of his pants. He would dance, and with all the other shit going on on stage it really looked like the guy had three legs. Jerry Phillips, Sam's other son, he said, Dickinson, the three-legged man is just the best thing I've seen since the Bullet.

RG: The Bullet?
JLD: You don't know about the Bullet? Piano Red, back in the fifties, used to have a quadruple amputee that traveled with him who was "the Bullet," and the audience would be hip to this and they would scream,

Bring on the bullet, bring on the bullet! And they'd bring out this little guy, no arms no legs, and they'd sit him on a stool right in front of the microphone and he'd just scream, *Wahhhh*, and the band would play, and that was the Bullet. Piano Red had a great stage show in the late fifties. That was back when just everybody didn't have a stage show.

RG: The performance art aspect of the Panther Burns is pretty clear.
JLD: At the first Panther Burns gig, it degenerated into a jam where members of the audience got onstage to sing.
MLD: That audience loved it so much they wouldn't let Alex off the stage, and he had to take a leak, and finally he just did.

RG: He peed off the stage? Damn, then I was there at that show.
MLD: Oh, it went all the way across the room. He really did have to take a leak.
JLD: When they originally had the Panther Burns, [drummer] Ross [Johnson] knew about music but he didn't know how to play, and Gus would play in one tempo and sing in another. When they would start to find a groove, Alex would throw them something wrong and fuck 'em up again. And the band didn't understand that that's what was happening—for fully a year. It was just exquisite. He was there to strictly fuck up, to play things he couldn't possibly play on his own stuff. Gus can still sing and play in different tempos without knowing it, though, if he's properly encouraged. But Alex reaches a point in his production techniques where he likes to turn off or turn down the weird parts. Like on *Flies*, Lesa played a lot more parts than are now audible. It reached the point where he started to erase them.

Lesa Aldridge, Alex Chilton's muse during much of the 1970s and 1980s, at the Well, circa 1978. (Courtesy of Dan Zarnstorff)

MLD: Think that was partly jealousy?

JLD: Sure it was. Because she could play so much more worse than he does. But it's the same thing with Gus. Gus can play with complete innocence, Alex is jealous of it, so he turns it off or down. Do you know about the Klitz? The all-girl punk band?

RG: I saw them at the Well once, and Tav's girlfriend threw a Heineken bottle at his head.

JLD: You've got to have the element of danger. This is my description of the Klitz: They didn't know what the notes were, they knew *when* the notes were.

RG: Any reason why you haven't had a record of your own since—

JLD: Oh I've been ready to make another one since I was through with *Dixie Fried*. Nobody asked. And I like to be asked. Everybody has to get off on something.

RG: What's your thought on Memphis today?

JLD: When Stax went down, it was sixty million dollars on paper, so I figure you can double that. And I figured Memphis would never recover from that. But I'll be damned if I don't think it is. The suckers for one thing—near record people. And that's what pays for the big wheel to turn, near records.

RG: What do you mean there, "near records"?

JLD: Well, Panther Burns is not quite a near record, but it would be if I wasn't involved. A near record is just beyond a vanity project. Bread-and-butter jobs that someone pays for. They may not be a real talent, but someone believes they are. One of my partners in Mud Boy, the bass player Jim Lancaster, he used to produce records in Mississippi at the Whitfield sanitarium. Because, as he maintains—which I heartily agree with—those inmates have a right to make records too. There's some pretty interesting sessions as a result of that. I don't see any difference between those sessions and the Replacements sessions. It's the same process, and you have to honor it. If you honor the process, then you have something that stands a chance in the overall moral struggle of the world.

I DROVE HOME from that interview exuberant. I'd long witnessed the public appearances of the Memphis underground, but Jim took me to the catacombs, laid bare a place where the spirit of the amateur was more prized than technical skill; where record sales were welcome but not as the criteria for success. "Hits are in baseball," he said. "Your royalty lives in a castle in Europe, and fair is where you go to see the pigs race."

There was popular aesthetic, and there was Memphis. Hadn't Sam Phillips kept the takes with the technical mistakes—bum notes, phones ringing—because the spirit was present? Tav Falco's approach to music was similar: "Here was an art form that I could participate in by just picking up the instrument," Tav told me, "like a Kodak Instamatic camera." Capturing this spirit wasn't about the force of spewing one's guts; this was an artistic process to honor. The chaos of *Like Flies on Sherbert* was intentionally developed. Memphis wasn't about getting it right or wrong, it was about getting it.

As a writer, I've learned that sharing that captured moment takes careful reflection. Bum notes in a song can bring pleasing idiosyncrasy, but in writing they've caused me much regret: choosing words that are awkward or flat-out incorrect, getting facts wrong, mistakenly betraying what an interview subject understood to be a private moment. Jim and I talked about that too—the business of recording, of capturing time. It can be so unforgiving, displaying mistakes. It can also prolong a beautiful present.

Years later, Jim made passing reference to his old house on Yates Road in Memphis. He, it turned out, was the hippie in the house behind the one we lived in when I was about six. My younger brother and I would hang on the cyclone fence we were not as tall as and stare at the cadre of long-haired freaks going in and out. The Memphis beatniks—my people! They frightened as much as intrigued; I remember many a stoner wandering in their backyard like something out of a *Monty Python Flying Circus* episode opening. I remember not just the volume of the music but its physicality as it boomed out of that little shack of a house, refusing all constraints.

Jim died in 2009 and I miss him all the time.

ERNEST WILLIS

IN HIGH SCHOOL, I'd learned that the ordinary Memphis surrounding me was full of extraordinary history. I'd heard Furry Lewis, I'd seen the powers of Jim Dickinson. Then I found out about the man who lived in a trailer beneath the old Mississippi River bridge. Nothing would make you turn your head if Mr. Willis walked past, but if you engaged in only a few minutes of conversation, you'd realize how extraordinary was the life he'd built.

I had an early interest in local traditions, and in high school I began to volunteer time at the Center for Southern Folklore. (What's not to like in a name like that?) I met Mr. Willis when the center's director, Judy Peiser, had me help disinter one of his hand-built fishing boats from the bank of the Mississippi River. She wanted to display it at her upcoming Memphis Music and Heritage Festival. Four of us successfully unearthed the boat on a humid summer afternoon. Someone remarked on all the cool river water flowing past, and the irony of it being too dangerous to enjoy; there are stories every summer of people swimming in the Mississippi and drowning. (Of the turbulent undercurrents, locals say that if you heaved a big log deep enough into the water, it would as likely surface a mile upriver as down. Another: Locals say the Mississippi is too thick to drink and too thin to farm.) Mr. Willis showed us a place where we could "safely" cool off in the Mississippi, which we did, though with great trepidation.

A camaraderie had developed over the course of the day's work. Not long before departing, I followed Mr. Willis out his trailer's front door and he halted, looking off at the huge span across the Mississippi with pylons larger than barges. He was in a reverie. "When they were building this bridge," he said, "and they were pouring concrete into those pylons, a man fell in."

"Fell into the river?"

"Fell into the pylon, buried in the concrete. They couldn't get him out."

He was almost unaware I was still there. He continued, "Sometimes I lay in bed at night and wonder about that man."

I stood still, sensing he was about to express something deep, an abiding concern.

But someone who'd been helping with the boat saw him at the door and hollered. Mr. Willis's head snapped, and as he answered, the mood was broken and I was left to ponder.

Not long after, I arranged to visit again. I brought a friend with me and told her the story on the way over: If the conversation should again go to that moment, we should not say a word but let the thought bubble up unsullied.

We sat in Mr. Willis's living area, beneath the thrum of bridge traffic, and talk turned to the river, then the bridge, and when he told the story about the man, he fell into that same trance, said those same words: "Sometimes I lay in bed at night and wonder about that man." My friend and I exchanged glances and our breathing slowed.

But Mr. Willis just stared off.

And we waited.

But he just stared off.

Realizing I'd never find out otherwise, I asked in a hushed tone: "What do you wonder about him?"

He replied with a practical urgency that completely broke the tone of the moment: "When Jesus comes, how's he going to get up out of there?"

Mississippi Reverie
Previously unpublished, 1985

Ernest Willis sits in his brown vinyl chair and looks out the window of his house trailer. In his front yard, the Mississippi River is rolling past. Willis's face is as calm and serene as the water itself. "I've done so many things," he says, shaking his head. His brown eyes seem to be looking at something that happened many years ago. "A book wouldn't hold it all."

Willis, seventy-eight years old, lives in a trailer on the Arkansas bank of the Mississippi River, beneath the three old bridges. He has lived there for the past thirty-six years. "I came here on July 4, 1949. I had a twelve-by-twelve-foot tent, a dirt floor, a kerosene stove, and an old army cot. I drove a 1940 Chevrolet touring car and pulled a two-wheeled trailer that held a boat I made. That was all I had."

Today, Willis lives in a trailer with two rooms. He has furniture, electricity, and a telephone. He has lifetime property rights to a small plot of land. He has a lawnmower. He has thirty-six years of river memories.

His yard is a touch of suburbia amid the wilds of the riverbank. Behind him is a huge soybean farm. Beside him is the overgrowth of the bridge's right-of-way. In front of him is whatever the river recently washed up. In the very center of Willis's yard is his trailer. A lush, well-groomed lawn surrounds it. A cottonwood tree that he planted on the day he arrived now towers over the yard. A floating shed, tied to the cottonwood with rope as thick as a man's leg, contains Willis's fishing gear. It sits at rest on the bank, awaiting high water.

Willis surveys it all: The automobile bridge overhead with its constant rumble of cars and its steady roar of tractor-trailers; the intermittent thunder and screech of the train bridge; the fleet of rusty, empty iron barges docked several yards below him; the third largest river in the world. These are his home. They belong here. The candy wrapper from a workman on the bridge does not. Willis walks across his yard to pick it up.

Ernest Willis does not look like he's almost eighty. Lean, with powerful arms, square shoulders, and a straight back, Willis's body would look normal on a man half his age. "The doctors say I have the body of a forty-year-old man," he says, showing a toothless grin. Though retired from channel fishing for the past three years, Willis has never been inactive.

If you were in West Memphis this morning, you may have seen him. If you were there this afternoon, you may have seen him. Every day, Ernest Willis is outdoors: six- to eight-mile walk in the morning, four- to six-mile run in the evening. He runs in races and fund-raisers. People offer the old man physical assistance. He politely refuses. They are shocked when he passes them in the race.

Running is a triumph for Ernest Willis. In 1911, when he was four years old, his right leg was severely burned in a fire. The doctors told him he would never walk again. Though the scar still covers his thigh today, Willis has been proving the doctors wrong for more than seventy years.

He was a Golden Gloves boxing champion in the 1920s, then he began training as a runner. He excelled. "I was one of the greatest athletes of my time," Willis says. He competed with the national team and was primed for the 1936 Olympics when a dog bite on his calf prevented him from running. "It like to broke my heart," he says. Willis was in the hospital looking at the stitches in his calf while Jesse Owens was in Berlin taking all of the honors.

Running has been just one way that Willis has kept his body in good shape. His life as a fisherman was active and full of adventure.

Ernest Willis in his younger days. (Courtesy of the Center for Southern Folklore)

His typical day began with a cup of coffee at four A.M. After that, if he was fishing in the Mississippi River, he would haul his motor down the bank to his boat, load all of his gear, and set out. If he was fishing elsewhere, he would carry everything to his truck and drive to his location.

In good times, he ran his nets twice a day. In flood times, his lines were laid closer to his home and he checked them four times daily. In lean times, he ran his nets only once.

He knows fish and knows how to catch them. "Fish is kind of like hogs," Willis muses. Hogs in a field will follow a certain path. "Sometimes fish will hit a point here, then they'll cross the river. Just like hogs go through fields, fish go in paths."

In a typical day of fishing, Willis traveled up to twenty-five or thirty miles in his boat. Eight to twelve hours later, the fishing done, the first half of Willis's workday was over. At his trailer, Willis ran a dock and sold his fresh catches. He returned with his fish, set up shop, and earned his keep.

People from as far as Pine Bluff, a hundred fifty miles away, were his regular customers. Fish were weighed in a big washtub that hung on a scale from the roof of his shed, which floated in the water. He primarily sold catfish, buffalo, carp, and drum.

He started his business the day he arrived, and continued until the day he retired. He never advertised. In the beginning, his business was slow, but word spread. After four months, he built his dock. After four years, he bought a trailer. After thirty-three years, he had many friends.

Fishing kept Willis busy. Besides catching the fish and running the dock, he weaved his own nets and built his own boats. He'd learned to fish from his father, who also taught him these crafts.

"I used knitting blocks and needles. I made the blocks out of cedar." The blocks are small, very smooth rectangles with one curved edge. "They have to be smooth so you can slide these meshes off them." Using three blocks and a needle whittled out of pecan, Willis weaved nylon nets. "It takes me a day to knit a net."

In the center of his nets, Willis wove a large mesh. Toward the outside, the mesh became smaller, "to catch smaller fish." Thus, his nets brought him a full catch. "I make them so much better than you can buy them."

The boats that Willis made were also much better than those made in factories. He recalled once buying an aluminum boat. Every time Willis used it, the boat rocked in the wind, making it difficult for him to work. Upset, Willis would strike the boat with the paddle. "I broke so many paddles," he says, smiling. "When I finally gave that thing away, it had a big U-shaped dent in the back of it." His arm makes a U in the air and he laughs. His gums show and his eyes shine. "Them boats in stores just don't work for commercial fishermen."

Had it not been for his handmade sturdy boats and his physical strength, Willis could never have brought in some of his catches. "I caught one in Pine Bluff that weighed 137 pounds, a blue cat. *Ooo-wee.* I weighed exactly what the catfish weighed. I carried him over my shoulder and his tail drug the ground." A 137-pound fish was not easily coaxed into a boat. Willis fought him. "That fish got so tired pulling that line and weight that he wore himself out. Then I just rolled him in on top of me."

Willis brought the big cat back to his dock, where he showed him off. He sold him to the Pine Bluff jailhouse. Big fish were not unusual in Willis's yard. "I'd have alligator gars laying around here like cordwood." He sold a 212-pound gar for five cents a pound.

Willis looks at the cottonwood tree in his front yard. "I dug it up and planted it there. It was thirty-six years old the Fourth of July." When the tree was first big enough, Willis put a table under it. At the table, he sometimes conducted business. Sometimes he sat there with girlfriends. Sometimes he climbed up onto the table and napped in the cool shade of the tree that he had planted with his own hands.

The river has not always been the friend it could be. Ernest Willis has had many arguments and battles with the Mighty Mississippi. Some battles he won.

"In 1963, that was the worst fishing. Fish, shrimp, everything died." Living on the river, Willis saw the pollution levels getting out of control. "It was terrible. The bank was lined with shrimp, dead. Everything was trying to get out on the bank."

After being quoted in a newspaper article about pollution, Willis was contacted by the government. He began the river cleanup. Although the water today is still too dirty for Willis's liking, he is proud and pleased of the work he has done to save the river life.

Some battles, he knows, cannot be won. Every spring, the river rises and floods. Every spring, Willis's yard is submerged, sometimes in twelve feet of water. Hence, every spring for the past thirty-six years, Willis has hitched his trailer (or packed his tent) and moved to higher ground.

He recalls the first flood. "I was living up above the bridge in a tent. I woke up one morning and the river was rising. I started to get out of bed, and I put my feet in the water. You ought to have seen me getting out of there!"

To escape the water, Willis moves to the paved highway behind him. Sometimes, the river chases him from there. Willis moves. The river wins.

Willis suffered one loss to the river that was mightier than them all. In the winter of 1937, he was living in Pine Bluff with his father and step-family. While Willis was helping his father haul cotton from an island in the river, the boat overturned.

Ernest Willis works the river. (Courtesy of the Center for Southern Folklore)

"I went down in about twenty-feet of water, and the only thing that saved me was I sat on the bottom and got my boots off. I got my feet under me and I kicked real hard. I came up right by a sack of cotton. I threw my arms onto the cotton sack, kicked my feet, and went over to a sandbar."

He was rescued on the sandbar, and then he went to look for his father and stepsister. He found the girl. She was floating in the water, drowned. The next day, sick with pneumonia, Willis got back in a boat and dragged the bottom of the river with a trotline. He found his father. "That hurt me worse than anything that ever happened."

Willis was the last person to pass through the Tennessee Chute. The Corps of Engineers built a dam that would prevent that branch of the Mississippi from washing away a peninsula that could—and did—become a slack water port and industrial area. Willis was out running his trotlines. He did not see "the engineer people waving red flags, trying to get me to stop" until it was too late. "I done started in there, and there wasn't no way in the world I could start back."

Willis survived the waves by using the river to his advantage rather than fighting it. "This is where your experience comes in." He shifted all of the weight to the back of the boat, let the waves break under the boat, and rode through it. "They thought I was gone," he says.

"I've had some narrow escapes. I've been in storms out there. I was almost took under by a big whirlhole." Whirlholes, he explains, suck from the top to the bottom, the opposite of tornadoes. "I've seen logs shooting out of whirlholes like bullets."

The Mississippi has made him many friends, but it attracts all kinds of people. "This river was full of thieves." He recalls one man who "would steal the nickels off a dead man's eyes." He continues, "I've had them steal my trammel nets, my barrel nets, my run nets, everything else."

He has had a few trespassers. His trailer was broken into once when he was away from home. Another time, a man on a dune buggy tried to run him over. That man wound up in the hospital. The loud noises from the bridge have never bothered him, but "if you step on a stick outside," he says, "I hear that."

While there are some inconveniences, Willis likes the piece of river life he now occupies. The *Island Queen* blows her whistle for him, and Willis comes out and waves to the tourists. Visitors stop by to meet him. Newspapers from all over the country—New York, Los Angeles, and Canada—call and visit him. *Sports Illustrated* recently contacted him.

Willis sacrifices many amenities for his perch on the river. For one, he has no running water. He always keeps a supply of drinking water in the trailer. When he wants to bathe at home, he must haul in water and heat it on the stove.

Hauling water means going to town. Going to town means driving on his driveway. Driving on his driveway makes Willis think of this past winter. "Oh this last winter, I'm lucky I got in and out of here."

To get from his trailer to the highway, Willis must travel a dirt road that winds along the bridges. Farm vehicles also use the dirt road and they tear it up, sometimes leaving it treacherous for travel. In warm weather, the road is bumpy. In rain, it becomes a mud hole. In winter, it is too much. "Sometimes I'd get stuck. I'd have to get out and jack my car up and build under the wheels. I like to froze my hands. The hide come off all on the end of my fingers. I'm lucky I got the feeling back in them."

In recent years, Willis has been required to make more frequent trips to town. Besides getting supplies, he has had to visit doctors. Some years back, an anchor tore through the scar on his burned leg. "It wouldn't heal. That went into skin cancer." After two months in the veterans' hospital and several skin grafts, he was cured.

Three years ago, he was told he had cancer of the bladder. After an operation and continued treatment, he is today cured. The cancer has, however, kept the doctors concerned. In recent years, he has had another operation and several stays in the hospital. He will have more doctors' appointments.

Willis is weighing the beauty of his river life against the potential turmoil and hazard of another winter on that dirt road. He does not want to move.

He sits back in his chair. He looks at the cottonwood tree, points to the top branches. They are browning, beginning to die. He points to the bottom of the tree. The cottonwood still stands strong, but the river has eaten away at the bank. The roots are exposed, groping for dirt. Willis postulates that two, maybe three more floods will pull the tree away.

"I don't want to stay here until the water washes me away, bank and all." His eyes are wide, his face is serious.

Ernest Willis knows the strength of the river. He knows the Old Man must always be reckoned with. It is stronger than him. Willis has given a large part of his life to this river, and the river has taken more. And the river has provided—a living, and thirty-six years of beauty. Ernest Willis appreciates the Mississippi River. And it may be just this appreciation that tells him it is time to go.

MOSE VINSON

I KNOW THE YEAR because the bar served Billy Beer, the cans endorsed by President Jimmy Carter's brother. It was 1977; I was sixteen, in tenth grade, a passenger in a car when I spotted a new bar sign: BIRTH OF THE BLUES. Sounded like a place I and my friends needed to go. It was across the street from the Ritz, a movie theater turned concert hall. We weren't old enough to enter either place, let alone be served, but we became frequent patrons, stumbling from one to the other when bands went on break. The bartenders knew us well.

Furry Lewis had piqued my interest in the original bluesmen and blueswomen, these living links to another time and culture. At Birth of the Blues, the band was all elder players, a great thrill. After the core group would wind down, barrelhouse piano player Mose Vinson would stay late, playing in the bar's picture window. Because that's what born barrelhouse piano players do. His keys had long propelled a night's diminishing party, and as the waitresses cleared tables, we last revelers gathered close around his piano bench, shouting encouragement and dancing the white middle-class boogie.

I didn't get to know Mose like I did Furry, but Mose was younger—he lived until 2002—so I got to hear him a lot more. He didn't record much, but fortunately Judy Peiser, who was giving Mose regular employ at the

Center for Southern Folklore, got with producers Knox Phillips and Jim Dickinson and they made the *Piano Man* recording happen. (Sun Records alumnus Roland Janes engineered.) I was honored to write the liner notes, and it's a disc I still play often.

No Pain Pill
Liner notes to *Piano Man*, 1997

"You ain't got no pain pill, is ya?" asks Mose Vinson, having turned all the blues in the room into a joyous sound. Bringing relief is his personal sacrifice, and he takes on the woes, like he's always done.

"I was born playing, Holly Springs, Mississippi," he answers, when asked what he would like listeners to know about him. "The good Lord give me that talent, and I play that talent behind the good Lord. I didn't learn from nobody, he give it to me."

Short of the new supermarket off the town square, Holly Springs—and especially the outlying area—fairly resembles how it was in 1917 when Mose was born. Which means the good Lord had to do some serious driving on backcountry winding roads to find Mose for the delivery of this gift. Thank you, Lord.

Mose, eighty, began his musical career when he was five years old. "First thing I saw was an organ, an old-time organ what you work your foot on the pedals. That's what I started playing, then I left that to the piano and I played a whole lot better. Organ was too soft for me." Behind the force of his piano keys, you can almost hear the din of a drunken juke joint, almost see an organ turn to toothpicks.

Those hands were made for music. When his peers took to the cotton fields, Mose joined a touring show and established a life in music. "I just play my own style," he says. "I never did practice anybody else's style." That style has defined the man. In the days when everyone had monikers—Dishrag, Butterfly, Turkey Hop—Mose Vinson was known as "Boogie Woogie." And while he can make a piano jump like a fat lady wearing thin house shoes on hot

Mose Vinson, boogie woogie piano player. (Courtesy of Axel Küstner)

concrete, *boogie woogie* is much too constraining a term. There is a strong jazz element that runs through his playing, and the gospel that is so near his heart never gets away from his fingers.

There is great humor in Mose and in his music. He punctuates his sentences with piano notes, running his big hands over the keys. He smashes notes together like a piano Impressionist. "I go up there and get the black keys, then come on down and mix it with the white keys. That makes my music sound pretty good."

It also sounds pretty good when, in contrast to his rumbling vocals, Mose adds a giddy "yeeeh," hearkening back to the abandon that prevailed in juke joints. "During that time when I used to play for nightclubs, they drink corn whiskey," he says. "People come in and stay all night long, tell me to play the blues, and I played the blues too. Ole country, way way back old dirty blues. All night long. They be shooting dice, those women get drunk, three, four o'clock in the morning, those women would have me play some dirty blues. Stay up all night playing dirty blues. Have a ball all night. Daylight in the morning. Five, six o'clock, I was through, do it again."

When recording settled into Memphis, Mose went to Sun Records for a job, and he ended up sweeping the floor. "Cleaning up, stuff like that. I'd play a few pieces." Sam Phillips auditioned him a few times and Mose lucked into the occasional released session (James Cotton's "Cotton Crop Blues" and "Hold Me in Your Arms").

As you'll hear during the discussion that intersperses *Piano Man*, Mose comes from another world. "He dead now," becomes an all-too-familiar refrain. His mother is dead (his father, a gambler, was shot when Mose was eight), his brothers are dead, his sister is dead. His friends and his rivals are dead. Some of my interview, in fact, took place among the barely living, in a convalescent home with Mose seated at the piano in the activity room (he was the only one wearing shades indoors), and when he began to play, the number of wheelchairs in the room increased, the attendants passed out tambourines, and suddenly two doctors came rushing in because (I swear) a bedridden patient was up and dancing.

There is nothing mournful about these blues. Mose Vinson absorbs pain, transforms it into music that, despite its sadness, evokes joy. Yeah, I got a pain pill. It's about five inches in diameter, it fits into a CD player, and it's got Mose Vinson's name on it.

THE FIELDSTONES

AFTER MUD BOY's near riot at the 1977 Beale Street Music Festival, I tried to hit all the civic concerts. One blues band caught my ear at a downtown summer event as the 1970s were becoming the eighties. The group was tight, sounded modern and urban, but they also conveyed a strong sense of traditional blues. They told me their regular gig was Friday nights at the J&J Lounge.

This was long before GPS was available. The phone book pointed me to Mississippi Boulevard. A more organized person would have brought a map. My friend Cam McCaa (a three-lettered poem of a name) and I crisscrossed streets until we found Mississippi, drove one way on it and then the other until we found the club. We returned regularly, never bringing a map, and never doing daylight reconnaissance.

The Fieldstones recorded only two albums, both for the University of Memphis record label, High Water. That enterprise was fueled by ethnomusicology professor, author, and jug band revivalist Dr. David Evans. Were it not for High Water, many of Memphis's great bands from the 1980s would have been lost. (On their million-selling album *Raising Sand*, Robert Plant and Alison Krauss recorded an almost-to-the-note version of the song "Let Your Loss Be Your Lesson" as rendered by High Water artists the Blues Busters.) The Fieldstones cut some very deep blues, a few tracks evoking their Saturday night gig. The release of the second album, *Mud Island Blues*, was subject to university budgets and delayed twenty years. Most of the band did not live to see it.

That first night I experienced them at J&J, the Fieldstones became one of my all-time favorite bands, and then their second home, Green's Lounge, became one of my all-time favorite clubs. Both really spoiled me: They were that hard to beat and that easy to access. I cherished them in their time, bringing friends from all over to share the experience. Their demises—the band's and the club's—have been like the death of family, a yearning for one more experience, one more sound, one more moment in their presence.

Got to Move on Down the Line
Liner notes to *Mud Island Blues*, 2005

My buddy Cam was already tanked when I picked him up just before the liquor stores closed. It was near eleven P.M. on a Friday night in 1980, summer, and we were driving from the more-monied suburban East Memphis to the less-monied inner-city neighborhoods we didn't usually go to, looking for the J&J Lounge.

"Hey," I'd shouted the weekend before to a man who'd just left the stage at a Memphis blues festival, "Y'all sound good, where do you play?"

There was only one J&J Lounge in the phone book, so, after buying a fifth of Kentucky Tavern, Cam and I set out. We found the J&J and would return often; the bar's exterior was never well lit, and our landmark became a large Victorian home with red lights glowing from behind all the drawn window shades. You paid the cover charge and bought your beer in an anteroom; the club was through a door. It was hot that first night and we decided to cool off with a couple beers before we hit the whiskey. (Play it in any key—play it in whiskey!) We laughed when the barman, to our suburban white-ass surprise, set out two quarts. Me and Cam, with three bottles glinting in the club's dim light, stayed popular that night at the J&J.

The Fieldstones were in mid-set, their warm, welcoming blues—so narcotic—enveloping us. The stage, unlike the club, was not barely lit; it wasn't lit at all. The music poured from the darkness like night from sky.

The band moved to Green's Lounge, where they developed an international reputation. It was not uncommon to meet people there who spoke no English but understood perfectly what was going on, and brought their own guitars to prove it. Green's Lounge was nothing but a double-shotgun

The Fieldstones at Green's Lounge. Left to right: Mr. Clean (dancing, left), Boogie Man (rear, of the Hollywood All-Stars, sitting in), Chester Chandler, aka Memphis Gold (guitar), Joe Hicks (drums), Lois Brown (bass). (Courtesy of Erik Lindahl)

building made of cinder blocks, half the front dividing wall cut out to create a U shape, allowing more audience to see the band and easily reach the bar. Sometimes the kitchen served food. People were always dancing— real, real dancing, dirty dancing, leaving little room for imagination or for the neighboring couple. As Green's increased in popularity, selling more quarts of beer, they got more popular with their distributor, and not long before the roof burned off, lighted beer signs were illuminating the dark corners, diminishing the mystery.

The band. The Fieldstones weren't known for their solos. The music came out as a whole, even when one member stepped forward. Joe Hicks, the vocalist / drummer, used to say, "Time to move on down the line," and he'd tap the snare a couple of times. He'd say it in between songs and always to start a set. "Got to move on down the line," *tap tap*, and the Fieldstones would fall back to their instruments. Bobby Carnes played the keyboard, and he rarely spoke, leaning into those fat church chords instead, the ones still smoky from Saturday night. Lois Brown, she played bass and had a beautiful smile. If the band got hot, she'd tug a string for the ceiling fan without missing a note. Lois was tough, and when acting as the band's manager, she brooked no jive. But her playing made the music lithe. She

Toni the drummer, left, and Rose, the proprietress of Green's Lounge.
(Courtesy of Huger Foote)

didn't move a lot, a little rocking to the beat, but there was a touch, a jump to her jump, that made the bass—and that band—so sinuous. People who never danced would dance to the Fieldstones. One guitarist's spot rotated, mostly between the soul band veteran Clarence Nelson and blues original Wordie Perkins.

The star of the band was Will Roy Sanders. For a while, he got a job driving a truck and was out of town on many Saturday nights. Without him, the gigs were good—hell, if you didn't know about the possibilities of Will Roy, they were great—but he could take the band to a higher, or lower, or deeper place. He had a long rubber face and he sang out of the side of his mouth; you could film a tight shot of him singing and, with the audio turned off, be entertained all night. He'd step up to the mic, wail out an opening verse or line or word (like he does on "Put Your Loving Arms Around Me"), and the band would kick in like your favorite tractor getting its first spark on a warm engine.

For their third set, the band would invite guests on stage. Saxophonist Evelyn Young would often show up—the young B. B. King had modeled his guitar parts on her solos; Evelyn didn't have to wait for the third set. Little Applewhite was a regular, but he never sounded more late-night than he does here on "That Ain't Right." A woman named Toni was always around, bumming drinks and dollar bills, sitting in on drums. One night, a wispy third-set bass player named Shorty who'd been sitting in for years sang a gospel song of such stirring beauty that the band had to quit for the night. Albert King sat in, Teenie Hodges, and a lot of those visiting people who couldn't speak English. The Fieldstones made everybody sound good. Their blues swallowed you.

Week after week they played world-class music until two or three in the morning. Whenever I took their Saturday night presence for granted, hearing them would refresh my wonder. For a long time, the oversight seemed indecent: Such huge talent, such obscurity. I wanted them to get wider recognition, to be heard by millions. But fame is relative, and in some ways this weekly gig was the best kind of success. It put extra money in their pockets, it gave them time in the spotlight, it drew people from all corners of the globe to their Saturday night home, to the community they had made within those unassuming cinderblocks across from the automobile graveyard.

The years have not been kind to the Fieldstones. Making this music was not glamorous. The last time I saw Lois, her health was failing seriously; I heard she lost a leg to diabetes. Joe Hicks had a series of light strokes; Clarence died; Wordie sobered up and, I think, works in a factory. Last time I dropped Toni off at her place in the projects, she borrowed fifteen bucks and has been hiding from me ever since. Evelyn Young passed, Applewhite has had serious kidney trouble. After Green's Lounge shut down in the mid-1990s, Will Roy purchased it and ran it with his wife, Dorothy. That's when a fire shuttered it.

I've waited nearly twenty years to hear this album. I bought their first one the day it came out, and it livened up many a party. Week after week I'd badger them for information on the release of their follow-up, and they'd say it was in the can and they hoped it would come out soon. Now that we've got it, here's my suggestion: Get one forty-watt light, maybe two. You'll need either a smoke machine or a convenience store's worth of burning cigarettes, definitely a cooler full of beer quarts, also setups—a maraschino cherry on top of a hotel ice bucket, napkins stuffed inside tiny drinking glasses. Find a real diverse group of humans: large, small, very fat, quite skinny, black, white, others. Put a sign on the wall that says NO DOPE SMOKIN', then ignore it. Hire a skinny old man you could push over with a sneeze, give him a loaded gun, and let him frisk everyone as they enter. Call me and I'll pick up Cam on the way. Turn up *Mud Island Blues*. Dance.

LEAD BELLY

I N ADDITION TO encounters with live musicians, I've also had good luck
buying used records. The cover of *Lead Belly's Last Sessions, Vol. 1* features white-haired Lead Belly, eyes closed, face intent, and you can almost
hear him humming. And how could a blues singer with a name like that
be bad? It turned out to be not only an encounter with a folk music master but also an invitation to a private dinner that never ends, that never
gets cold, that continuously whets my appetite.

The more I learned of Lead Belly, the more my admiration grew. He
came to the public's attention through folklorist John Lomax (and his son
Alan), who first recorded him in a Texas prison, 1933; after being previously pardoned for murder, Lead Belly was in this time for a non-fatal stabbing. His relationship with the Lomaxes was complex and fraught. They
managed his singing career and made him popular. They also hired him as
their driver and valet. In a 1935 *March of Time* newsreel, Lead Belly wears
prison stripes and is made to reenact his previous year's liberation from
jail into the care of the elder Lomax. It's like the 1966 televised interview
with the American POW in Vietnam, Jeremiah Denton, whose favorable
answers about his responsible care by his captors were belied by his blink-
ing in Morse code *t-o-r-t-u-r-e*. Lead Belly recites the script's lines, but his
exaggerated shucking and jiving conveys the relationship's deeper truths.

By the time of this recording, more than a decade after the newsreel, and only a year before his premature death in 1949 from Lou Gehrig's disease, Lead Belly seems to have made his peace with the world (though not necessarily with his wife, Martha).

Nobody in This World

Oxford American, Summer 1999

You are sitting next to strangers—on a city bus, or maybe in a doctor's waiting room. The space is close and would be claustrophobic, but you begin to overhear conversation—a riveting tale, an old man's life, a world away from your own. The one you thought was his son next to him, or his niece on his other side, are strangers, and this man is talking not to them but to everyone, and unlike the crazed rants from which polite folk avert their eyes, his story holds the room rapt.

Such is the effect of *Lead Belly's Last Sessions, Vol. 1*, a revelation of another world in song.

I have been listening to my copy for more than twenty years, and I continue to learn from it—not only about Lead Belly's life and American song but also about musical arrangements and production and about my own life and what I don't know.

This album is no *Sgt. Pepper's*, no high-tech layering of sound. In fact, it could hardly be more lo-fi. It is only Lead Belly singing, joined occasionally

"You can almost hear him humming." (Courtesy of Robert Gordon)

by his wife, Martha—no instruments. They're not even in a recording studio but in a New York apartment. A friend, jazz scholar Frederic Ramsey Jr., had invited them to dinner, and afterward he retrieved a tape deck from the closet. We hear dishes being cleared, beer bottles being opened. Then, Lead Belly sings 'em as he thinks of 'em, moving from early twentieth-century field holler to contemporary protest song. There are gospel and army songs, pop tunes, and plenty of blues. Over the course of an hour, Lead Belly sings more than thirty. Some get introductions, others flit past.

I had a hard time finding my way into this record when I bought it as a teenager in 1977. ALL USED LPS $1.88 read the store's banner out front. I knew nothing of Lead Belly except what the cover photo told me: He was black and old. The LP was also old (I was buying the 1962 reissue of the 1953 original release), on thick vinyl, and the sleeve was of heavier paper stock than the glossy Boston and Kiss albums that overflowed from other bins.

Instead of opening with the hook of a great pop hit, *Lead Belly's Last Sessions* begins with muffled conversation and hard-to-understand words, making us eavesdroppers. Once the singing finally begins (no guitar, no piano, no harmonica whipped out from anyone's pocket), it's a far cry from the push and pull of teenage amour:

> *I was standing in the bottom*
> *Working mud up to my knees*
> *I was working for the captain*
> *And he's so hard to please.*

I remember reeling around a few tracks later when I heard him sing "Liza Jane." We'd sung that in kindergarten. Then "Jimmy crack corn and I don't care . . . ," then "Bet on Stewball, he might win win win." I recognized "Bring Me a Little Water, Silvy" from a Harry Belafonte record my family played on car trips, and just before the first side ended, I got a roots-rock surprise. There was a hard-rock radio hit at the time by some group, Ram Jam, called "Black Betty," and here it was again, just Lead Belly's voice and his handclapping—one clap per measure, smacking like a bullwhip:

> *Black Betty had a baby*
> *Bam ba lam*
> *Little thing went crazy*
> *Bam ba lam.*

The link across time hooked me. I still didn't like Ram Jam's version, but I no longer laughed when I heard it. I returned to Lead Belly less hesitantly.

After one tune, Ramsey says, "That's an old, old song, isn't it?"

"Way back," says Lead Belly. "Way back."

"They made a record of it recently," says Ramsey.

"Mm . . . hmm," responds Lead Belly, "but not like that they didn't."

BORN IN LOUISIANA in 1888 to former slaves, Huddie "Lead Belly" Ledbetter served time in a Texas penitentiary for murder. A composer of such facility, he wrote a song for the visiting governor that won him early release. Then a stabbing incident put him in Louisiana's Angola prison. Song collector John Lomax heard Lead Belly there in 1933 and the following year he arranged to have him released to his oversight. Lomax made Lead Belly a popular singer, and also his manservant. Lead Belly's relationship with John's son Alan Lomax was more egalitarian. Alan's defiant response to his landlord's anger at his hosting Lead Belly and his wife inspired one of Lead Belly's most enduring songs, 1938's "The Bourgeois Blues."

Last Sessions was recorded in late 1948, when Lead Belly was approaching sixty. He'd soon be diagnosed with ALS and would die in late 1949. He's in a reflective mood, remembering songs from his days working the fields with other convicts, days when the heat beat down so relentlessly that they took it personally and named the sun:

Go down old Hannah
Please don't rise no more
And if you do rise in the morning
Set this world on fire.

The song is slow and heavy, a tempo for the long haul. Ramsey says, "That's the first time I've heard you sing that many verses."

"Oh well," says Lead Belly, "you can just make 'em right on up."

Periodically throughout the evening we hear Lead Belly pause or slow in his singing, groping for a rhyme or idea. Once, he makes "anywhere" rhyme with "car."

He sings a series of field hollers, wherein individual words are dragged over many notes. His bass tones are thick and humid like summer. As important as the words are to one alone in the field ("I don't know you / What have I done?"), the sound of the voice is supreme, the calling forth of the rumbling from deep within, cajoling it from the pit of the soul through the belly and along the gullet before it flies from the throat to the open sky and Hannah above, where its dissipation is so vast as to make the plaint totally ineffective. *The sun won't feel that rumble, no matter how deep I go.* The futility builds belief in the process, in the making of the sounds, in the emotion with which they are vested. *Forget Hannah, if she don't hear my plea, I feel better having made it.*

Lead Belly pauses after these hollers to speak a few quiet sentences in his deep voice to Ramsey: "I be around home sometimes and do that one. My baby, she says, 'What's the matter, you sick or something?' When you get the blues feeling, I be washing dishes, keep her from having to wash 'em. I love to wash dishes . . . Well, I know you got it running and you want something else, let me see what I can give you," and without hesitation, as much for himself as for the listener who has been left on the floorboards, he cannonballs into the excitement of "Rock Island Line." The power of a train as a means out of a bad place, a promise not of freedom but of escape, is overwhelming.

NOT UNTIL WELL into the evening do we hear from Lead Belly's wife. During "Old Ship of Zion," Martha joins in, the additional voice giving new dimension to the material. Their voices were made for blending; even when their harmonies are off, they are on. She contributes to the next song, then she returns several times, but like a sitar or a studio effect, she's on only enough cuts to make us want more.

Much later and a couple verses into an old army song, Lead Belly says, "That's the part you can catch; come in there." Obligingly, like a weary soldier, she joins him on the chorus. "That's pretty good, your coming in there," he drawls, and continues. After the fourth verse, when she again adds her mournful harmony, he interjects, like a dope fiend who's taken a good hit, "Oh good God, it's killer."

> *The biscuits that they give you*
> *They say they're mighty fine*
> *But one jumped off the table*
> *Knocked down a pal of mine.*

They do a few more, her voice turning the bread to cake, and after the last one, Lead Belly speaks the closing flourish: "Wow!"

The comments that he sprinkles throughout the album are as integral as the melodies. They are about timing, mood, and effect, like horn lines in

Martha Ledbetter, left, and Huddie Ledbetter, aka Lead Belly. (Courtesy of the John Reynolds Collection, Smithsonian Folkways)

a soul song. Between verses of one holler, Lead Belly creates whip sounds, the captive's cry, and the captain's gleeful retort—in the same breath. The contrast, the ease of delivery, and the way these asides make the lyrics stand out have helped me understand how complex songs come together from various elements.

HIS PROTEST SONGS reach to the same authority as his gospel:

If the Negro was good enough to fight
Why can't we get a little equal rights?. . .

One thing folks should realize
Six feet of dirt makes us all the same size

Well, God made us all and in Him we trust
Nobody in this world is better than us.

That song leads right back into the next:

We're in the same boat brother
We're in the same boat brother

And if you shake one end
You're gonna rock the other.

He drags the second "same" like a trombone's blue note, at once gleeful and woefully sad. There's also handclapping, which, after the lack of accompaniment, is thunderous.

Lead Belly may attend church and may join in a protest song, but he's never far from the street. In "Mistreatin' Mama," each verse is a short story, the next line building on the previous one, so that a song that begins (belted out like Ethel Merman), "Mama, Papa's got the blues" leads to

Don't bother me
I'm just as mean as can be
I'm like the butcher coming down the street
I'll cut you all to pieces
Like I would a piece of meat.

The songs blend together, trancelike. The occasional discussion, at a lower volume, becomes the soft part of the symphony, preparing us for an explosion of song. And like the melody of hushed violins, Lead Belly's quiet discussion takes hard listening; then it reveals its complexity. It took years before I distinguished an argument between tracks. A conversation is silenced by the sudden presence of Martha's thin voice, sounding a beautiful weariness:

I'm thinking of a friend
Whom I used to know
Who wandered and suffered
In this world below
I—

But she stops short and says, "I forgot."
Lead Belly: "Go ahead and sing something. Christ. You started."
The song returns to Martha's mind, and she continues her elegy.

What are they doing in heaven today
Where sins and sorrows are all done away.

She makes it through the chorus once before Lead Belly interjects, "That's good, let loose on that thing. Sing it, let yourself on go." She forges ahead, and he quiets.

There was someone who was poor
And suffered in pain—

"Let loose," Lead Belly says, no longer playing the between-line turn-arounds but sabotaging her song, the only one she leads. She *tsks* her tongue and says, "I wish you would leave me alone."

"Sing it, honey. You done all right now."

"I can't. If you talking—"

"All right, I'll lay low. But you were doing good. Come on, what's the matter with you?"

"I'll sing later," she says.

"Don't pay me no mind. Just think about what you're doing."

"I can't! I'm trying to listen to you. How I'm gonna—"

"Don't listen to me. You're singing. Somebody says something to me and I'm singing, I don't listen to 'em. You watch and see if I don't."

"You do it all the time."

She quiets, and everyone quiets. "Just pour it right on there," says Lead Belly as if nothing's happened, as if he's not, like the butcher in "Mistreatin' Mama," mean as he can be. "That was a good piece. Special too." Martha is done.

With the next-to-last track, Lead Belly changes his tone, launching into a sermonette built around the repetition of the phrase "in the world." Purposely disjointed and mumbled, only occasional words are decipherable ("I met an old man . . . a different type of man from our world . . . I walked into a bar . . . in the world and asked for a drink in the world . . .") until the ending, which is stated clearly: "We all got to get peace together because we're in the world together." It's Lead Belly producing the record, giving a final meditation, a closing convocation. "I'm sleepy now," he says, "I want to go home. I'm going to have to go home."

But there's still a hot coal on his fire, and ever the professional, he knows to leave 'em singing, so he makes the thought into a song. "I Want to Go Home" sounds improvised, and it is light and fun, but its plea for freedom, refracted through the evening's material, evokes the captivity of the slave, hearkens to the subjugation of every recording artist to both the recording tape and to the recording company.

The quiet that follows the record's completion is huge, and puzzling. The initial distance from the artist has completely disappeared. It's not as though we were sucked in close but, rather, we crawled willingly, song by song, nearer my God to thee, and his sudden absence leaves us wanting. Here we are, after all, in the world we know, far from this other place we couldn't invent, yet that drips from our being, so recently immersed in it.

This album is a testament to the nature of song, how lyrics and music live, how they can transcend time to resonate to a man born soon after the Civil War and also to a man born a century later during Vietnam. This album spreads itself across a life, with some songs belonging to childhood, some to adolescence, and many yet to reveal themselves. Most studio recordings fail to capture the personality that makes this night so eternal. The ease of the situation draws him out, and he seems to sing for the sake of the song, not for his own personal gain. The living was hard, but the art is fun.

ROBERT JOHNSON

I GOT SERIOUS ABOUT writing after college. To get out of the nightclubs, I took a job as a baker, reporting to work when the opening act would be taking the stage. I'd wake early afternoons, sit at my manual typewriter for several hours, then sneak a falafel into the repertory theater before punching the bakery's clock. I wrote a novel that way, got practice in long-form narrative arcs, and developed discipline. (I could afford an electric typewriter, but the authenticity of the manual let me commune with all the greats. And I liked the sounds it made. And here's two writing lessons from college: 1. You can't pay the rent on inspiration. Meaning: Writers write. Sit in the chair even when you don't want to. And 2. Avoid adverbs. If you have to describe the action, then the setup hasn't been developed. A third rule I think I always knew: If you can say it in fewer words, do.) The bakery job was not happenstance. Writing was a risk, and if I failed, if nuclear fallout hit, if the economy crumbled—we'd always need bread. I can, today, put my hands on the recipes, measured in pounds of yeast and sacks of flour.

Soon into the magazines, I hit my short-form stride, delivering 300- to 1,500-word articles many times a week. Some pieces were for them, some for me. I was getting the drill down, my eye on making a living at it.

This Robert Johnson piece was different. Until this point, I'd mostly written profiles and album reviews. In music journalism, there's plenty of room to write creatively, to research important history, to share the power and impact of someone's life. However, and especially with older recordings, it's ultimately subsumed by the corporation—boosting their sales. With this article, I experienced a deeper kind of journalism: Poor people entitled to money weren't getting it, and everyone who might be responsible claimed it wasn't their fault.

The Complete Recordings marked the first time that all the known tracks by the Delta blues great Robert Johnson were released, and it promptly earned gold-record status—selling more than half a million copies. There was much rehashing of Johnson's Faustian legend and analyses of his musical prowess and spare, elegant storytelling, but nobody wrote about the royalties.

Follow the money, right?

Like so many other good ideas, this one began with Peter Guralnick. I met him toward the end of the 1980s. He was in Memphis beginning his research on the Elvis biographies, and I was making a blues short, *All Day & All Night*. The producer invited him to the edit room, and when we were introduced, he asked if I was the guy who'd written a small piece on Al Green's collaborator Teenie Hodges for *Spin*. I was flattered that this authority noticed my article, and impressed with how he kept up; *Spin* was not where you'd find a lot of roots music writing. We began a correspondence, and when I was doing archival newspaper research for the 1995 publication of *It Came from Memphis*, I'd mail him interesting Elvis bits. He'd come to town and I'd take him to funky places for fun, food, and listening. (The bond was sealed after he ordered and consumed a heap of deep fried chicken livers. Respect.) Peter's always had a generous spirit, and that empathy comes through in his books. It makes him a good guy too. He was too far gone with Elvis to write this piece, but he called me, said the *LA Weekly* would allow the newsprint space this might need, was I interested?

The *LA Weekly* editor RJ Smith schooled me. This story had many characters, byzantine business transactions, and was about—blues. To make it accessible to a wide audience, RJ had me ease the reader in, slowing to paint the pictures needed, pulling wide every now and then—an establishing shot for each new scene. He had me considering images that open a paragraph, the weight on which a paragraph closes, the implications of putting a name near an event (meaning, even if I don't connect them, the reader will, which is useful for insinuation but can be a danger for unintended innuendo). We spent hours on the phone, working through the meticulous process of getting the details in and keeping the article moving. I did two more features for RJ over the following year, Charlie Feathers and James Carr. When we were done, I felt more like a writer.

Hellhound on the Money Trail
LA Weekly, July 5–11, 1991

The sun did not shine, but it was hot as hell the day a memorial stone was unveiled for bluesman Robert Johnson near a country crossroads outside Greenwood, Mississippi. About seventy-five people filled the tiny Mt. Zion church, a row of broadcast video cameras behind the back pew and a bank of lights illuminating a hoarse preacher as he praised a man who reputedly sold his soul to the devil.

There was no finality in setting the stone. The attention came fifty years too late, and even if his memory is more alive today than ever before, Johnson's rightful heirs still have nothing but the name. This service was not about the body of the bluesman, which lies in an unmarked grave somewhere in the vicinity; it was about the guitar-shaped wreath provided by Johnson's current record label, and about the video bite that would be beamed into homes around the country that April 1991 evening.

Johnson's recordings captured a spirit, a desperate, maniacal, even existential spirit, but so have other recordings. Leroy Carr, Kokomo Arnold, Tommy Johnson, and people whose names we don't even know have weeds instead of memorial stones on their graves. But Johnson has the myth.

When he first played around Robinsonville, Mississippi, his skill was so poor that other musicians made fun of him. After traveling for a year or so, he returned and talked his way into playing a party while the great Son House took a break. "He was so good! When he finished, all our mouths were standing open," recalled the late House. "I said, 'Well ain't that fast! He's gone now!'" Many people were suspicious of his sudden improvement. Whether Johnson himself told others or whether it was whispered about him when he was not around, the possibility was generally accepted that he had sold his soul to the devil.

His fatal poisoning at age twenty-seven in 1938 also stokes the myth—the murderer and the means remained unknown for decades. His mystery was so great, it was not until the midseventies that researchers knew what he looked like; no photograph had ever been found. Johnson's racked, cryptic voice, and the drama of his guitar playing have influenced countless musicians (When Keith Richards first heard Johnson, he asked, "Who's the other guy playing with him?").

Only in the last year have fans been able to hold the myth in their hands. *Robert Johnson: The Complete Recordings*, a boxed set released in August 1990, has triggered extraordinary interest in the mysterious bluesman. More than six hundred thousand sets have been sold worldwide; the box reached as high as eighty on *Billboard*'s pop charts, generating an initial royalty payment described by a source at Columbia as a "chunky six-figure check." (Using a standard formula for royalties, that would be approximately $420,000.) With the next payment in September, Johnson's combined royalties could amount to well over a million dollars. Johnson won a Best Historical Album Grammy in 1990, but in 1991 he is a contemporary pop phenomenon. He's been on the cover of numerous magazines, been featured as the lead story on *Entertainment Tonight*, and been the subject of talk around Hollywood. Robert Johnson is a growth industry. For somebody.

To date, Robert Johnson's family has received no money from *The Complete Recordings*, no money from cover versions of his songs, no money from the publishing of the singer's photograph.

DECADES BACK, WHEN a folklorist for the Smithsonian Institution named Mack McCormick chanced upon information concerning Robert Johnson's death, the mysteries of the bluesman's life began to open up.

"In 1971," says McCormick, an authority on Texas blues who had been pursuing Johnson since 1948, "an ex-wife and Johnson's children were located." The following year, he found Carrie Spencer Thompson and Bessie Hines, two of Johnson's half sisters. Among their documents were the first two photographs of Johnson ever discovered by researchers: a studio picture of Johnson and a nephew and a dime store booth shot. McCormick signed agreements with both sisters granting him first publication rights for the pictures and for biographical information to be used in a book already under way.

Soon after meeting the sisters, McCormick contacted Columbia Records' John Hammond. In the course of the legendary talent scout's career, Hammond had worked with Don Law, the producer of Johnson's two recording sessions; he was also a passionate Johnson fan, and a key source for McCormick. By the time they corresponded in 1972, McCormick was giving the strong impression the book, *Biography of a Phantom*, was imminent.

But in the summer of 1973, blues entrepreneur Stephen C. LaVere also found Carrie Thompson. (Bessie Hines had died.) LaVere asked Thompson about Johnson memorabilia, and she presented him with a photograph different from the two she had given McCormick. LaVere remembers: "She told me, 'You know it's really strange that I didn't have this picture when Mr. McCormick was here.' And we both took that as a sign of Providence that the good Lord just didn't want Mack McCormick to have that photograph." LaVere went to Thompson's attorney and had a new agreement drawn up, assigning him ownership of her photographs and, as long as God was on his side, ownership of Johnson's copyrights. Thompson died in the early 1980s.

"As the last known surviving heir," says LaVere, "Carrie Thompson was the holder, the common law copyright owner, of all Johnson's compositions. My arrangement is a full and complete transfer of all right, title, and interest to me. I am now the copyright owner . . . Now that she is gone I have an obligation to pay her heirs, and when I'm gone, my heirs have to pay her heirs. And it goes on, as long as money is collected, money will be paid."

Money is being collected, but money is not being paid.

LIKE THE MISSISSIPPI River that constantly eats away at its banks, the Robert Johnson myth consumes fans, critics, and scholars. Eventually, everything at the edge of the river falls in. Everything becomes mud. "It's almost part of the Robert Johnson myth that as you become involved with it you decide you own it," states Jim Dickinson. A producer and musician who has worked with people as diverse as the Rolling Stones, Sleepy John Estes, and Sly and Robbie, he is a longtime Mississippi resident. "It comes with the territory."

When screenwriter and filmmaker Alan Greenberg was beginning his screenplay for *Love in Vain*, a fictional account of Johnson's life, McCormick invited him to peruse his research files. "The summer of '77 I was in the Delta," Greenberg recalls. "By the time I got to Houston, I had been skipping meals and nursing the gas pedal just to get there. I get to his house, he invites me in, everything is very nice, he gives me a drink, which got me very drunk just from the first sip because I was starving, and when I got to the point of saying, 'Okay, where do we begin with all the research stuff,' he said, 'For $35,000 and six and a half percent of the profits of your film, I'll show it to you.'"

A record collector tells of a time he was riding on a California highway with LaVere in the midseventies. "I had a tape of Lynyrd Skynyrd's live album, and I asked him if he had heard it. And he went nuts when he heard Johnson's 'Crossroads.' He said, 'Pull off at the first place you can where there's a phone.' And this is like nine o'clock at night, out in the middle of nowhere near San Diego. It would have been midnight on a Saturday night in New York. He called some people back in New York and started screaming how he was going to sue 'em and all this kind of stuff, wanted a cease and desist order immediately on the record and wanted them to pay him royalties."

Both LaVere and McCormick were fans of the blues before Robert Johnson came into their lives. But when these two men, from distinctly different backgrounds, found Johnson, they found a calling.

Robert Burton "Mack" McCormick, the first Robert Johnson author-ity, lives in Houston. The son of X-ray technicians, he has worked on a chicken farm in Alabama, been employed by the National Park Service, and shilled for a Las Vegas casino. By the 1960s, McCormick was writing about jazz for *DownBeat* and producing records for people like Lightnin' Hopkins and Robert Shaw. In 1965, he took a group of Texas prison inmates to the Newport Jazz Festival. He has worked in various capacities with the Smithsonian Institution.

"He's an excellent field-worker, an excellent writer, and an excellent idea person," says Ralph Rinzler, assistant secretary emeritus at the Smithso-nian, and the man who brought McCormick to the Institution. "He's meticulous and determined in his pursuit of information." Among his other achievements is an enlightening ten thousand–word essay that accom-panies the 1974 album *Henry Thomas—"Ragtime Texas."* Other writing projects, however, have not fared as well. He collaborated with author Paul Oliver on what was to have been a definitive history of Texas blues, though it has yet to be published. McCormick is also a playwright; one of his scripts was produced in England.

A very private person, Mack McCormick rarely grants interviews. After two weeks of receiving phone messages and a Federal Express package from this writer, McCormick's "brother" finally responded. Claiming to be a lawyer, the "brother" provided much information about the search for Johnson's family, including firsthand observations; apparently, he often accompanied Mack on research trips. The "brother" asked not to be quoted. McCormick's quotes come from articles and press releases.

Stephen C. LaVere, the son of a Los Angeles piano player who worked with Jack Teagarden, is a longtime record collector who started out work-ing in record stores. He narrates his background, like he describes his cur-rent work, in a smooth and patient voice, his tone conveying an ordered world with everything in its place. "I produced a number of records for the Liberty combine—Imperial, Blue Note, World Pacific, those labels," he recalls over the phone from his Los Angeles home. Sunnyland Slim, Shakey Jake, and the Muddy Waters Blues Band are some of the performers he recorded. "I was very close friends with Bob Hite and Henry Vestine of Canned Heat. We had a brainstorm one day and came up with the Legendary Masters Series, which was a very successful series for Imperial, reissuing a lot of early blues."

LaVere went south in 1969 to work at the Memphis Country Blues Festival. "I became acquainted with Furry Lewis, Bukka White, Piano Red, Sleepy John Estes, and all those people, and it was just mind-staggering. I couldn't believe the wealth of blues talent that was just laying there going to rot, getting one festival a year and a gig here and a gig there. I was there until May of 1975 working with the old cats."

A job with Sun Records, then recently acquired by music industry entrepreneur Shelby Singleton, led LaVere to independent research. He turned up new information about bluesman Joe Hill Louis and rediscovered Harmonica Frank Floyd and Jimmy DeBerry, as well as a few other neglected musicians.

His former employer at Sun, Shelby's brother John Singleton, has not forgotten LaVere. "He kept some of our tapes, which rather perturbed us," recalls Singleton, who now runs the label. "I think it's well known in the industry that several of our things showed up on bootleg albums not too many years after that. We've really had nothing to do with him since." (Among tapes said to have come into his possession are Howlin' Wolf sessions and a famed Jerry Lee Lewis conversation about the devil. LaVere says about the accusation: "No, that's not true.")

"One of my oldest and closest friends" is how LaVere refers to photographer Ernest Withers, who has documented Memphis's African-American culture for five decades. In the 1960s, according to Withers, LaVere took an extensive collection of photographs and negatives from his studio without permission. Recently, a Memphis museum obtained photocopies of LaVere's collection of Withers's material. "When I saw that stack of pictures, I realized: Here's a man who robbed me. There's collections of dead folk, church people, people he don't know. All he knows is Elvis Presley and Bobby Bland," says Withers. "Here's my wife with Count Basie," he continues, holding a photocopy of the image. "Do you think I'd give him that?" And though Withers vehemently states, "I have never signed a contract with him," LaVere wrote in *Living Blues* magazine:

"The shot of Howlin' Wolf [in the boxed set booklet] is my copyrighted photograph by Ernest C. Withers."

Withers is contemplating legal action. "It was a verbal agreement," says LaVere. "He said just take 'em with you and if you make any money off 'em, share it with me."

"LaVere used to run this little shop on Cooper," recalls Jim Dickinson, "a curio shop, used records and that kind of shit, and Nazi stuff. I mean for real Nazi shit." The store was called the South Cooper Street Curio Shop; after LaVere left Memphis, the building was destroyed in a fire that may have been set by striking firemen. "That's where I first saw the pictures of Robert Johnson. And he had dogs that he kept there all night because he was paranoid someone was going to steal from him what he had stolen. He was here for a good many years, all through the seventies. Used to drive an old Buick."

("Oh yeah," says LaVere, "we sold all kinds of stuff, anything that would sell.")

"Outside behind the old Home of the Blues," continues Dickinson, referring to another Memphis record store, "they used to throw away the old 78s, and I've seen LaVere and [folk guitarist/folklorist] John Fahey stand behind Home of the Blues and if there were three of a certain thing, they'd take one each and they'd break the third one. I saw that personally." The rarer the records, the higher the value to collectors.

LaVere returned to California, where he "spent seven or eight years in the insurance business." By selling policies door-to-door, a record collector can gain entrance to peoples' homes—and to their music collections. The residents can unload some clutter and get a little spending money; the collector can find, literally, lost treasures.

Documentarian and musician Randall Lyon was active in Memphis's country blues renaissance. He too met LaVere. "At the time, white people didn't like us playing black music, and black people didn't like us invading their communities.

"When people started realizing money could be made on this music, this guy came along who smelled a buck, he lived in Los Angeles and all, and he really creamed us. We were just a bunch of naive redneck hippies.

"We were so involved with getting people to trust us that we didn't even see [LaVere] sneaking up on us. And finally, when all our records and all our paraphernalia was gone, we realized what he'd done."

Since 1983, LaVere has been a dealer in rare records and has established a small photo archive. "You have to do what you think is right, try to make a living for yourself in this world," he says. "There's lots of ways to do it, and you have to be inventive, you have to be creative if you want to do what you want to do. I don't want to sell insurance, I want to deal in the music business."

Now THAT HE had Carrie Thompson's agreement in hand, in 1973 LaVere approached Columbia Records with an idea: to package together all of Robert Johnson's recordings. John Hammond immediately hired him as coproducer of *The Complete Recordings*, a version of which jazz and blues producer Frank Driggs was already compiling.

The first time Robert Johnson's music was available in anything but old 78s was when Driggs packaged *King of the Delta Blues Singers* for Columbia in 1961. Featuring sixteen of Johnson's twenty-nine titles, this album helped create a new generation of fans. *King of the Delta Blues Singers, Volume 2*, released in 1970, had the remaining titles. Both sold better than Johnson sold in his entire lifetime, and both continue to sell. By 1973, demand was such that Columbia was packaging them together.

On the back of the second volume, Columbia printed a minor statement worth major bucks: "The selections are in the public domain." For all the years that Columbia sold Johnson, they never paid song royalties, thinking that nobody owned the copyrights.

Whoever owned them would be entitled to payment every time one of Johnson's songs was heard on the radio, played on a stage, or covered by another performer. Record labels often make a practice of obtaining the copyrights, or a percentage, so that they are paying themselves. The more of the copyright they own the less they have to pay the artist. Since before the thirties, many a blues musician was offered a hot meal and a few dollars in cold, hard cash for their signature on a copyright agreement.

LaVere says his 1973 offer to Carrie Thompson included two copies of her half brother's recordings, and a fifty-fifty royalty split.

A song's copyright has a certain lifetime, and when it expires, it goes into public domain. So when Columbia labeled Robert Johnson public domain, they were guessing; Johnson's contract had never been located. The label in effect made a public announcement that they didn't own his songs and they didn't owe anybody royalties.

He could not be sure, but Columbia producer Larry Cohn claims in the May/June 1991 issue of *Living Blues* that Johnson signed a contract giving him a flat fee up front and no royalties, as was "the standard procedure for that time period." Such procedure produced broke musicians and rich executives, and the system has yet to be overhauled.

(McCormick claims to have found a contract signed by the Chuck Wagon Gang, who recorded in San Antonio the same day for the same label as Johnson. That agreement assigned them a royalty, he says; however, the Chuck Wagon Gang's archives in Nashville claim no knowledge of this document.)

Though it appears he did not own them, Hammond (a friend of LaVere's father) nonetheless signed away the copyrights to LaVere in 1973. "LaVere got a deal such as nobody I've ever heard of getting in the history of the business," recalls producer Frank Driggs. "I have no axe to grind with him, but it boggles the mind."

Driggs cites a CBS contract made by Hammond with blues singer Ethel Waters in the 1960s as the precedent for LaVere's contract. She was still alive when Columbia was releasing a three-record compilation of her material. "Hammond called Waters and said, 'We're going to make up for the fact that Columbia didn't treat you right,'" recalls Driggs. "He always did it on the basis of conscience. She was not entitled by contract to royalties on some of those songs, so we made an overall arrangement whereby she got royalties on everything."

"I not only also represented the copyrights, both musical and photographic, but Johnson as an artist as well," LaVere recently recalled in *Living Blues*. "Consequently, CBS had to be very forthcoming to satisfy me." Whether they had to, CBS assigned the money owed the heirs to a third party; putting the royalties in escrow would have been easy enough, but Columbia took LaVere's word that he would pay Johnson's family.

The Complete Recordings was compiled and mastered by LaVere, and awaiting release in 1974.

In satisfying LaVere, CBS necessarily dissatisfied McCormick, who learned about the deal in a 1974 phone call from, of all people, LaVere. McCormick contacted Hammond, who claimed not to know him. (Hammond's associates have noted that he had suffered a stroke and his memory was affected.)

McCormick pursued his case, writing Columbia's chief legal counselor to question the validity of LaVere's contract: "Please be advised that by agreements signed July 8, 1972 with Mrs. Carrie Thompson . . . I purchased rights for exclusive first publication of all documents, photographs, memorabilia, and other material from their family collections and / or personal reminiscences . . . I respectfully suggest you examine whether you do in fact have proper title."

The specter of a legal battle loomed, and CBS ultimately shelved the completed project.

"It got to be a running joke," says former Columbia A&R person Jim Fishel, who picked up the dormant project in 1976. "We used to go to a product meeting every week, the various departments. We'd get to Robert Johnson and they'd look at me. We'd start to laugh and they'd table the discussion and it would go on to the next meeting. I had the same cover [as that released in 1990] on my wall in my office back in 1977. It was done, just sitting and waiting. It had catalog numbers and everything."

McCormick's letter to Columbia frustrated LaVere. "It was a bluff," he says. "[McCormick] would have never sued CBS because he didn't have a leg to stand on. I mean, I have all the documents I need to file for song copyrights, photo copyrights. And Mack never did have that. Whatever he claimed as purchasing rights is invalid because it wasn't a legal contract."

He acknowledges that McCormick beat him across the finish line, but he says that his contract makes him the winner. LaVere says his is binding, even though McCormick's predates his.

In fact, LaVere's fundamental premise—that Carrie Thompson was the "sole-surviving heir"—might be flawed. Johnson's mother was definitely alive when he died, so according to Mississippi intestate law, she precedes the sister as an heir. Thompson's claim is no stronger than that of any of her nine siblings, or her nieces or nephews. Further, Johnson's children or a widow would precede the mother, so if McCormick has in fact found either, Carrie Thompson could not sign away her rights because she never inherited any.

(An attorney for Thompson's heir contends that the contract between LaVere and Thompson may be null and void. "Based on factors relating to Mr. LaVere's alleged non performance," says Jay Fialkov, "efforts were made in the early eighties by representatives of the estate of Robert Johnson to rescind that agreement.")

LaVere admits that if McCormick has found heirs, his case would be damaged. "He says he's found a large extended family of Robert Johnson's, but he has never identified anybody. He's only just made that claim."

McCORMICK HAS MADE that claim and many others. In the slim field of Johnson scholarship, he is well respected. "[He] doggedly pursued the most tenuous leads and . . . has gone a long way toward filling the enormous void of knowledge surrounding Johnson's life," writes music historian and author Peter Guralnick in his *Searching for Robert Johnson*. McCormick was the source for—and in large part the subject of—that book.

While in Mississippi in 1970 riding a "rolling store"—a truck that serviced farm workers—McCormick's inquiries into Robert Johnson's history produced the response, "You must mean Robert Spencer." That same year, in Dumas, Arkansas, he logged the first two eyewitness accounts of Johnson's murder.

"Finding the facts of his death—the end of the story," McCormick wrote in a 1988 article in the Smithsonian's *American Visions* magazine, "brought with it a fresh compulsion to learn the rest of it . . . I decided to write a book on Robert Johnson under the working title, *Biography of a Phantom*. It evolved as a detective story." That the dead man went by several names makes it that much more suited to the genre. Learning of the death, the gumshoe—McCormick—attempts to uncover the circumstances, which leads to an investigation of the man's life. But this detective has yet to turn over his evidence—after forty-two years of research McCormick's book is still not published.

In the 1970s, McCormick told Guralnick that the book was in the hands of an academic press and a trade press and he simply had to choose between them. Since then, he has said he could not publish until after the murderer's death. In the 1988 article, McCormick claimed his sources feared repercussions if they revealed their information. "They finally spoke when I offered a signed document stating that what they told me would not be published until after their own deaths."

More than forty years since McCormick began making inquiries into Johnson, and more than twenty years since those first substantial clues, McCormick's reputation as the preeminent Johnson authority remains based on trickles of information shared with only a few journalists. His scholarship remains locked up in his files.

The aura of mystery that clings to McCormick befits a Johnson scholar. Much like the power Johnson has gained from the unanswered questions that surround him, McCormick's seclusion has become his strength. Should he release his information—whatever information he has—McCormick becomes a bona fide authority, but at the expense of his mystique. After so many years of essential silence, McCormick's secrecy seems intimately tied to the force that he found in Johnson. In his attempt to master the Robert Johnson myth, the myth may have mastered McCormick.

In 1976, Guralnick visited McCormick while working on a story about Johnson for *Rolling Stone*. It was one of the few times that McCormick divulged any of his research, and in that article, he referred to LaVere's information as "pirated." By putting family members and other sources in touch with one another, McCormick made the work easier for future researchers.

"I had no doubt that he had found the sisters first," says Guralnick, "considerably before Steve LaVere, and that he had made an agreement with them which precluded LaVere from selling the photographs to Columbia. I have no doubt of that today. But what seemed to me to happen after my story came out was that Mack used the story as ammunition. He argued even more vigorously that Columbia had no right to use the photograph without his permission, which they probably didn't—and essentially that was what tied up the album's release for fifteen years."

Neither man made any major moves for the next decade. In 1982, Guralnick published his "Searching for Robert Johnson," initially as an extended essay in *Living Blues* and in 1989 as a book. LaVere wanted Columbia to interpret that article as the fulfillment of McCormick's contract with Thompson to publish her information first, despite the fact that the photographs were not used and McCormick was not the author. Columbia did not agree.

Greed wasn't likely LaVere's original motivation. When he proposed the *Complete Recordings* package in 1973, neither the blues audience nor Robert Johnson's popularity was very large. Johnson wasn't making anybody rich. In the beginning, LaVere was, probably, just a fan—an energetic, obsessive, hustling blues lover. But as Johnson became a bigger part of his life, LaVere began blurring the line between fan and artist. By putting his copyright on the songs and photographs, LaVere owns the Johnson that survived. In his arrangement, Johnson's relations must come to him for their money, as if he were the artist returning from a gig, his pockets jingling.

THE SUN CAME up on LaVere's fortunes the summer day in 1990 that he got a call from Columbia executive Larry Cohn. "He said, 'We want to release the package just the way you envisioned it.' And I said well halle-fucking-luyah, it's about time.

"Since the CBS record has come out," continues LaVere, "it has been very advantageous for [me], because we can now say that CBS recognizes that my publishing company is the legitimate copyright owner. With one big dog like that in our corner, we have a chance at going after some of the other big dogs."

The dogs could be set loose on anybody who covers a Robert Johnson song and does not pay LaVere. Such acts include Cream, Led Zeppelin, Johnny Shines, Cowboy Junkies, Bonnie Raitt, the Kronos Quartet, and John Hammond Jr. Johnson has even been sampled on at least one rap record. When the Rolling Stones covered "Love in Vain," they attributed the song to "Woody Payne." Though obviously not the author, the invention was an attempt to avoid becoming embroiled in copyright disputes. "We have to go after them," says LaVere, whose company has begun receiving royalties, but he won't say from whom. "All sales from this point forward should be contributing to my publishing company."

In 1986, LaVere was approached by *Rolling Stone* about publishing, for the first time, one of his Johnson pictures. "So much time had gone by since Mack and Peter Guralnick initially published that research," says LaVere, "I figured well, why not." When the photo came out and there was no complaint from McCormick, the marketing of the pictures began: calendars, postcards, posters, magazines.

In his attempt to control how the public sees Johnson, LaVere has vigorously pursued payments for the publishing of the photographs. Thus, he has billed *Musician* magazine, which used a photograph and put an illustration of Johnson on their cover. "There's nothing in their article that is a direct promotion of the LP," says LaVere about the cover story. "The emphasis of that article is the influence of Robert Johnson upon the musicians of today." Cartoonist R. Crumb drew an image of Johnson for *78 Quarterly* that also ran on the cover of *Rock & Roll Disc*, an independent, small-press magazine. "Our article was completely a review of the boxed set," says Tom Graves, publisher of *RRD*. "LaVere has sent us confrontational letters with a threatening tone. He implied a suit and told us to contact his lawyer."

R. Crumb received an unsolicited contract for his use of Johnson's image. "LaVere was telling me if I did anything else with this drawing," says Crumb, "I would immediately have to pay him five thousand dollars. He wanted to keep the original drawing I did as part of the deal so he would have exclusive proprietary rights to that. I never gave him any."

CBS professes ignorance of LaVere's actions. According to Columbia spokesman Robert Altshuler, "What LaVere does is entirely between LaVere and who he does it to."

IT WAS BOUND to happen. As the royalties mounted, so would the claimants. On a June 1991 day in the tiny Leflore County courthouse in Greenwood, Mississippi, infighting began among Johnson's relatives. "The court listened to testimony," says attorney Jay Fialkov, who earlier this year represented Annye Anderson, a retired schoolteacher and half sister of Carrie Thompson. "The judge became aware of allegations which suggested a potential dispute concerning who the heirs of Robert Johnson were. It was impossible in one brief hearing to get a full sense of everything that has happened so far concerning the estate and everything that needs to be done. And for that reason, he appointed his chancery clerk as the temporary administrator of the estate."

Craig Brewer is the Greenwood attorney representing the temporary administrator. He has spoken with LaVere's attorney and happily reports that "LaVere was coproducer of the *Complete Recordings* and may have been a corecipient of the Grammy . . . He apparently has a wealth of information about Robert Johnson. LaVere's willing to pay money into the estate, they just don't know who the rightful heirs are."

LaVere further established his benevolence by presenting a sum of money to the court. "[The funds] were tendered on the basis that they represent royalties owed and collected to date by Stephen LaVere," Brewer explains. When asked if the check from LaVere was (as the Columbia source indicated) in the "chunky" six-figure range, Brewer was dumbfounded. LaVere's check to the court: $46,968.39. Brewer said, "It would almost appear that somebody slipped a decimal."

If Brewer considers LaVere a potential source of information, Anderson tends to view him more skeptically. She is contemplating a suit against him.

LaVere explains that mere details delayed his payment to his contractual partners. "There's [been] a matter between me and the heirs that needs to be settled," he says. The "matter" is a third photograph of Johnson, once in McCormick's possession and described in Guralnick's book. "If [Thompson's heirs] have it, I want it," says LaVere, claiming it was mentioned specifically in his agreement with Thompson. "And if they don't have it, then tell me so. But I haven't received any correspondence from the lawyer at all."

"It's just jive, he's just making up a story to justify his grief," responds a lawyer associated with Thompson. "There is no holdup."

The last fair deal has yet to go down. While Thompson's heirs attempt to establish their rights and prepare their case against LaVere, and while those heirs known by McCormick remain a mystery, this writer turned up at least one heir-claimant who knew nothing of either historian when he copyrighted twenty-eight of Johnson's twenty-nine titles in 1973. (The title he overlooked, "Dead Shrimp Blues," was later claimed by LaVere.) Though that is the same year that the Columbia dispute began, Ken Johnson, who says he is the bluesman's grandson, apparently acted independently of both researchers when establishing his Queens, New York–based Horoscope Music Company with the United States Copyright Office.

Ken Johnson may not be entirely reliable. To other people he has claimed Robert Johnson was not his grandfather but his father. Also, he has said Robert Johnson was still alive but horribly disfigured and an embarrassment to the family. Further, four months after its release, he was unaware that Columbia had issued *The Complete Recordings*.

Columbia spokesman Bob Altshuler again: "This company always pays royalties to the person who the royalties are due. Other than that, we don't discuss our royalty payments on any artist."

"CBS IS GENERALLY off the hook," says CBS project coordinator Gary Pacheco. "Steve LaVere, through documents he presented us, assumed responsibility. The agreements give CBS indemnification. We've done a number of things that have proven we have nothing but the most altruistic goals here." The label's good deeds, according to Pacheco: They "get this guy's music heard," an act of charity also known as "selling records." And they gave $17,000 to the fund that erected Johnson's memorial stone.

The owning of the myth. Like the hamster that eats its children to protect them, McCormick will not reveal the identities of the heirs he says he's found. He not only wants to preserve their knowledge for his book, he also wants to protect them from exploitation. But if he is protecting them, he is also depriving them; their information and photographs have been worthless since they met McCormick. His protection parallels LaVere's proprietary notions.

McCormick is reportedly working on a film in Mexico now, while he awaits the death of Johnson's acquaintances. (If anyone knows the whereabouts of a man named Tush Hog or his two daughters, last heard of near St. Louis, conveying the information to McCormick might expedite publication.) *Biography of a Phantom* has no publishing date.

Though Johnson may make LaVere a millionaire, it took the recent Greenwood court hearing for him to even make a token compensation. Ironically, LaVere's selfishness has had a public benefit—the rerelease of the music. McCormick's archives remain his alone, while LaVere makes his bread basket available to the public for an offering.

While talking to him on the phone one day, I asked LaVere something I'd been wondering for a while: How did he choose the name of his publishing company, the name of the concern which collects Robert Johnson's royalties. Considering his role as paymaster to Johnson's heirs, the name LaVere picked, King of Spades, has some unsettling connotations.

He responded immediately, as if he'd already posed the question to himself. "In all of Johnson's words I could find only one reference to him in the third person, and that's in 'Little Queen of Spades.' 'You are the little Queen of Spades and I am the King.' So I thought, well, King of Spades. Makes sense to me."

★ ★ ★

THIS ARTICLE FOCUSED attention on the Johnson case and prompted new reporting from the *Washington Post* and international magazines. But it was light with no heat, no change in the shady dealings between the music business and blues musicians. Many artists, especially from the first half of the twentieth century, had neither the knowledge nor the wherewithal to protect themselves and their families from corporate exploitation. They signed the deal, pocketed small change, and the corporations made the money.

In 1998, seven years after this piece was published, Mississippi courts determined that Robert Johnson's heir was Claud Johnson, a son not born of Johnson's wives. Claud was in his seventies and working as a gravel-truck driver in Crystal Springs, Mississippi. His wife ran a BBQ stand. If the blues had been falling like rain, the weather changed: Claud Johnson received a hefty payment from the escrow account. When he moved his family to a nicer house, he kept his gravel truck, a reminder of his life's hard work. He died in 2015.

Court battles continue, but the publishing money flows steadily to the Johnsons of Crystal Springs. The Mississippi Supreme Court, in 2014, secured their ongoing income from photograph licensing.

Now here's the twist: By creating the publishing company, Steve LaVere created payments that Sony would have to disburse, of which he'd pocket an uncomfortable amount, and then the remainder would wend its way to a family who otherwise would have known no wealth. The corporation keeps less, and one dispossessed family is enriched—collateral benefits of LaVere's work. Later, LaVere sold his King of Spades publishing and it has since changed hands again, its value increasing. LaVere cashed out. The Johnsons of Crystal Springs continue to cash in.

And as for Carrie Thompson, she got the blues. She preserved the photos all those years, shared blood and company with Robert Johnson, empowered LaVere as the presumed heir—until she tried to rescind the contract, or became uncooperative, or was somehow replaced by the Johnsons of Crystal Springs—and all she and her heirs got was LaVere's hundred bucks.

Mack McCormick died in November 2015. His books have yet to be published. Perhaps it was all that potential for proprietary research in blues heaven, but five weeks later Steve LaVere followed Mack's trail.

JUNIOR KIMBROUGH

I'D HEARD OF Junior Kimbrough from the High Water releases that were coming out under Dr. David Evans's auspices at the University of Memphis. I'd seen him perform too, at the Center for Southern Folklore's Memphis Music & Heritage Festivals. The key, however, was I knew never to decline a party invitation.

The accessibility of these happenings never ceases to amaze me. When I was writing *It Came from Memphis*, my then-new friend Danny Graflund told me a line I've since used often: Memphis is the town where nothing ever happens but the impossible always does. Junior Kimbrough's juke joint was an impossible experience, and available every Sunday. A musical nirvana. Rapturous. Plunk in the middle of a social and economic disaster zone. But there it gathered those seeking a stronger jolt, higher wattage, a more intense escape. Like a church, Junior's joint was a room pulsating as one. What a rave must be like but with older people on different stimulants.

Mississippi Juke Joint
Previously unpublished, 2005

Before we'd slammed shut the car doors, a drunk woman came spilling out of Junior Kimbrough's house. Drunk, or maybe crazy. Crazed, certainly. She was shouting, her words indistinguishable, her tone sharp, her finger pointing at our hearts. Her body was doubled over as she jabbed, stumbling and squalling. She ignored others and looked at us, through us, her rampage unrelenting. We three were the only white people in evidence.

Junior's house was in the middle of a cotton field, the cabin a structure only slightly more handcrafted than the long rows into which the field had been furrowed. You could take a wide view and in all that you saw, the house was the only thing that wasn't a cotton plant, its wooden brown stood out against the crop, still green and bursting all around us. It was a home filled with humans, all seeking a state of exalted rapture.

The crazy woman was half-dressed; technically, you could say three-quarters. Her shirt was unbuttoned—or had lost its buttons—and her brassiere was loose. Her head was swathed in a do-rag, her feet slipped into something that once had been house shoes. She was older than forty, but younger than a hundred. And as astonishing as her appearance was, her tone was making the impression: a scolding, a warning, an admonition. It

Junior Kimbrough at home in Holly Springs (not the same location as the cotton field). (Courtesy of Dan Ball)

was so personal, so intimate, that while I couldn't doubt it was at us, I did look behind, expecting to see her children or her sister or someone she knew. But this woman at that moment was knowing no person. She was out of her mind and soon lurching out of our sight, and we entered the door she'd exited anticipating a taste of some of whatever it was she'd had, with a result not dissimilar.

JUNIOR KIMBROUGH AND the whole of the droning north Mississippi sound have become such a part of me that it's hard to remember when I first became aware of it. But around 1988—within the first few months of my return to Memphis (following a decade of only visiting home)—I was riding around Holly Springs, Mississippi, and stumbled upon Aikei Pro's Records Shop, a store with overflowing shelves of blues 45s and LPs run by a storyteller named Mr. Caldwell. The Aikei (pronounced "Ike-ee") had old records in great shape from Chess and Stax and kept current releases from north Mississippi groups, few though the choices might be. And Mr. Caldwell told it like it was, stories that day were about being a black man with blue eyes and the mixed heritages that belie our skin tones.

I returned there with a couple friends visiting from the cosmopolitan Northeast to show them how quaint and charming a small town in Mississippi could be. My Yankee friends finished inside the store before me, and when I came out, they were in casual discussion with one of the locals. He was a big man, like a football player, with an air of quiet violence,

Junior Kimbrough at Aikei Pro's Records Shop, Holly Springs, Mississippi. (Courtesy of Axel Küstner)

Junior Kimbrough could keep the dance floor packed at his famous
house parties, 1994. (Courtesy of Bill Steber)

simmering sexuality, and raucous good times. His eyes were big, like they'd
seen things we wouldn't believe, and though he was welcoming, he also
seemed to have a live 220 current running through him. He was Junior
Kimbrough.

Junior invited us to his house party, to be held Sunday afternoon, the
following day. Giving us directions, he said, would be pointless as his
place was impossible to find; he instructed us to instead ask anyone who
loitered at the Aikei to lead us. So the next day, we did just that, and then
we stopped at the Sunflower grocery to pick up a case of beer, some of
which we gave to the guides as payment. We followed several middle-
aged black men in a pickup truck, making turns on winding roads that
had no visible names until the lead truck slowed in a wooded area, a hand
coming out the passenger window and hooking over the truck's cab, pointing us to the woods on the left. The opening in the trees wasn't apparent
until we'd almost passed it, and the turn in was a hairpin; they'd slowed
dramatically, made sure we caught it. The drive ran down a hill, the curtain of trees thinning to our right, another hairpin turn at the bottom
unfolding into the red dirt field where, floating in its middle, we saw the
house where all the action was.

THE PARTY AT Junior's was in the large front room, and I only recall two
other rooms. A few chairs and a sofa were pushed against the living room
walls, creating as much dance and band space as possible. In the bedroom

to the right, all the other tables, some chairs that didn't fit, lamps, and other furniture were stacked floor to ceiling, leaving only the bed untouched and ready for falling into. Back in the main room, a door at the rear led to the kitchen, but that door was split horizontally. The lower half stayed closed, and behind it was seated a woman, wide and stocky, massive in her density, like she was made from the missing upper door: the house lady. She sold drinks, woke sleeping drunks, and maintained order. No one wanted to cross the house lady.

I have a confession to make. When I first ordered a beer from her— we'd set down our case and all the cans had disappeared as if into a hole in the bottom of the sea, which pleased us (and it didn't bother the house lady, who never had enough beer anyway)—she offered me a choice of canned beer or Junior's homemade fruit beer. I can't imagine why I didn't leap at the opportunity to taste the fruit beer, except perhaps that the words *fruit* and *beer* together were so unexpected—sort of like the time at Mardi Gras in New Orleans when I stumbled upon a woman at a card table in front of a bar; she had a large, clear jug of something soaking in pinkish water, and so startled was I when she said, "Pickled pig lips, fifty cents," that I dug into my pocket, saved from the awful treat by the lack of a quarter (she wouldn't sell just the upper). Fruit beer—in all my visits to Junior's house and his later juke joints, I was never offered it again, and by the time that day I'd loosened my mind enough to go for it, she was sold out. "No fruit beer, just regular." I'm sure I answered, "Yes ma'am."

The band was a trio, with Junior seated on a folding chair, a guy named Cotton on the bass, and the drummer's kit always a hodgepodge, salvaged from the Salvation Army's bin of the unsalvageable; one time a drum was a cardboard box reinforced with duct tape. They had amplifiers for the guitars and a vocal mic, but everything was so close and intimate—the musicians repeatedly pushing revelers off them—that what they played was felt every bit as much as it was heard. Music filled the house like water in an aquarium.

And the music never stopped, the players handing off their instruments and joining the audience. Half the people there were musicians, and they all played all the instruments. Junior played only guitar, and he'd play whenever he felt like it, breaking into the song he was best known for, "All Night Long," as often as he liked. With its familiar opening wail, its gradual build, and then the funky gallop of the song's body, it was the crowd's favorite, and Junior never tired of giving them what they wanted. He could draw the song out for an easy quarter of an hour, and people danced the whole time, with partners or without, whether they were

Junior Kimbrough, playing the blues, 1996. (Courtesy of Bill Steber)

lingering from the last dance, rising at the song's first notes, or lunging up when overtaken by the spirit in midverse.

Everyone danced. This sea of people moved not as one, but like a riptide, and it was amazing how blindingly bright it was outside and how dark within. I once tried to shoot some Super 8 film at Junior's house, but even with the lens all the way open it was barely possible to capture a distinct image. As the afternoon wore on, people passed out in chairs, on the porch, in the bed, and in the field. Might've been the fruit beer.

I RETURNED TO Junior's several times, once with my longtime friend Belinda Killough. "When you told me about Junior's Sunday blues jam," she said after her first visit, "I thought it was going to be in somebody's small backyard with bowls of Fritos and stuff."

Belinda continued, "We must have gotten there about one P.M. or so, after church service, because I remember ladies in dresses with church fans. The crazy lady wore a pair of stretch shorts and a long-line bra, and you said she wasn't even *the same* crazy lady that had been there before.

The band was all young guys wearing Batman T-shirts even though they couldn't afford a movie ticket. We must have stayed there twelve hours."

Soon Junior moved the party into a former barbecue shack called the Chewalla Rib Shack, then to a final location in Chulahoma. A converted church, it was heated by a wood stove. It burned down not long after Junior Kimbrough's death in 1998.

R. L. Burnside lived next to that joint, and he played there often. R. L. and Junior became the heart and soul of Fat Possum Records; they recorded at the juke joint. Though fruit beer was never offered at the Chulahoma place, I did taste all kinds of white lightning, some of which was quite smooth and appealing. More memorable is the worst white whiskey I ever tasted. It was a full-moon night and a group of us were cooling off out front, a mixture of locals and visitors. Two white guys in hunting camouflage opened a jar and passed it around. They were leading a discussion about coon dicks, the penises of raccoons made into necklaces and worn for good luck. I was not interested in the coon dick they offered me, but I did taste their whiskey. I almost gagged, but my scientific impulse won out and I quickly tasted it again to confirm it was as bad

R. L. Burnside outside his home, 1978. (Courtesy of Axel Küstner)

as it had at first seemed, which it was. Its bouquet was of freshly mowed lawn clippings, and it went down like long thin shards of glass, with an aftertaste of rusted barbed wire. "Rusted" may be assigning it too much character.

My own memories get foggy about the end of that night, but Belinda saw it all: "The crazy lady continued to get really drunk and later at night somebody took her in a back room and put some pajamas on her and she came running out like a little kid even though she was full-well grown. She asked me for my lipstick and I gave it to her."

I was there often enough for Junior to recognize me, and I got on a first-name basis and had a couple adventures with Cotton. But I never got to really know my fellow revelers, nor my host. I didn't know their struggles or their loves, their lives, their particular strains of boredom or despair. But each time I went, we were unified in our release from all those things. We all shared equally in escaping with the blues. We all got real real gone.

I LOVE WHAT's in this piece, but I have misgivings about what's not. When I was hanging around, it was for fun—not reporting. I captured the good times, but there was another side. At Junior's, we all escaped into the blues, but our escapes out were not the same. At day's end, I would go home to my comfy bed in an insulated house, romanticizing the missed opportunities of fruit beer. And Junior and all his friends would go home to shacks where the wind blows through.

That first time at Junior's, when I opened that bedroom door and saw all the furniture stacked, I instantly recalled a description of a "rent party" from a college class on the Harlem Renaissance. Tenants who needed to make rent would throw a party where they lived, pushing all the furniture back to allow more room for dancing. Everyone paid at the door and bought food and drink inside, helping the residents raise the payment. Junior's party had its economic purpose too—the house lady sold those drinks (though I don't recall paying to enter). But the party also struck me as a way of reminding the worn and the weary of the reasons for living, a way to reinvigorate the spirit in the face of a week of otherwise abject poverty and grueling manual labor. The thin walls may be poor shelter from the cold winds, but they can still harbor the collective heart, like the blues.

CHARLIE FEATHERS

"No one expects an abstract thinker to come out of rockabilly."
—Ben Vaughn

THIS PROFILE ON Charlie Feathers put me in an ethical quandary, and I didn't come out so clean. I'd read an interview where Charlie gave a startling quote about his theory of Elvis Presley's lineage. The notion was kind of ludicrous, certainly outlandish, and I was, even at the mature age of thirty, taken by the idea of the potential controversy his statement might provoke.

I wanted the quote.

Charlie was about to turn sixty and was, for the first time, going to have a record on a major label. He'd gotten his start at Sun Records in the 1950s and never stopped releasing songs and albums on a variety of small and independent ventures. His dedication to rockabilly endeared him to a select group of pomaded, cuff-jeaned fans the world over, and his remarkable voice expanded that base, slightly. In early 1991, he would have his first major label release, an opportunity like he'd never had.

I drove across town and was having a really great visit with Charlie. We sat in lawn chairs in front of his house, situated in a post–World War

II middle-class neighborhood of modest but sturdy structures. The summer air was unseasonably unoppressive. Charlie was feeling the lift of success when he'd no longer imagined this kind of exposure. He'd been embittered by the music industry—a business that's always looking to toss aside talent and loyalties for the next new thing—and this late-career praise was pleasing him, even if he didn't like to show it.

Ambition was impairing my better angels and I wound the conversation toward his old labelmate Elvis. Charlie had genuinely great musical ideas, but in the wider world, he was distrustful. Functionally illiterate, he had to be wary. Even the previous year's contract signing with the Warner Bros. imprint Elektra / Nonesuch had nearly derailed when Charlie learned it said right there on the contract that there was nonesuch company. But if you'd been ripped off as many times as Charlie Feathers—by the music biz, by show promoters, by the power company and the auto mechanic and every dad-blamed person in the world, you'd be suspicious too.

The Onliest
LA Weekly, August 1991

The Rebel Inn is on Highway 78, once a major thoroughfare linking Mississippi cotton land to the Delta's big city of Memphis. The old motel's neon sign no longer functions properly, and the parking lot these days is more of a teen hangout than a place for weary motorists. James Earl Ray is said to have slept in the Rebel Inn the night before he shot Martin Luther King.

Conspiracy has long haunted Charlie Feathers, who lives on a dead-end street behind the motel. The rockabilly great never really made it, never became the star that might seem natural for a friend and inspiration to Elvis Presley. Feathers's modest house is not very different from any other on the block, but it is worlds away from the stature of Graceland, the mansion of the rock and roll King.

Beneath a shade tree in his front yard, Charlie is seated in a black rocker. Wearing a faded flowered shirt, the brightest ornamentation is the pouch of Red Man chewing tobacco poking through the top of his chest pocket. Despite the fact that it's August, his Christmas lights are still up, the sign of a man thinking about both the past and things to come.

"Rockabilly is the beginning of the end of music," the genre's greatest enthusiast pronounces. "It is the *onliest*. It'll be the last; there's no more after rockabilly."

It's a grand statement with an elusive meaning, but the subject gets Feathers excited, worked up like an evangelist in a gin joint. He is a rockabilly preacher, a fundamentalist when it comes to this blend of country and rock and roll that thrived briefly in the 1950s and has been often revived. Charlie has to pause, partly to gather his thoughts and partly because he's had a lung removed recently (that's why he chews instead of smokes his 'bacca) and he's not supposed to get palpitated. Words frustrate Feathers, they limit him.

"It's–just–no–more–music," he says, his hands punctuating the rhythm of the sentence to drive home the point to his congregation of one. "Rockabilly comes from cotton-patch blues and bluegrass music. Ain't nothing else exciting left, you see. I seen some guys the other day on the television. They're sickening to me. I watch them boys with the big hats on, unh-uhmmm. The world ain't gonna move backwards!"

SOME WOULD SAY Charlie himself needs to study this last statement. His rockabilly cohorts found success when they moved to rock and roll (Elvis, Jerry Lee, Carl Perkins), country (Johnny Cash), and the sappiest pop ("The last band Elvis had was dime a dozen. Get 'em anywhere. He was just singing because he already had it made. The dadgum rockabilly made him."). Charlie stayed with the dadgum stuff, working new ideas into the old genre. He has just released his first ever major label record, part of the initial installment in the distinguished American Explorers series. The album includes an updated version of his "I Forgot to Remember to Forget," which became the back side of "Mystery Train," Elvis's first major hit. (Alas, Charlie sold his ownership in the song when money was tight.)

It is more than thirty-five years since Elvis Presley released his first rockabilly record. "Blue Moon of Kentucky" was a fusion of blues and bluegrass, and Charlie Feathers feels he's never received proper credit—for bringing the song to Elvis, for coaching him on his vocals, for helping fuse the genres. He was hanging out at Sun before Elvis or any of the other hillbilly cats came along, talking shop with Sun founder Sam Phillips and trying to tune in the music both men heard in their heads. Feathers demoed material for the label and wrote songs, including "Gone, Gone, Gone" and "Get With It."

Feathers speaks conspiratorially when discussing why fame has eluded him. Sam Phillips passed on his "Tongue-Tied Jill," so Charlie took it across town to Meteor and had a minor hit. "Sam said he was going to hurt me, and he did," says Charlie. "He said that because I left after Elvis left. He could see hisself going out of business."

The reasoning seems far-fetched; Sun still had Johnny Cash, Carl Perkins, and Jerry Lee Lewis on its roster. But Charlie is ablaze, his face all the redder against a full shock of white hair and thick white sideburns. He accuses Phillips of withholding his best material. "Sam's-got-the-main-cut," he says about songs recorded thirty-five years ago, believing they'd be hits today if Sun would turn them loose.

For the first time in decades, as many people as desire can hear his new album. *Charlie Feathers* is a slam-bang rockabilly record, pairing him with former Sun session men. It's got its feet in the past and its head in the present. "We Can't Seem to Remember to Forget" mourns the passing of rockabilly, Feathers singing, "That time it slipped away / And that's something we don't want to forget." The irony is that Charlie wanted to record it with his son Bubba's band, giving it a more modern punch.

Feathers's voice is itself like a band. The hiccups, yips, and other vocal eccentricities punctuate his lines like guitar fills, adding depth and excitement. He keeps your attention by switching from a growl to a whisper. ("That's your rockabilly when you slow it down, lower it. The dynamics. Music is made to make you sit up, so damn much stuff going on.") His oddest vocals are on "Uh Huh Honey"—he begins in a voice thick and deep, then takes an inspiration from Ralph Armstrong's piano solo and leaps into a tone like helium escaping from a Donald Duck balloon.

But Feathers is not all gimmicks. For the verses to Hank Williams's "I Don't Care (If Tomorrow Never Comes)," Charlie contrasts the weary tone of a downhearted, abandoned man against a tender but propulsive rhythm section (Stan Kesler, a regular Sun bassist, and J. M. Van Eaton, Jerry Lee Lewis's drummer); at the chorus, he gives the song a twist, looking on his loss as a freedom and singing like a new man. Chris Isaak's guitarist could take a few lessons from Roland Janes's swampy vibrato.

Feathers is the first to admit—to insist—that *Charlie Feathers* is not a pure rockabilly album. "Rockabilly ain't got room for drums," he says. "That train song, 'Pardon Me Mister,' me and my son Bubba run through it down there and it was so outstanding with just the rhythm and the electric guitar. They put the drum on it and killed it." All songs deserve such delightful and exciting deaths.

BENEATH THE TREE in his front yard, Charlie has turned the rocker so as not to spit tobacco juice on his guest. He is still talking about the possibilities in rockabilly, illustrating it with a dream project of recording an album of ten different versions of "Roll Over Beethoven." "They say

Charlie Feathers at home on his porch, relaxed and comfortable. (Courtesy of Trey Harrison)

[on the *Charlie Feathers* liner notes] I won't do a song twice the same way. Yes I will, if they say that's the way they want it. I'll do it another way if they don't say nothing. I could cut 'Roll Over Beethoven' ten different ways with ten different voices. I can mess around with a song, man."

"He's so far into music that he is, in my opinion, a genius," says Ben Vaughn, who produced the new album. "Like we think of jazz greats: Sun Ra or Mingus or Monk. No one expects an abstract thinker to come out of rockabilly. But that's exactly what Charlie is. He's never given up on rockabilly, and he continually redefines it in his mind."

Feathers remains a devoted apostle of Elvis Presley, despite his contentions of unrequited appreciation. Challengers to the throne are met with disdain. "Elvis sang so damn hard, man. People think of the Beatles and all that—*ohhhhnnn*. Any mama that washes dishes in the kitchen could sing the same way the Beatles did. 'La la la.' It's not singing from down here [the guts]. They could stand there and sing thirty days and thirty nights, and never hurt theyselves."

Charlie pauses, and when he continues, his voice is lower, softer, as if someone might overhear. He told Ben Vaughn that Elvis was half African American, and he tells me, "The truth never came out about Elvis. I don't believe Vernon was his daddy. He kicked Vernon out of the house the minute his momma died. Elvis wasn't black-headed, you know that. He had albino hair, yellow as a baby duck. He'd play a show, the minute the show would end, he'd run to the bathroom, wet his hair down with water. If it started drying, it'd kick up like a little yellow baby duck. That's the truth.

(Courtesy of Trey Harrison)

And his nose was down just like that, flat. I think he done something to his nose later on. I don't want to say too much about it."

Beads of sweat have formed on Feathers's forehead, whether from the afternoon sun or the heat of the conversation. Rosemary Feathers, Charlie's wife, has served us sweet tea and the ice is now melted in the glasses. A bird dog in the neighborhood is baying and it sounds like a car alarm. "I'll always write songs," says Charlie. "I'll be laying in there and I know damn well I'm asleep, but a whole damn song will go through my mind. I open my eyes, by the time I get up, damn, somehow or another it'll slip away from me. There must be another world beyond this one. There's got to be, man, I don't understand why I can't quit."

In this other world, rockabilly is king and Charlie's ideas are respected and appreciated. It's a world where Feathers is Elvis and Elvis lives behind the Rebel Inn. The tone of his voice reveals his conviction.

"Craziest damn thing I ever seen is this music business," he says. "You don't think nobody cares, and yet you meet people from all over the damn world; they come here and they care and they know. I don't understand it, man, I do not understand it." Then he gets a twinkle in his eye and the waning excitement ratchets up a notch. "I got a song that Dean Martin could sing and it would be a smash hit. I got one right now that Jerry Lee—I went out there and *give* it to him. He never listened to it, he never heard that son of a bitch. In two weeks' time, I guarantee that he would have a number one hit in the nation . . ."

★ ★ ★

CHARLIE PHONED ME immediately after the piece had run. In Memphis, the local weekly ran it as the cover story. He hemmed and hawed, mumbled some. I could tell he was bothered and tried to draw him out. He said, "You'd better talk to my wife."

Rosemary Feathers got on the phone and gave me what for. She didn't like the way I'd presented some of Charlie's ideas about Elvis's parentage. Did he say that to you? she demanded about his assertion that Elvis was half-black, her question getting exactly to the crux of the matter, and I admitted that he did not, he only implied it. I drove there immediately. Charlie was in the front yard on a lawn chair beneath the tree chewing tobacco. Aw it's awright, he told me, and I apologized again for my slight. Rosemary had appeared outside, and I can't recall if she also said it was all right, but the way she stiffly walked back inside let me know that it wasn't.

Eight years later, a small label in Austin, John Fahey's Revenant, compiled and issued most of the singles from Charlie's early career. Titled *Get With It: Essential Recordings (1954–69)*, it is a beautiful package, with a booklet featuring many photos, and liner notes from Peter Guralnick, Nick Tosches, Colin Escott, and Jim Dickinson. The two CDs present Charlie's genius in a shimmering light. His voice, his voice, his goddamn voice. It sounds heavenly, it sounds Hawaiian, it's a violin, a saxophone, it's a perfectly tuned instrument that he lets waft in the warm breeze. The fiddle bow draws across the strings, the metal slide on the pedal steel yodels with glissandos, and Charlie pinches his vocal cords, managing a high pitch from the bottom of his gut:

> *I've been deceived*
> *There's no use denying*
> *I was fooled by kisses*
> *Your sweet talk and your lying*

You can throw around your comparisons to Hank Williams and Bill Monroe, but you don't need to know the sound of anybody or anything except for birds singing in trees to appreciate the purity of Charlie's voice. He's about art, not about blasting rave-up energy. Charlie Feathers vocals are sculptures.

Charlie, built stocky and broad, what you might call a powerhouse, could be feisty and uncooperative. He'd been through the record business ringer, a major talent who managed not to get real heard. He got early guitar tips from Junior Kimbrough, a bluesman who would achieve prominence in the 1990s. As kids, they both hung around the Slayden, Mississippi, cotton gin where the older Junior showed Charlie some licks. When Charlie was nine, he saw bluegrass greats Bill Monroe and Clyde Moody perform in a tent.

The blues and the bluegrass set him up perfect for Sam Phillips, who had recorded Howlin' Wolf and Junior Parker, and would soon find Elvis Presley and Johnny Cash. Charlie was at Sam's Sun Records in the very early days. He could be cantankerous; not being able to read or write compounded his frustrations. He didn't feel like Sam gave him the proper push, and Charlie went through Meteor, King, and some smaller labels, even winding up with Sam Phillips again at Holiday Inn Records. The music was great throughout Charlie's career, the distribution was not. He jumped around a lot.

With this new release, I wanted to visit Charlie again, but I was intimidated by my past errors, and by Charlie's wife, Rosemary. I needed the connection that my friend, photographer Trey Harrison had—he had the power of the pig. "After the Revenant release I called him up," Trey relates, "and talked to him about coming to his house to make some pictures. He was resistant, and he said, 'You got to talk to my manager.' While I had him, I mentioned this duplex where I used to live, and that Charlie's son Ricky lived on the other side. Charlie said, 'Ain't that where Ricky had that pig?' I said, 'Yeah, Ricky and I buried that pig in the backyard.' Charlie goes, 'Why'nt you come over tomorrow about ten o'clock.'" It was set. I'd ride with Trey.

Charlie lives in a small post–World War II-era house in a neighborhood right off the Memphis highway that leads to the north Mississippi hill country where he was born. He's lived there long enough that people driving by slow down and call his name. He greets them all with a wave, and sometimes a few words.

"You seen Marshall?" one asks.

"Ain't seen Marshall," Charlie answers.

As the car drives away, Charlie says, "That boy Marshall, he's messed up on drugs."

We sat in the living room for a while. Charlie wasn't much interested in talking about old songs. But he was enthusiastic about the duplex. One morning, Trey found his front door open and his six-year-old son seated on the porch next to Charlie Feathers, who was wearing big pink slippers and had just come out of the hospital, where one of his lungs had been removed. Trey did not interrupt their discussion.

Charlie also remembered sitting on that duplex porch. He faced an awning across the street that he'd hung when he worked for an awning company. "Would have been in the forties," he told Trey. Rosemary's voice piped up from the other room: "It was the fifties."

Charlie was ready for a chew, so we retired outside. He had an old wooden rocking chair on his porch that hadn't moved for a thousand years. Charlie sat in it and reached for his pouch of Red Man chewing tobacco. Trey reached for his camera.

"I wouldn't stand there," Charlie told Trey. "That's my spitting spot."

Trey took several giant steps in the other direction, and then Charlie settled in. "A chewing man attracts women like no other," Charlie said. "They just swarm you, man. Women love it. I think it's the smell or something."

Charlie was relaxed. His Red Man was handy, his previous pouch twisted and empty nearby. He talked about fast-pitch softball and drag racing. In passing, he mentioned that the rockabilly era was very competitive. "It was a style," he explained, almost a formula to which songs had to adhere. Trey asked him what he thought when he first heard Chuck Berry. "All our jaws dropped," Charlie said, "when we heard his guitar."

Trey snapped some photographs. I mostly observed. It was August, and hot, with Charlie sometimes shooing away insects, saying, "I guess they want their picture taken." After about half an hour, Charlie stood. He'd loaded up that spitting spot; it was all wet. He said, "Well I guess you got it by now." We thanked him. He said to Trey, "I'll tell Ricky hi for you. I'm gonna go sit in the air-conditioning."

Less than two weeks later, Charlie Feathers suffered a stroke and fell from the rocking chair. Several days later, on August 29, 1998, he died. The funeral was held in Holly Springs, with a Memphis burial. There was no Charlie Feathers Day. The funeral wasn't broadcast live on the radio. Celebrities did not rush to town. Charlie was buried like he lived: surrounded by those who loved him.

AFTER THE PERIOD covered by the Revenant CDs, Charlie Feathers released occasional recordings on a variety of labels in a variety of countries. He traveled to Europe, where audiences appreciated what Americans had dismissed.

Dean Blackwood, from the Revenant label, remembered preparing for *Get With It* by going through tapes and tapes and tapes Charlie had in a closet. "He was worn out and so was I. We didn't expect to find things quite so consequential. But we found the tracks he recorded with Junior Kimbrough, which are included in the package."

The Revenant release came about two months before his death. "He was excited by the response," says Blackwood. "He wouldn't admit to it,

Ricky Feathers in the front yard of the duplex, frying a late-night supper.
(Courtesy of Trey Harrison)

and he groused and grumbled, but he was excited to have people care. Whatever role he did or didn't have with the Sun sound, he's the real deal. When it comes down to what's there in the groove, he's as good as anybody that ever did it."

TREY SAYS RICKY Feathers used to go fishing all day, and when he'd come home at night, he'd fry fish on the duplex's front porch, shaking it up with flour in a brown paper sack to coat it. "He had a big metal bowl full of oil and he ran a line from a propane tank in the back of his pickup truck. He always parked right in the front yard. It was a red truck, with flames painted on it."

Ricky had learned hospitality at home. I remember the smell of food in Charlie's house, and I can visualize Rosemary in the kitchen. Their house seemed real comfortable, everybody happy and surrounded by good scents. Seems to me it was pies, but it may have been fried fish.

JAMES CARR

Vocalist James Carr was revered in Japan, Europe, all over the world—except at home, where he was just another minority dude on welfare. When my friends at Easley-McCain Recording alerted me that he was coming in to record, I landed an *LA Weekly* assignment and made the ten-minute drive to James's garden apartment. There was no garden, not a flower to be seen; all the doors opened from a common exterior walkway that overlooked a train track. James was pleased to have company, to be recognized by a Memphian for his artistic merits. I was honored to give him that recognition.

James was known to suffer from mental health issues. I'm unaware of any formal diagnosis, but in my encounters with him, it always looked like he needed medication or was on something heavy (and not necessarily prescribed). The recording sessions proved both thrilling and disturbing—it was magnificent to hear him break open his voice when he would, and it was unsettling to see how, echoing the words of one of his earlier hits, messed up his mind was.

Way Out on a Voyage

LA Weekly, May 22–28, 1992

When it was built in the 1950s, Memphis's Mid South Building was probably stylish and sleek. Today, the blocky turquoise exterior pales next to the snap of the nearby fast-food joints. The elevator moves slowly to the third floor. The hallway to the Goldwax Records office feels institutional, with no natural light and a musty smell. The tiled floor reflects the dim ceiling lights. The yellow paint is not sunshiney.

The walls of the office are mostly bare, the blue carpeting subdued. The fax machine in the corner seems like a futuristic anachronism. Only the large coffee table littered with music magazines indicates the nature of the office's business. That, and the two men who now run the company, Elliott Clark and Quinton Claunch.

Quinton Claunch founded Goldwax in 1964, at the same time that nearby Stax Records was breaking out with Otis Redding. By then,

Quinton Claunch's Blue Seal Pals were a radio country and western band, not unlike the Slim Rhodes Band, seen here on their 1950s Memphis TV show. (Radio was much less of a production.) (Courtesy of Preservation and Special Collections Department, University Libraries, University of Memphis)

Claunch was established in the local scene as a radio musician, Sun session man, and producer of regional hits. Though he's played and performed all his life, Claunch would be the first one in a crowd of a thousand people you'd assume was *not* in music. Coke bottle glasses and arms crossed uncomfortably, he speaks in a Mississippi drawl that is at once rushed and clunky. His tan polyester pants and plaid shirt are more suited to his forty-three and a half years as a tristate supply company salesman, peddling steel products, heating and air-conditioning supplies, and sheet metal. Nothing about him indicates a man who discovered and produced some of the greatest soul voices ever recorded. Claunch's Goldwax originals included the Ovations, who achieved brief fame with "It's Wonderful to Be in Love"; Percy Milem, whose "I Slipped a Little" was recently revived as a beach music hit; and Ollie Nightingale, a vocalist who later had modest success on Stax. Some of O. V. Wright's early material belongs to Goldwax as well, including "That's How Strong My Love Is," which was promptly covered by Otis Redding at Stax. Goldwax has an impressive roster, but what gives it real weight is the presence of James Carr.

Carr's place in soul music history is assured with his 1967 original version of "The Dark End of the Street," the version to which all others are still compared:

> *I know time is gonna take its toll*
> *We have to pay for the love we stole*
> *It's a sin and we know it's wrong*
> *Oh, but our love keeps coming on strong*
> *Steal away*
> *To the dark end of the street*

It's one of pop music's great cheating songs, a full concession to the truth, no justification, just continued intent. Carr's deep voice is tremulous, conveying the difficulty of pursuing the wrong, and his dedication to doing so.

James Carr is often referred to as the World's Greatest Soul Singer, though certainly other great soul singers are more renowned. From the mid- to late 1960s, he established himself with sad songs, singing with desperation, like what his life depended on was gone and what was left was these songs.

Like many of his peers, Carr has been influenced by the gospel tradition. Unlike Otis Redding, however, he is not a roller and shaker whose energy reflects the hand–clapping and swaying of the choir. Nor, like Sam and Dave, does he work into a frenzy through call-and-response. Carr has always been a quiet person, and his best work is with slower material, ballads. His father was a Baptist preacher, and one imagines Carr as a youth in church, eyes trained on his father, observing the hysteria but absorbing the solemnity.

Goldwax had just gotten started in 1964 when Claunch met Carr, who had yet to release a record. "About midnight one night, there came a knock on my door," recalls Claunch. "I opened the door and there stood three black guys. Roosevelt Jamison, James Carr, and O. V. Wright. They said, 'Man, we got some tapes we'd like for you to hear.' They didn't make an appointment or nothing, they just knocked on my door. They had their little tape recorder, portable, and I said come on in, and we sat right down in the middle of my living room floor and, man, we started playing those dang tapes of O. V. Wright and James Carr, and I really got hooked then." Goldwax released Carr's first two singles that year.

Carr and Wright had been singing spirituals together in the Redemption Harmonizers, and Jamison was enlisted to help them cross over to the more popular and lucrative soul music; the gospel group's manager did not truck with the secular world. Jamison is a tall man with a soft voice, and he exudes courtesy. He composed Carr's "That's How Strong My Love Is," which the Rolling Stones also soon covered. Jamison remains devoted to Carr, despite being ousted as his manager in 1966. That's when they were appearing at the Apollo Theater in Harlem. "I really became conscious of his imbalance right after he started working on the road," says Jamison. "When we were in New York, James told me he was going to sign with Phil Walden and Larry Uttal [a soul music label head]. Phil managed Otis Redding, and they promised to make him bigger than Otis. Later, I went up to Phil and Larry's office, and they gave me $3,200 for James's contract. I came downstairs and gave James $1,600 and told him he better hold on to it, because I didn't know which way it was going from then on, but I was going back home."

A couple months passed before he heard from Carr. "After they pushed me out, James got super sick and he came to me. He always kept my number in his mind, and if he was lost at an airport, drifting around the streets, wandering around, he would call and ask me why wasn't I with him."

Jamison's voice becomes hushed as he finishes this story. "He managed to make it to my house one cold morning. There was somebody knocking on the door, and my wife asked about it. When I went to the door, snow

James Carr. (Courtesy of Tav Falco)

was everywhere, and he was sitting down on the steps. He said, 'Man, I kept looking for you and looking for you, where you been so long?' "

WHEN ELLIOTT CLARK got involved in revitalizing Goldwax in the mid-1980s, he assumed James Carr was dead. Clark, an avuncular black man in his fifties, is the label's director; Quinton Claunch, a decade older and white, now serves as president. Put these two in the same room and they will fill it up. Clark laughs like your best friend, and his demeanor says he's seen it all and knows that laughing is better than crying. "Million seller" dots his conversation, the way veteran music biz people talk. Clark has managed soul artists, produced tours, promoted concerts, and owned labels.

James Carr is a priority for the new Goldwax. Claunch and Clark need a hit and, like forty-niners, they believe there's still gold in them hills. Claunch knows better than others how mental illness has dogged Carr's career, so he's approached the prospect of new work with care. "In 1990," says Claunch, "I decided to do a demonstration thing with him, see if he could still sing. Rather than spend a lot of money, I figured I'd go to a little studio down in Iuka, Mississippi. So I picked James up every Saturday morning for eight weeks. If I'd known he was going to sound that good, I would have used real musicians." The result was *Take Me to the Limit*, not a great record—synthesizer backing tracks—but it proves that Carr still has a voice, and that, after twenty years, he can even create feeling from a lifeless keyboard program. The new Goldwax is ready to invest further in Carr. They have pulled master tapes from older, previously released songs on other artists; the band tracks are strong but the vocals aren't, so they're going to replace the old vocals with new ones by James Carr, inexpensively creating a new album.

Claunch is working at Easley-McCain Recording, which is the first structure in Memphis built from the ground up to be a recording studio. It was designed for hitmaker Chips Moman—he produced Elvis's "Suspicious Minds," King Curtis's "Memphis Soul Stew," and hits by Wilson Pickett, Neil Diamond, and dozens of others—and he co-wrote and engineered

Carr's "The Dark End of the Street." The Bar-Kays, when they filled 1980s dance floors, owned the studio for several years after Moman; under Doug Easley and Davis McCain, it has been the site for albums by Lydia Lunch, Alex Chilton, and other perverse underground characters. The studio maintains a somewhat obsolete 16-track tape machine and that's the format of Goldwax's tapes from the 1970s and '80s. When I walk in, the equipment is being properly dusted off. James Carr is sitting behind a cloud of tobacco smoke in the corner.

The oxides on the old tapes have deteriorated, and while the engineers are threading the machine, Claunch launches into an explanation of how he's baked the tapes with a light bulb for seventy-two hours to make them playable. The control room is not small, but between the number of people and the frenetic explanation that nobody quite understands, it's getting claustrophobic.

The first baked tape is loaded. It plays fine, and a soft hum wafts from the smoky corner of the control room. By the second verse, the hum has assumed more definite characteristics, and by the next chorus, James Carr is belting out the words like he's about to audition for the New York Metropolitan Opera. In the half hour of setup time, the music has focused him.

Carr, fifty, is handsome in his sports jacket, though he is a wisp of a man. He has high cheekbones, thinning hair, and extremely long fingernails. In the corner with cap and sunglasses, he looks like a movie star.

Ready to record, Claunch sends Carr out onto the studio floor. Except for a spotlight over the one microphone, the room is dimmed. Carr puts on headphones and stands in place—there's no music yet, and it's hard to tell whether it's Carr there or just his shadow. When the tape rolls, he nods his head, coming in on cue and singing the entire song in one take. Claunch tells him that it was good, but he wants to do it again. Carr sings it several more times, usually all the way through, and the improvement is the difference in how a car runs if it's driven on a cold engine or has a chance to warm up.

The overdubs go quickly. Claunch occasionally pushes Carr, waving his arms from the control room and telling him to give it more punch. The spoken direction he gives is "Put more James Carr in it" or "Give me some more of that preacher." When the track is done, Claunch asks, "Think you can do any better?" Carr declines; he's done singing that one.

Everyone is pleased. If Carr's voice is legendary, so are his depressions. At the last of the original Goldwax sessions in 1969, Claunch had him recording in Muscle Shoals, Alabama. "We had four good songs lined up, including 'To Love Somebody.' And that's the only damn song we got on the session. He just sat up there and looked. Man, I wanted to take a bottle and knock him off that stool. Time was going, we got all them high-priced musicians, and we finally got that one song. I don't see how he ended up singing as good as he did, but, man, he sang the whole thing through, didn't have to overdub or nothing. And we didn't get anything else, didn't get nothing."

While they are cuing up the next song, Carr intently smokes Kools in the control room, pulling drags that leave half-inch coals glowing. So far, the session's been a piece of cake. If the first track was not a hit, it was suitable filler, which is all Claunch and Clark intend it for. They are anticipating a James Carr series, fleshing it out with more of these old masters. Their series will mix the good with the not as good, keeping Carr visible for some time to come, and generating steady income for the company.

Trouble starts when the second song rolls. Carr can't remember the words, and after several tries, Claunch is getting steamed. "I gave him these two songs to learn a month ago," he says, "and I told him we wouldn't go in 'til he was ready. He told me he knew 'em, but he don't know this one."

Carr sings words out of order, repeats lines already sung, and the song lacks not only feeling but also sense. Take after take, the producer hears his artist almost get it. After nearly an hour, I'm sent out on the floor to feed him lyrics, saying them aloud during the musical break that precedes each line. But the lyrics I've accumulated are from the jumbled mess Carr's been singing. He misses the cue for the first line, one he'd previously gotten every time. Communication between the control room and the floor gets mangled by the frustration, and James and I are not always sure what verse they're playing. For two hours, Claunch plows ahead, line by line, and finally a finished take is pieced together. Whatever merits the first song had, even as filler, this one lacks.

On a break in the lobby, Carr is calm, though I may be projecting my own sense of relief. The cloud of smoke, the sunglasses, the reticence, even his kidding about the role I've just played—somehow it seems he knows everything that's happened, even orchestrated it. Claunch and Clark have had enough and they shuttle him out the door. The sudden silence that fills the studio is broken by our nervous laughter.

AFTER ANOTHER DIFFICULT recording session, I arrive at the Goldwax office with mixed feelings. I've been bothered by an impression of small-time graft, of men in the know trying to squeeze one last hit from someone out of the know. Something to retire on. Their conversation doesn't clarify their intentions.

"I dare to say, if he got a hit record right now, he couldn't handle it," says Claunch. "If he had a million dollars today, a month from now he wouldn't have a nickel."

"So why," I ask, "are y'all trying to help him have a hit?"

Clark answers. "We thought that we could help him. Most of the reasons for people being in a bad environment is because they don't have the finances to support anything other than that. But if you got him in the right environment, I really believe he could come back."

"I've been knowing him since he was nineteen years old," says Claunch. "Thirty years. And I just think where he could be—in [the wealthy suburb of] Germantown in a mansion. Rather than skid row. He's got talent."

Clark: "But I just don't think he could handle it. Naw, naw."

For the past eighteen months, Claunch and Carr had been in almost daily contact, culminating, last April, with Carr's first New York engagement in perhaps two decades. Claunch drove him up, got him to the rehearsal on time, kept him away from the bar before the gig, and didn't let him get sidetracked with women during the evening. His performance at Tramps—a live band, familiar songs, an appreciative audience—was a personal and professional triumph.

Returning to Memphis, Claunch sat in Carr's kitchen and paid him, heard Carr say he was going to help his sister cover some bills. Then Carr vanished. Three weeks later when he called, he was broke: "He didn't even have no money to buy no cigarettes," Claunch says. "From now on, we're giving the money to his sister."

"Before 1990, he was gone, nobody knew about James," says Clark, "but we've got him notoriety. They're calling from all over the world. We put James in all the major magazines, bought ads, journalists wrote good articles on him, gave him good reviews. Here's a man who could make a half a million dollars a year right now."

"I think it's a physical problem," says Claunch. "He's on medication, and man he goes off somewhere for three or four days and don't take his medicine, he starts sliding back."

"If he stays on his medicine," says Clark, "he's just A1. What's so frustrating is, when we've got him set to come back, all it takes is a good record and the man is set for life. We maybe can get another good song, but he can't make that transition back to reality. When you're playing with the big boys, you can't screw around. When I was a kid growing up in the country, they'd shoot you for going in the watermelon patch."

James Carr. (Courtesy of Tav Falco)

Claunch: "One of my neighbors caught a couple guys in the watermelon patch; he brought the double-barrel out there, made them eat two watermelons, rind and all."

Clark: "So if you didn't plant it, don't pick it."

Claunch: "'There's the watermelons, just have at it. When you done eatin' that one, you're gonna get that 'un too.'"

Clark: "That's business. A lot of people don't understand that. This is the music business, and the ones that's making it, they do business. It's not so much talent as it was back then. It's hype. Like those *Billboard* charts. Half of those records are hyped to number thirty anyway. Ninety percent of 'em. You get above there, then you got a record. All those forties—" Elliott Clark laughs hard. "When you start getting up in those twenties—" again, laughter.

"Why do you think Crest sells so much toothpaste," asks Claunch. "Ain't no better than Pepsodent."

"Look at Coca-Cola," says Clark. "Got to promote, *got* to promote."

"I really feel sorry for him," says Claunch. "What he could have done. He can't hardly write his name, but he done it."

JAMES CARR IS waiting for me outside his apartment, ready for our lunch appointment at a nearby greasy spoon. His eyes are focused. I can imagine what he was like appearing at Claunch's home in the middle of the night. You might just think he was quiet.

At CK's Kitchen, he chooses a booth next to the large picture window, our images reflecting. He discusses his New York gig, and he's pleased. He tells me that he and Claunch recently wrote a song together; he can't remember what it's about, but, "I know Quinton can think of it; he'll never forget." And he laughs.

"I've been learning songs and recording them," he continues. "I really like sentimental songs, I can really feel sentimental songs. But I've been recording all types, country-western, blues, rock and roll. Sometimes the band puts the tracks down when I'm not there. I like for the band to be there. You can get together more of it, knowing what everybody is gonna do and knowing what you gonna do too. But if it's already done, you just have to catch ahold to it and go on and do it."

"Dark End of the Street," he says, was cut live with a band. I wonder aloud what makes that song so good. "It's really simple," he says. "It's really a simple song. Just sing it the way you talk." And then James Carr sings the whole first verse and chorus of his biggest hit, with plates clattering in the background, silverware falling on the floor, and conversations at nearby tables uninterrupted. With each line, he makes our presence in the diner more ridiculous; this voice should be on big stages. When I think he's through, he continues, and I imagine that the whole diner will be suddenly still, then burst into applause. I'll look at the newspaper on the counter and the headline will read, JAMES CARR IS BACK. People will know.

He finishes singing and waits a beat. "It's just easy," he says, "and I arranged it by the way I read it, the way I read the words." Our food plates clatter onto the table.

Carr makes eyes at a girl seated in a booth across from us, and also at our waitress. "If I had a hit and made a lot of money," he says, "I'd put it in the bank. I don't know if I need a house, but I know I need a place of my own. Can't have no privacy living with my sister. Whenever I get ready to do something, I have to go to a hotel. So I might get me an apartment, but I think I'd rather stay at the hotel where them womens be at."

In the course of our conversation, I ask him about a notorious 1979 Japanese tour, a comeback event that, despite several good performances, is notorious for the one gig where he stood on stage catatonic, unable to perform. "I really wasn't ready," he answers, and his tone is definite. "We didn't have nothing really right, me and the band. We just thought about some songs we could do, but I don't think it was what they were playing. I sung my heart out, but it wasn't that good."

Roosevelt Jamison remembers the Japan tour. "I've got the tape, and it's not as bad as they said. One of the shows he couldn't finish, but he finished the others. He was sick as a dog over there, mentally and physically. He had a fever and was stopped up in his chest, his throat was sore." When he continues, he is hushed, reverential, slowly building back up to a fatherly bluster. "I saw James on that stage being whupped, but he was too much of a champion to give up. I could feel his agony and pain out there. His temperature was sky high, his chest was clogged up. But he stayed there and he took the beating, and I was proud of him. It made him a champion, made him realize that all the good that the stage had been to him, he also owed the stage something."

Jamison's story reminds me of an earlier conversation, from the day after I first met Carr. I'd expressed concern about his condition and Jamison told me that Carr was fine, he'd just been doing a little drinking earlier that night and was quiet. This deflection made it seem like Jamison felt himself responsible for Carr, like he was a coach refusing to admit his champion's weakness. Having invested his life in the singer's career, maybe Jamison needs Carr every bit as much as Carr needs his longtime friend.

Quinton Claunch has made a similar investment. Carr quit his job on an assembly line making tables when he started performing in clubs thirty years ago; music is all he knows, and he's made his best music with Claunch.

And when I'm up close to Carr, his clear love for Claunch and all they've done together apparent, I think that what looks from a distance like graft is also the fundamental nature of the record business: Claunch has had success exploiting talent, and Carr has had success from Claunch's exploitation. They've both signed up for another round.

JAMES CARR TODAY doesn't see himself as the man who made the Japanese tour, or the man who sang the early hits. He looks in the mirror often, as if seeking to confirm his presence. Coming back from his years of emptiness—which, despite his good days now, are certainly not over—has made him a different person. "Lost in a dream," he says about the past twenty years. "Way out on a voyage."

In the car after lunch, I show Carr a photograph of himself when he was about twenty-five. He looks at it and is silent. "All I am," he finally says, "is a voice."

Then he tells me a story, in the same strong tone he's held all day.

"After I was born I went to sleep and I woke up other people," says James Carr.

"What do you mean you woke up other people?"

"Some of them was parading, some of them was performing, some of them was doing actions in movies, stuff like that. So I woke up with them and carried on their duty, their performing. For that short period of time, when I was first born.

"They put me to sleep, and I woke up then, woke up in midair, in rain, woke up the rain, the rain was hurting, hurting me, yeah it was hurting me, it was hurting, I could feel it. Snow. Stuff like that."

He continues. "I was hurting too. I could feel the rain hurting, but it wasn't really me. I was there, in sight and soul and everything, but my body wasn't there. My body was at home."

Home is where we are, and Carr hits me up for some cash. Then, money in hand, he asks for a ride to the corner store, where he buys a quart of beer. As he exits the store, he pauses and asks me, "Do you want a beer?" I don't, and I drive him back, to home, where body and soul can rest.

That ending—there's more to it. After that meal, we were in my car, still in the diner's parking lot. I pulled out the album *World's Greatest Soul Singer*, which has a portrait photo of him on the cover, and, not thinking too much of it, I asked where the photo was taken. The fall through the looking glass came then. I couldn't print it while James was alive—he had too much to overcome (I had learned *something* from my Charlie Feathers experience). James died in 2001, and I hope that sharing this now shows a little of what was going on behind the sunglasses that were clouded in smoke. Myself, I keep going back to it, trying to catch ahold of something.

ROBERT GORDON: Where was that photo taken?
JAMES CARR: At a recording studio on Chelsea and Hollywood in Memphis. That's where I recorded "You've Got My Mind Messed Up," some other songs. I don't feel like the same person that I was when I had this picture made.

RG: Do you feel like you're the same person you were when you went to Japan?
JC: Yeah, I'm the same person.

RG: But not the same as this one?
JC: No. *[Pause]* Do you believe another person can switch bodies with you?

RG: I've thought about it.

JC: Do you believe it? Well I do. I believe it.

RG: Did it happen to you?

JC: Yeah, at the airport.

RG: What happened?

JC: Well, there was a guy there that looked just like me, and I was in New York at the photo company, and they said, "We gonna steal you." I didn't say nothing, and somebody I walked by, I walked by, and it looked like something switched us. And uh, and I said, "Gyat damn," did like that, "Shit." Then myself started running, said, "You'll never get this back." *[Laughs]*

RG: Wait a minute. This was in the airport?

JC: No, I was leaving from the airport. I was on my way to Jamaica. I met them, and the guy that look like I do now. And this guy got money, had his picture on it. Looked sorta like I did. They told me they were gonna steal me, tried to get me not to go, but I didn't pay no attention.

RG: Okay hold on, man.

JC: Because I didn't know nothing about that kind of stuff.

RG: So I'm confused now.

JC: I heard him telling me they'll be waiting on me at the airport. Going to Jamaica. Mm hm.

RG: And there was a photo studio.

JC: No, this was in New York.

RG: The guy who looked like you?

JC: Yeah.

RG: He said he was going to steal you away?

JC: Yeah, he said, "We gonna steal you."

RG: He told you that in the airport?

JC: No. Yeah, he told me that at the airport too, but they hadn't done it then, you know.

RG: Where did they do it?

JC: When I got back to Memphis and passed by this barbershop. No, it was in Miami. There was three of them, it was two of 'em. And they called me down, said, "Come'ere." I was upstairs at the hotel. I came down, they had on suits like mine. One of them hollered, "Switch 'em." And they switched us. I said, "Gyat damn." That hurt my feelings, because he didn't feel too good. Then again, it happened when I was on my way to somewhere, and I come walking down Florida Street, passed by the barbershop and they switched us. And I was really sick then, whoever it was was sick. I said, "Gyat damn." Then I heard them say, "Put this in 'im, he won't be sick." So they put it in me and I wasn't sick. But I just couldn't make it, and I would walk down the street and I turned around and went the other way. I think it was a woman, though.

RG: That they switched you with?

JC: Yeah.

RG: So when they switched you, did you ever switch back?

JC: Not since I've been looking this way, I never switched back. But they said they'd be waiting on me.

RG: Wow, man, that's a pretty wild story.

JC: It's hard to believe, but it happened.

RG: So when they switched you, they left your voice with you?

JCL Yeah. Seems like that's all I am, a voice.

RG: I want to go somewhere and let you tell me that story again. In order. Is that all right?

[He nodded, and we drove to the apartment that James shares with his sister. A sheer curtain covered the large window, but it was gloomy inside. We sat in the living room.]

RG: So when did this happen, about how long ago?

JC: It's been about, um, it's been a pretty good while. That's the reason I stopped singing for a while, 'til I got myself back together.

RG: So when they switched, what did they switch?

JC: Body.

RG: Why do you think they wanted you?

JC: Their body was running down, I guess. Something wrong with 'em, I guess. I don't know. I really don't know. I wish I knew.

RG: Who do you think it was?

JC: I can't say.

RG: Do you have an idea?

JC: No.

RG: Do you think something similar happened to Roosevelt [Jamison]?

JC: No.

RG: But you think the Roosevelt you're dealing with now is not the same one you used to deal with?

JC: No, they just know one another. I don't know if they brothers or what, his son or what. I don't know. But anyhow, they knew one another before I met them.

RG: Is Quinton still Quinton?

JC: Well, there's two of them.

RG: Two Quintons?

JC: Uh hm. You can tell when you get around the real one because more money is involved and he seem more important in every way. But, around this one, it seem like he's just trying to find something to do, something to get into.

RG: The real one's got a real feel for what you do and can get songs done and stuff for bigger money, and this one kind of fishes around?

JC: I really don't know what he do. We talk a lot. We go out and have a sandwich or something, mess off the time. Don't mess with women. Every once in a while we might go out to the hotel or something, meet a woman, but it seem like the other one be with me then. *[Long pause]* Want to look at a little TV?

RG: I got to get going. So that switch, man, I'm going to be thinking about that.

JC: I don't let it worry me too much. Might not get myself together, might die this way. It's hard to tell.

RG: What does your sister think about it?

JC: She don't know. I ain't never discussed it with nobody. You're the only one I've discussed it with. I don't know why I feel like talking about it.

RG: What was the cause of the switch?

JC: Lost in a dream.

RG: That's the way the past years felt?

JC: Yeah. Lost way out on a voyage. All I do is look in the mirror these days.

I FELT AS helpless hearing this story then as I do reading the transcript now. He needed more help than I could give him, more than Quinton Claunch or Elliott Clark could give. He needed health care, dependable doctors, and reliable medications.

However, and though it's a stretch, more than two decades after the fact, I see a logic to James's madness I'd never considered: James Carr contributed powerful art and important songs, and when his talent faltered, America dumped him. Unable to keep up, he was "switched," spat by the side of the road. His recordings live on, forever youthful, while James ages. Many soul stars make their best records in their later years, but America didn't give James that chance. He died of lung cancer before he turned sixty.

OTHA TURNER'S FIFE AND DRUM PICNIC

O THA TURNER'S FIFE and drum picnic is what you'd want to see if you could go back in time. When I feared that to find work I'd have to leave Memphis, the experience I knew I'd miss most was the summer fife and drum picnic. There were two, both in Gravel Springs, Mississippi—a town small enough not to be on most maps. One picnic was in July behind L. P. Buford's crossroads store—I've lost my flyer pulled from a pole on a desolate gravel road that announced, "There will be drumming." The other picnic was around Labor Day in the nearby side yard of fife player Otha Turner's farm. These picnics seemed ineffable even when standing in the middle of one, like trying to touch an echo.

Otha's picnic was decades running. His farm, with its leaning tarpaper shack, the small barn behind, a large garden for personal crops, a white horse with its tail swishing—it was like a movie set of a small independent farm. Neighboring trailers and homes were far apart, and at night in Otha's holler, dark quiet encircled everything. When Otha played the fife—he called it a "fice"—it was just a change in the air, his breath through a piece of bamboo pushing into the dust and night that hung so close. It was like a bird's beautiful chirp, an ascension, a dawning, and when the drums fell in, sticks beating on animal skins, the simple music assumed massive power,

Otha Turner and the barn behind his house. (Courtesy of Yancey Allison)

making listeners fall in the line that falls behind the piper, to dance with Gabe, the archangel.

These notes accompanied the first album by Otha Turner and the Rising Star Fife and Drum Band. Many people assume all of Mississippi music sounds like the blues made famous in the Delta, but the north Mississippi hill country has a distinct tradition. Music is the aural expression of place, a geyser emitting sound instead of water. Time was, the way a person sang a song—"61 Highway," "Joe Turner," or any of what we call "folk" songs—was like a spoken accent; it told where in the area they lived. The vast, alluvial Delta sounds very different from the nearby hill country, where the land is stony and arable only in patches instead of huge swaths. Driving through the Delta, the long tilled rows and the limitless horizon have a way of suggesting Robert Johnson's forlorn blues and Son House's piston-fired guitar strokes. In Tate and Panola counties, Mississippi, it's dust and trees, and the fife and drum sound seems sprung from them. (In Junior Kimbrough's Marshall County, they drone.) And this is not your Revolutionary or Civil War martial music, even if the instrumentation is similar; the black rural fife and drum sound evokes an African connection like no other American music.

As Jim Dickinson's sons, Luther and Cody Dickinson—the North Mississippi Allstars—grew up, they helped organize the picnics. Soon there were three stages—a flatbed for the electric bands, a porch stage for the acoustics, and the parched middle for the fife and drum. Otha wore a wireless lavalier microphone so the fife sound was amplified, piercingly pure in that night air. Guests paid a cover charge, which assured Otha's family was getting some real return on all their effort.

Guns in Mississippi. Guns in America. (Courtesy of Yancey Allison)

My passion dimmed after two gun incidents, both at the L. P. Buford's location, not Otha's. The first was at nighttime. Suddenly two men were in a tussle, their forearms locked and forming a tall triangle, a pearl-handled pistol atop like a Christmas tree star. The man on the right was trying to bring his forearm down 90 degrees so the pointed barrel could kill. The man on the left worked hard to keep that arm up, and the opposing exertions swung them circular, like clumsy dancers. Locals separated the men. Time moved thickly through the scuffle. I don't recall a shot fired, but the party was over.

The second incident was a summer or two later, in the early 1990s, during broad daylight. Crack was at epidemic levels across America, and part of why I'd left the Northeast was the random violence the drug created in the big cities. Turns out, backwoods Mississippi was not immune. In a very big crowd in the middle of the afternoon in a wide-open field, one local walked up and put a large bullet from a loud gun into the heart of another. My friends were feet away, felt the heat of the flash, said the young man thudded to the ground, instantly lifeless. I was in the rear field, where the music was to resume, and my recollection is not of hearing the gunshot but the thunder of the dispersing crowd's feet. The party emptied like the kid's life left his body. It was there, then it was gone.

Otha's picnics were nearby Buford's, and while there'd never been a fight at Otha's, I'd seen guns there too. Once, shooting night video, I focused on a glinting belt and didn't realize until the later playback that it was a gun tucked in the small of someone's back. But at Otha's, unlike Buford's, I never saw even a fistfight. I liked to believe this was due to Otha's standing in the community; it's what I told myself when I brought my three-year-old.

My passion also waned when, several years running, multiple documentary film crews descended on Otha's. The picnic had grown by then, which meant Otha would make more money and probably sell more CDs. (For R. L. Burnside and Junior Kimbrough, popularity moved them from the area fields to the world's stages, rewarding them with increased earnings in their later years.) The larger crowds were fine, the growth had been organic—but the film crews were different. They broke the mood. Their signs advised Otha's longtime neighbors that they were now on a film set, and that felt like a violation of personal space—who the fuck were *they*, who'd never been here before, to dictate to the locals? The crews hit trouble when, on the dusty land, in the deep darkness, electricity was not readily available. There was no convenient place for their snack table. Then, the fife would *pip* from across the field somewhere; the fife performances occurred irregularly, and weren't scheduled or announced. So the film crews stumbled and shoved and shouted to save their shoots, killing the feel they were trying to capture. Their refusal to listen was loud, their extension cords spread like kudzu vines.

But am I writing about myself? I've brought video cameras to places not usually documented. If I've done my work well, with pen or camera, I've invited the kind of growth I'm reacting against; am I disdaining my presence at many of the places in this book? Maybe. But I do think it's possible to become enveloped in the audience, to minimize the intrusion; even a camera—which tends to objectify—can be used with tact. And I hope that has been my way, though I can't know for certain.

At Otha's, when he hit the fife, people would encircle him and the drummers, dancing and snaking with them. Many people took photographs. After the documentary crews, the locals with cameras seemed different, a sea of arms raised over the performers, lenses angled down and peering from all around. The whole tenor was off. The cloak of night was lifted and I felt exposed, angry that their presence had wrecked what had been a beautiful gathering. I wonder how Otha felt.

At one of those overexposed affairs—within five years the swarm departed and a local feel returned—I tried to buy some hooch from Otha. He kept it in his barn and over the course of the night I'd see him making forays there, returning to huddle close with one of his neighbors. Otha was known for his smooth white whiskey, and in the past I'd easily bought a jar. But this night, when the picnic was filled with so many strangers, he was trusting no one, the fear of being busted as old as the paths into the hills. I was glad when the picnics got smaller. Otha probably made less money, but I believe he enjoyed them more.

Let Us Eat Goat

Liner notes to *Everybody Hollerin' Goat*, 1998

A stretch of interstate. You are between two cities. It is night, and quiet, and each rural exit proposes the idea of what's beyond, or suggests an emptiness far from your own thrumming world.

On a hot night in late August, less than an hour on the highway south of Memphis, you take an undistinguished exit onto roads so remote their names are not posted and drive less than fifteen minutes from the truckers and the travelers, passing maybe a dozen domiciles on a gravel road before you reach a sunken area off to the right and find yourself in Otha Turner's backyard.

An old wooden barn leans. A white horse swishes its tail. Otha's mule brays.

A fife and drum picnic. There may be five or fifty-five people milling about, blacks, whites, others. In 1970, fife and drum music was being played in Waverly Hall, Georgia, and in Otha's area around Como, Mississippi. The tradition seems to have withered in rural Georgia, but at today's picnics in Mississippi, when Otha Turner blows the dust from his cane with a flourish of trills, generations of Turners can, like the shamans, create spiritual music that divines the self from the self.

The side yard at Otha Turner's during a picnic. From left, Lonnie Young, Chip Daniels (with microphone), Kenny Brown on porch with guitar, Otha Turner (overalls, back toward camera), Cedric Burnside on drums. (Courtesy of Yancey Allison)

Drums is a calling thing. The mighty pounding rings out through the dark Mississippi night, drums chasing the fife like dogs on a rabbit, and people step outside their homes and know Otha's having a picnic.

Neighbors and friends materialize from the night, appearing first as the sound of crunching gravel, then as shadows on the dirt driveway, then fleshed beneath the electric lights that Otha has strung through his side yard. Beneath the lowest branches of giant trees, the yard has an embracing warmth, becomes a lair.

The picnics start on a Friday evening and end sometime on Sunday. On Friday, a couple goats will meet a hatchet, and the horse and the mule sigh with relief that they were not on this earth as goats to become three-dollar sandwiches at Otha's picnics.

Friends have already started to collect, though it is just midday and the picnic hasn't actually begun. Moonshines are compared. The goat must be barbecued, and with it a pig. A load of beers must be purchased for resale that night, some off-brand sodas, never enough ice.

Otha is ninety years old and powerful. His friends call him Gabe, like the archangel who blows the horn. His daughter Bernice has been playing since she was a child, and her teenaged sons—Andre, Rodney—and her nephew Aubrey (everyone calls him Bill)—they all blow the fife and beat the drums. But when it comes to family fife blowing, no one blows like granddaughter Sharde Thomas, who is eight and has been blowing the fife since she was five. She stands firm-footed like her granddad, holds

The community gathers for a fife and drum picnic.
(Courtesy of Yancey Allison)

the fife with authority, and blows "Shimmy She Wobble," which also happens to be the first song Otha learned.

"I WAS ABOUT sixteen years old [making the year about 1923] when I started blowing the cane," Otha told Luther Dickinson, his friend (and producer of this fine album). "It was an old man they called R. E. Williams, tall slim man. We would all come out of the field when it rained, too wet to pick cotton, and he'd be at his house blowing the 'fice.' I didn't know what it was. I say, 'Mr. R. E., how you make that? Will you make me one?' He say, 'Son, if you be a smart, industrious boy, listen to your mama and obey her, I'll make you a fice.' I wished it was tomorrow but it was about four weeks, he say, 'Here your fice.' I say, 'I sure do thank you.' He say, 'You ain't never gonna do nothing with it.' I say, 'But I'll try.' He say, 'Well son, don't nothing make a failing but a trying.'

"Everywhere I got a chance, I be trying to blow that cane. Mama say, 'Put that dad-blamed cane down, I'm tired of it.' Mr. R. E., he turned around blowing the cane and I just stood there watching him. And I learned how to blow it. I made my own songs.

"Then there's a man called Will Edwards, he owned some drums. One day, we heard 'em, say, 'Mama, I hear some drums.' She say, 'Y'all do your work, get ever'thing done so we come home tonight, I'll give y'all a bath and carry you up there.' We say, 'Yes ma'am, yes ma'am.'

"We do our work, she give us a bath, and we go up there. There's people standing around, old men down there playing drums, putting drums between their legs. They say, 'What you looking at, son? Getting down ain't it? You want to try it?' I say, 'Yes sir.' He say, 'Boy, don't you bust my drum.' I say, 'No sir.' I got that drum, mess around, be playing all around it. 'Listen at him, Will, listen at him, that boy yonder playing that damn drum.' After a while, he say, 'All right, young man, you been raring for this, you got a job, you one of my players.' And I started playing with other peoples. Guys found I could play the cane, they be hiring me, carrying me to different places.

"Then I say, 'I'm gonna buy me some drums and start giving picnics.' My kids say, 'Daddy, you gonna do that? You got nobody to play.' I say, 'I'm gonna hire somebody to play.' So I did, and my daughters, they kept a'watching me and wanting to try it. I say, 'Don't bust it!'

"So I was down at the field and I heard the drums at the house. I came back, asked my wife, 'Who's that messing with my drums.' She say, 'That's your children.' I say, 'You mean to tell me that my children messing with my drums? Y'all go get the drums and bring it out. I wanna see can you play.' They got them drums and played them drums. I say, 'Well hooray for y'all!' "

IN 1997, NEARLY all the fife and drum players in north Mississippi have learned from Otha Turner. Nearly all, in fact, are his kids, grandkids, some cousins, and lots of neighbors.

Every good session begins with Otha berating the drummers for playing too fast, or for playing too slow. He's got to whip the fire into them. He assembles each lineup like a barbecue chef selecting spices. He knows the nuances between the older players and the younger, between each individual. They'll beat the drums for a five- or twenty-minute stint, and everyone soloes and everyone plays together.

The players exchange instruments throughout the night, but performing at any one time there is usually one marching band bass drum, two snares, and a fife. Otha makes his fifes from cane the length of a bamboo segment and a half; they're longer than a foot but not by much. He bores out the middle with a poker heated on coals, then, by sight, bores five fingerholes. The drums are shouldered with straps, allowing the players to snake slowly when playing. Otha's fife is always kept handy in the back pocket of his overalls, at the ready like nunchucks.

The trance music begins as imperceptibly as a breeze, the sound of someone testing their instrument. Is it still there? It is still there. Another

Otha Turner made his own instruments from cane. He played smoking fife, 1998. (Courtesy of Bill Steber)

asks, Is mine still here? Mine is still here. Someone laughs loudly, buys another beer at Otha's makeshift bar, yells, "Play that thing."

The crowd gathers, thicker suddenly, as people spill from the darkness. Otha begins to march and the drums follow. Not fast. Not slow. Snaking, people fall in behind them and beside them, arms raised overhead and swaying, hips shaking over the county line, forth and back, side to side, grinding and doing the do. Men hump the drums and women hump the drums. The crowd shouts, spurring the players to take them higher and further, spurring the dancers to shake with more abandon. A lady in her sixties throws herself in a push-up position and makes love to the earth.

The sound goes through us and reverberates off the trees and in the hollows all around. We are at the mouth of a cave. We are in Morocco with the Master Musicians of Jajouka, on a second line in New Orleans, the funereal spirit entwined with the life spirit. "The old people taught me and told me that that was African," says Otha, "that way back in Africa, you played drums if somebody died. At the funeral, they would march behind the casket to the cemetery."

Time blurs. The drum pounds. The fife hypnotizes, human breath through an ancient piece of wood. Serpentine goes the line behind Gabe, serpentine. "You makes a fice do what it do," says Otha Turner, and he has the wisdom and the calluses that confirm this simple statement. "You know your cane with your fingers. You put that cane up and start to blowing, and you can put what you got through your mouth into that cane. The fice ain't got but two whistles to it, high and low; you got to catch something yourself. Then know how to know it, then blow it. You got to be patient with it. You gots to know how to know it."

MAMA ROSE NEWBORN

THE MORE I learned about the great jazz siblings Phineas and Calvin Newborn (and about their bandleader father, Phineas Sr.), the more I realized what a force their mother was. Both Phineases were dead—her husband and her son—and I realized Mama Rose (as everyone called her) was living quietly in the South Memphis house that Phineas Jr. bought her in 1956. I knew she had stories, so I got her number from her surviving son, Calvin. She invited me by.

I wrote this piece but never submitted it for publication. It's hard enough to find a magazine interested in obscure musicians; an article about the mother of obscure musicians? I couldn't face the odds. I wrote it for myself, then tucked it away. I paid her an honorarium for her time, which was the honor I cared about, and the one she did too, since publicity couldn't help with her heating bill.

Useless Are the Flowers
Previously unpublished, 1993

The sun came up on the morning of May 26, 1989, and when, around six A.M., it illuminated the sagging front porch of 588 East Alston Avenue in a crumbling South Memphis neighborhood, it shone like the spotlight that had always eluded Phineas Newborn Jr., seated in a chair outdoors and dead. Junior—as he was known to friends and family—had that night, as most recent nights, haunted the doorways of nearby Beale Street, then returned to the house he'd purchased for his parents more than three decades earlier, when his musical star was ascending. That was before he'd recorded his first album and when word of his awesome talent was being spread by awestruck musicians like Count Basie and Lionel Hampton. This night, he returned to his mother's upright piano and then retired to a porch chair in the pleasant Memphis dawn, where his soul departed from his fifty-seven-year-old body.

A few nights before his brother died, Calvin Newborn was awakened during the wee hours to hear Junior sitting at the piano. "I lay there and tried to figure out what he was playing and how he got that sound," Calvin recalls. "It was so eerie because it sounded like single notes, but he was playing fourths. The notes were so together it took me a long time to figure out what he was playing. He just played it once, that was all he played.

"Later, my mother said he was playing 'Going Home,' and I knew he was sending a message. He knew he was going."

"It's some rough sides to these mountains, I'm telling you," says Mama Rose Newborn, wife of the late Phineas Newborn Sr., mother of Junior and Calvin. "Yeah, man, I've come up some rough sides of the mountain, but I'm a happy old lady." Mama Rose is a petite woman, diminutive in body but gigantic in spirit. She is not a bitter woman, though she mourns the loss of her husband and her firstborn son—and each before their time. Phineas Sr.'s orchestra was, beginning in the 1940s, one of the most influential in Memphis. Among the artists who went through his band were saxophonist Hank Crawford, who became band director for Ray Charles during both "What'd I Say" and *Modern Sounds in Country and Western Music*; trumpeter Bowlegs Miller, whose own band became a starting point for many Memphis soul greats (including the Hi Rhythm Section, who would eventually be the core of Al Green's hits); Robert "Honeymoon" Garner, a stalwart Memphis jazz organist; and Herman Green, who played behind a young B. B. King and alongside John Coltrane. About his father, Calvin said, "He made Elvis dance and elephants dance. If you had a heart, he'd make you dance."

Junior, who was fluent on tenor sax, trumpet, and vibes, in addition to the piano, began touring at the age of sixteen. As a teenager, he joined Lionel Hampton's band. At twenty-five he made his album debut with Atlantic Records and that same year he stole the 1956 Newport Jazz Festival; he collaborated with Charles Mingus on the soundtrack to the 1959

Phineas Newborn Jr., circa 1956. (Courtesy of
Preservation and Special Collections Department,
University Libraries, University of Memphis)

John Cassavetes film *Shadows*. Before he was thirty, he suffered his first
nervous breakdown, and thereafter, mental hospitals became as routine in
his life as recording studios.

MAMA ROSE, AS she is known even to people whom she's never met, is
seated in the living room of the small Alston Avenue home. There are
handkerchiefs drying over the gas heaters, a couple crumpled one-dollar
bills stuffed for all the world to see into the stockings that she wears. She
has on a housedress and a colorful African hat with vertical stripes. "There
is so much you don't know," she says, referring both to people in general
and to me specifically, "could make another world."

The front room to Mama Rose Newborn's home is filled with posters,
awards, citations, photographs, album jackets, a piano, and other memorabilia of her husband's and sons' careers. This assemblage is for herself, because
she is proud. "The public don't recognize them like they should," she says,
"but I don't worry about it. I would like for them to, but I know how the
trends and things are." She reaches to a table beside her chair and pulls
down a large Bible, turns to the inside cover, and reads aloud the following
notation, one among many: "Bill Monroe, fifty years ago got a prize on
Grand Ole Opry. August 1991." Then she adds, "They still honor him.

Things like that is something that a lot of people forget. People ain't thinking about what was. Thinking about what is."

CALVIN NEWBORN HAS a gig in Memphis. He is seated on a stool so near the front door of the soul food restaurant that when customers walk in for dinner, the door almost bangs his guitar. The restaurant seats about twenty-five people. Calvin's accompaniment is a boom box. A karaoke version of "Feelings" comes on and Calvin shuts his eyes and plays mellifluous jazz guitar, singing the words so softly that not everybody in the small place can hear. He gives the song his all, much like he will at a gig in Chicago a few months later, where he will command a nice fee and draw a sold out crowd, and much like he will every night for a year when he's playing show tunes on a tour of Europe in the orchestra of a Broadway musical.

Unlike his brother, Calvin was not a prodigy. He knows the ticking of years that precedes proficiency, a knowledge that helped him falter not at all in his more recent pursuits of painting and writing. His book of his family's history, *As Quiet as It's Kept!*, includes some reproductions of his paintings. He also recorded some of his finest guitar work ever on what will surely be a hard-to-find and underappreciated CD by Herman Green, *Who Is Herman Green? His Music, Worthy of Note.*

Calvin, who has lived all around the world but keeps a room at his mother's house, now also has a studio apartment of his own in public housing at the end of Beale Street. He can be seen on some evenings darkening the same doors his father and brother passed through decades ago, occasionally playing on the bandstands where their legends still cast a shadow. Some of the club owners know who he is, but many of the bouncers see him as part of the rabble they're paid to keep out. One young band, Free-World, often honors him with a spot on the stage next to his old friend Herman Green. Calvin's legend is widely known, but he himself almost always requires an introduction.

"MY HUSBAND AND I came to Memphis with nothing but traveling trunks," says Mama Rose. "Up from Whiteville, Tennessee, where we were born, and we got a room in Orange Mound [Memphis's first suburban development built for African Americans]. We were poor people, and my husband had a bike. The trolleys was running on Southern Avenue, and he would take that bike up there and catch that streetcar, let it pull that bike all the way to State Normal [now the University of Memphis]. My husband was the cook's helper there; he was a good cook. And on his way back, he'd do

Calvin Newborn at home, 2002. (Courtesy of Chris Floyd)

the same thing. Later we moved from Orange Mound because he wanted to get uptown, close to the music."

Memphis was a place where, with a little ingenuity, small means could be grafted onto bigger ideas. Each family had been musical, the Murphys—Mama Rose's side—in the small farming community of Whiteville, fifty miles northeast of Memphis. And near Jackson, Tennessee, Phineas Sr.—he pronounced it with a long *i* and spelled it *Finas* on his bandstand and bus—and his brothers played in the high school band and at church, where they also sang.

The legacy began at least one generation prior, with Mama Rose's father playing guitar in the Church of God in Christ. With a long cord between his guitar and amp, he could wander all over the room. "Calvin's grandaddy would play gospel songs in church," says Mama Rose. "He didn't play this other music. He had the guitar, and you know how sanctified folks do, he'd be jumping up, hollering 'Glory!' and 'Hallelujah!'

"That's where Calvin got his movements from. He never seen him, because their grandaddy passed away a long time ago. But that's why Calvin's got to move. It was just in 'em both to move! And it was in their daddy and me too. I used to dance and play the piano, played organ at church. Just music lovers."

Just music lovers, loose in Beale Street heaven: block after block of clubs, filled at night with big bands and small combos, a mix of local musicians and touring acts like the Brown Skin Models, which was a medicine show with long legs as the cure-all.

Beale Street was a place for jam sessions, for cutting heads. If you thought you could do better than someone on stage, then the bandleader, the band, everyone in the audience wanted to know. Because no one was settling for second best. Finas's route into the coterie of players—and ultimately to the superior position of bandleader—began by challenging another drummer to let him beat the skins. He also worked as a roadie for the bigger shows that played the grand Malco Theatre at the corner of Beale and Main (now the Orpheum). Finas was a man who wanted to immerse himself in music.

"We'd keep up with who was coming to town and we would come uptown. He had a cousin lived up here; we would stay overnight, and, honey, Count Basie, Jimmie Lunceford, all them old musicians, my husband would help take out their instruments and get us some passes. He played drums with lots of 'em. I met 'em all.

"We didn't have no babysitter, we didn't have money hardly to pay the rent. We would have to carry Junior with us. I'd stay in the ladies' room until time for the music to start because I nursed by breast and didn't have no Pampers. When I'd get him dry, their daddy would take him and put him over behind the drums. He'd have to play or keep up some music, or else Junior would start to cry. Count [Basie] looked at Junior and said, 'Hey bright eyes!'"

Calvin was born a year behind Junior, and as their father got deeper into music, the kids kept up. They never knew otherwise. Finas turned down touring offers from Jimmie Lunceford and Lionel Hampton, opting instead to help raise his family. Calvin remembers, "I was about five years old and Junior was six, and we walked from Orange Mound to Beale Street for the first time. We had heard about the Midnight Rambles from my dad, he used to play those shows. So we followed the railroad tracks all the way to Beale Street, and we went in the theater and saw the shoot-'em-ups, cartoons, and all that stuff until midnight when the lights came on and everybody was supposed to leave. We ducked down under the seats, and when the lights went back out and the stage show started, two heads popped up with eyes big as teacups. But we saw the stage show, and it was exciting. That was the beginning. After that I knew that I was supposed to be in show business." Their proximity to Satan's music was confirmed when they were walking home from Beale and Calvin's foot got caught in a root across the path; he stumbled and hollered to his brother, "Help me, the devil's got my leg!"

Calvin and Junior were different kinds of players, different kinds of people. Calvin identifies himself as an extrovert and Junior an introvert. At the age of four, Calvin suffered a severe burn on his back, resulting in six months on his stomach beneath an infrared lamp. "The doctor told my mother I wasn't going to be as strong as other boys my age, but I refused to be weak. I played with the biggest boys, I did the dangerous things, I refused to be pampered. My brother was just the opposite. He practiced more or less eight hours a day. I concentrated on being more of a show-man, and he concentrated on playing."

"Calvin would throw papers, shine shoes, chop cotton," Mama Rose remembers. "Junior would be sitting up on that piano, *ding dong bong bong bing*! And Calvin would come home, Junior still practicing, not loud, just practicing. He'd say, 'You need to come and go with us. Essie Mae—' Calvin named the girls '—and all them were on the bus and we had our sodies and ice and wet our handkerchiefs and put them on our heads. You should come go, man, we'll have a lot of fun.' Junior would say, 'No, I'll take your word.' *Bing bong ding dong ding.* So Junior didn't do nothing but play music. He went into the army and his job was to get that trumpet and wake the soldiers. And after that, he'd go to the marching band. After that, to the officer's club. So Junior never done no kinda work but play music."

The extent to which this applies to Junior is illustrated by an anecdote told by his acquaintance, Memphis musician and producer Jim Dickinson. "One of Phineas's wives wanted him to pick up the laundry that was on the bed, get it out of the way. He said, 'My name is Phineas Newborn, piano player. Not Phineas Newborn, laundry mover.'"

IN THE COLLECTION of photos through which Mama Rose seems to be constantly browsing, she finds one of a young Junior in a bathing suit at the swimming pool. Phineas looks awkward, like maybe the sunlight and the outdoors are foreign to him. "Yeah," she says, "they stole his clothes that day. He came home with some pants on big enough for that dresser. I said, 'Whaaat,' and he said, 'Well I went swimming and I come out and I didn't have no clothes and I just went in the junk room at the swimming pool and put on something.' I said, 'Oh man!'"

Finas had been playing drums with the prominent Memphis band Tuff Green and the Rocketeers. As his kids grew older, he made them professional musicians as well. "When Junior and Calvin were in high school, they started playing with the old man," says Mama Rose. "They was at the Plantation Inn when they were children and going to Booker Washington High School in the daytime."

The Plantation Inn was across the river in West Memphis, Arkansas, and it featured black bands playing for a white crowd. Across the bridge, outside the city limits, all the rules were looser. "I started to high school in '48," says Calvin. "My brother had been there a year, and it was pretty tough going to school every day and playing from nine until two at night—even for teenagers. On weekends, we used to come from the Plantation Inn and stop sometimes at Mitchell's on Beale Street, where they jammed 'til daybreak.

"But I enjoyed it because my pockets stayed full and I was able to buy nice clothes at Lansky Brothers on Beale Street and Julius Lewis even [the high-end store for whites]. And I wore the best shoes. I would stop on the way to school and get my stumps shined every morning. There was a shoe shop right on the corner of Alston and Lauderdale, going toward the railroad track. My shoes stayed clean every day. They *stayed* clean."

Both Mama Rose and Calvin remember the diversity of the Finas Newborn Orchestra. "They played what y'all call blues, jazz, folk music," says Mama Rose. "They played all kind of music. That's the difference in music now and music then. My husband's band, they could read that music and they played any kind. At the Plantation Inn, they played 'Tennessee Waltz,' just like on the Grand Ole Opry, every night, and the owner and his wife would dance to it. My husband would teach them kids that you're supposed to satisfy the customers. That's the reason Calvin gets on his knees and all that. His daddy would tell him to play to the crowd. He'd keep guitar strings in his drum case, because when Calvin get through stomping and carrying on, he'd probably broke a string. His daddy was a drum beater, boy, and he taught 'em to play what the audience wants."

"My dad had a way with playing drums where he would lock you in," says Calvin, "and you couldn't go nowhere—you had to play right! And he had the foresight to see that television was going to be the thing. He had us play good music and give the people something to see at the same time. There was usually ten of us: four horns, four rhythms, a vocalist, and a dancer. You think James Brown is bad, you should have seen Baby Ray dance. He would line up chairs on the dance floor as long as a truck and turn somersaults over them.

"My dad also insisted that we stay abreast of everything new. Bebop was pretty hot on the East Coast, Charlie Parker and Dizzy and Miles. 'Moody's

Mood for Love' was one of the first songs that lyrics were put to a jazz solo, and it was taboo, really. They were doing it on the East Coast, but people here weren't accepting it. I sang it with Wanda Jones, and we only did it when my dad knew he wouldn't make the audience angry by playing bebop.

"And we had a family quartet within the band. Wanda, whom I married, was the vocalist. She also played trombone and piano. I arranged the music, my brother arranged, and my father arranged. We had quite a show.

"A lot of people think that there is no such thing as wrong notes. Dissonance can be beautiful—Monk proved that—but there is a certain way to play dissonance. And silence is beautiful. But if you're looking for it to be silent and all of a sudden"— he makes sounds like a pantry emptying— "it's a little much. Something too abrupt aggravates me. My brother was such a genius with putting music together so I guess I got spoiled. We did a lot of improvising; it was like spontaneous combustion. To create spontaneously is the highest art form on the face of the earth. And creative intelligence is very spiritual. I think that's as close to God as you can get."

UPON JUNIOR's 1955 release from the army, he returned to Memphis. His father had opened the Newborn Music Shop on Beale Street at a time when gods would meander through the door. "What was that boy's name?" says Mama Rose. "Howling Wolf! He came in the shop and Finas had his head on that little desk in the back. Howling Wolf came in talking, called me some sweet name. He said, 'You know what? You just would fit around—' Finas raised up, picked up his pistol, and said, 'Your head will just fit this thirty-eight too!' Howling Wolf said—" and here eighty-year-old Mama Rose Newborn howls like the Wolf in "Smokestack Lightnin'."

With Junior home, Senior was anxious to restart the family band. But Junior's designs were on broader horizons; Count Basie had promised him an introduction to his New York City booking agent. Calvin states, "When we shattered our dad's dream of having a family band by going to New York and forming the Phineas Newborn Jr. Quartet, we also broke his heart."

Before departing, Junior bought his parents the home on Alston. "I asked whose name should I put on this house," Mama Rose remembers, "and Junior said, 'Put Phineas Newborn Senior and Rosie Murphy Newborn, because as long as you and daddy got a floor and a door, I believe I got a place to live.'"

Junior and Calvin set out and latched their dreams onto Manhattan. Their playing was tight. Since they'd been kids, the Newborn brothers "could feel one another's emotions from afar, like mental telepathy," writes Calvin in *As Quiet As It's Kept!* "I stepped on a nail in the backyard and

Rosie Murphy Newborn and Calvin Newborn. (Courtesy of Calvin Newborn)

though he was inside the house, Junior said he felt it too. And when a window slammed down on his arm inside the house, though I was outside, I felt it." The tight synchronicity got them gigs. Promptly, they were booked to open Count Basie's run at Birdland. They sent for Memphis bassist George Joyner (later known as Jamil Nasser). "The toughest thing we had was keeping a drummer," says Calvin, "because my brother played so fast and had such intricate arrangements. We changed drummers very often."

When the quartet played the 1956 Newport Jazz Festival, Phineas Sr. was introduced in the audience. "Our dad stood up while the audience applauded, and as I stood on stage holding my guitar ready to play, I could feel his sadness," writes Calvin. "I knew he wanted more than anything to be playing drums with us." Sadness and disappointment would shadow Finas for the rest of his days.

THE PHINEAS NEWBORN Jr. Quartet was included on the 1957 Birdland tour, along with Count Basie, Sarah Vaughan, Lester Young, and others. Calvin was asked to keep his eye on pianist Bud Powell, who was not well.

"Our quartet came on before the Bud Powell Trio at the concert hall in Toronto, Canada. We finished our set, and on the way to our dressing room backstage I noticed that Bud was butting his head against the wall and stopped him. I went into the dressing room and put down my guitar and when I came back out, Bud was on stage playing his opener, 'Un Poco Loco.' After that he played the most prolific interpretation of the standard 'Like Someone in Love' I'd ever heard. It was supernatural! I knew how Junior loved Bud's piano playing, and though my heart was bleeding when chaperoning Bud, I'd missed something. Suddenly I knew why Junior dug Bud so. Though I had no way of knowing it then, some years later my heart would bleed for Junior just as it had for Bud."

Though the prominent critic Leonard Feather would soon proclaim him "the greatest living jazz pianist," Junior's talent provoked a heated debate among jazz fans. He was always praised for his technique, though some critics said his skill overpowered his emotion; they said the opposite about Calvin. "When I got to New York, I realized what I had been missing by not practicing. On the first record, they wouldn't give me a solo. We were with Atlantic, and they said when Junior got through playing there was nothing left to play. Someone suggested that I take some lessons from a CBS staff guitarist, Barry Galbraith, and I learned a lot from him. I learned how to relax mostly, because it was hard for me to stay still and play. I was used to doing like Magic Johnson—flying." The showman and the perfectionist; the extrovert and the introvert.

There is a picture of Calvin as a young man, his face contorted and intent on his playing; it is clear that this man is deep into what he's doing. And upon closer inspection, one sees that he is airborne, his legs pulled up higher than the nearby tabletops. "I was about six feet in the air," he says, "playing the guitar."

He pauses, then reveals, "As a matter of fact, I used to think I could fly."

He lets that image sink in, then continues: "I felt like I could make myself as light as I wanted to. I have jumped off a two-story building and never really hurt myself. I saw a lot of movies and I thought I was a stuntman. Even today, sometimes I dream that I'm just walking down the street and spread my arms and just take off and fly."

His father must have felt the same as that trolley pulled him through the streets of Memphis. And his brother's music reflects the same sense of freedom: Junior untethered the left hand, making it as integral to the melody as the right. It's clear in his arrangement of "Dahoud" from his first album, *Here is Phineas*, and it's clear in later original compositions, such as "Blues Theme for Left Hand Only." "Junior wrote a lot of contrapuntal stuff,"

Phineas Newborn Jr. performs at the University of Memphis for a class taught by visiting writer Robert Palmer. Randall Lyon, right, on Porta Pak for Televista Productions, circa 1976. (Courtesy of Pat Rainer)

says Calvin. "He had a lot of parts with me playing contrary to him, and it took a lot of practice to play together. Harmonically, he did a lot of things. Even before the Modern Jazz Quartet, he was doing that swing. He always believed in swinging hard."

Junior's little brother was right at his side, citing his own swinging influences. "Charlie Christian was a big inspiration to me," he says, "but my main inspiration was Wes Montgomery. The first guitarist who really impressed me as a kid was Nat King Cole's guitarist, Oscar Moore. Dad had some records of Nat; I used to hear his trio all the time and it just impressed me. Nat was in Memphis with Norman Granz's Jazz at the Philharmonic when we were little, and our dad played with Nat. Nat Cole's feel influenced me and my brother. Junior said that the reason he and Oscar Peterson sound so much alike is because they were influenced by the same people— Nat Cole and Art Tatum."

WITH HIS KIDS grown and gone, Finas finally accepted an offer to tour. This time he was not with the greats he'd known in his younger days. "When the children went on," says Mama Rose about her husband, "he started working for Paul A. Miller's Circus. My husband would be on the drums with that brush, and that lion tamer would be saying, 'Go on, Annie,' and the lion would get near that hoop. The old man knew when she got close enough, he'd hit that cymbal—POW—pow pow! Annie would jump through that hoop over that fire." When he quit the circus, just before he died, Mama Rose says they had to hire two drummers to take his place.

He never got over the idea of the family reunion, his pride in his children always tinged with an unfulfilled yearning. Junior left New York for Los Angeles in 1960 and his father came out to visit. "One night our dad sat in with Junior at John T. McClain's It Club," Calvin says. "When he finished playing, he had to be helped off the drum stool. The next day, with a firm grip on the monkey wrench he was using to repair the kitchen sink in his apartment, Phineas Newborn Sr. suffered his seventh heart attack. It was fatal."

Junior's health was also fragile. He'd endured the pressure of skyrocketing fame in his youth, then suffered through two failed marriages. In the early 1960s, he had a nervous breakdown and was hospitalized in California. Upon returning to Memphis, his diagnosis and medication were changed, resulting in another lengthy hospital stay. Ultimately, under the care of his family and close friends, like Memphis saxophonist Fred Ford, he achieved some stability.

His fondness for the ladies never changed. His standard pickup line for total strangers was "Do you like music? Give me a kiss." Mama Rose remembers how people would take advantage of him. "All these pictures setting up there on the piano, I came home one day and all the pictures was gone, frames and all. Junior was sitting in here alone, and there was a pile of stuff on the floor where this woman had emptied a box out. I said, 'Junior, what?' He said, 'I was around the corner there and they was playing the jukebox and somebody said, "This is one of the greatest piano players in the world, got all kinds of records." This woman said, "Can I go around there and play some?"' She got around here and she wanted a drink. He goes to the whiskey store, left her in here and when he come back she done took pictures, frames and all. He was just that kind of person, he didn't think. But I won't complain, because he's the one that fought the battle. I knew his condition and I just rolled with his conditions. But he didn't think. He just trusted."

Junior's love of the ladies nearly cost him his life. "Somebody beat him up once," Mama Rose says, and her countenance darkens during this story, as if she bears responsibility, as if his mugging is a tear in her matriarchal fabric because it was preceded by a fight with her. "They had him—well I had him really—put away. He'd drank this liquor, I guess it went to his brain quick. I cut the light out or something and he had nerve enough to get up and he slapped me. Honey, I hit him with this left and he hit that chair. I went next door and called the folks and they put him in the VA. He was already taking medicine. They told me, 'Don't tell him about it now.' After he got pretty settled, they told him. He said, 'Well if I done that to my mama, find me a new place.'

"They found him one, near some of them ofay brothers. Them white gals would be meddling with him and doing him. It had snowed and he had went down to one of them joints. And on his way back, a gang of them got him. They broke his fingers and messed him all up. Broke his fingers."

Mama Rose visited him in the hospital. "I told Junior, 'Work your fingers. Play CDEFG.' Junior worked C, D, E, F, G. I said, 'Junior, them fingers' gonna be all right.'" During his recuperation, Fred Ford arranged for him to be released evenings, and they recorded his Grammy-nominated album, *Solo Piano*.

Junior was better, but not well. Jim Dickinson recalls picking him up for a gig in the late 1970s, around five thirty in the afternoon. "He was asleep with his overcoat on. He gets up and puts his hat on, sits down at the kitchen table. Mama Rose is cooking him a fish for breakfast. She's had to deal with three generations of crazy musicians, Junior ain't nothing to her. She says, 'What do you want for your birthday?'

"'I want a pistol.'

"'Well, you ain't getting nothing then.'

"He says, '*You* got a pistol.'

"'Yeah,' she responded, 'I've got a pistol, but I don't run down the street going, 'Yeah yeah yeah.'"

Not only that, Mama Rose doesn't run down the street going, "No no no." Despite all she's seen, all she's heard, all she's endured, she still greets visitors at her small home, still sees it as a palace gifted to her by her gifted son. "I been all around, not just riding up and down the road," she says. "Music—I'm like my husband about that. Music ain't gonna lose nobody and it ain't gonna find nobody. You got to find it, and if you don't get it, that's your fault."

Calvin and Mama Rose live in the present, haunted by the past. "The other day, Calvin brought me flowers when he come by," Mama Rose says. "I sang, 'Give them the flowers while they live / trying to cheer them on / Useless the flowers that you give / after the soul is gone.'"

TOWNES VAN ZANDT

I N 1993, DOUG Easley and Davis McCain got a phone call from a young German guy, Peter Schneider, who wanted to record some Memphis groups as the heart of a compilation called *Love Is My Only Crime* and then organize a European tour around the record. Easley-McCain Recording was by then a hub for bands that wanted a fringier Memphis experience than Ardent offered (Ardent is where Big Star recorded). Easley-McCain maintained vintage gear and offered the analog tape option when digital was all the rage, but also it was about the atmosphere. It had a large, high-ceilinged recording room that housed good ghosts who made the work easygoing. If anyone checked the clock, it was to see if liquor stores were still open or if it was time for Al Green's Bible class.

The call from Germany confirmed the studio's growing reputation. They handled the recording and Peter and I coordinated the tour. We settled on a five-group bill, four from Memphis and Peter's personal pick of Townes Van Zandt. Townes is the Cormac McCarthy of songwriters; he deals in stories of powerful desperation and desolation, along with the occasional commercial hit, like "Pancho and Lefty." I traveled as the American road manager and became the show's emcee.

Davis McCain, left, and Doug Easley, with neighbors Eric and Chris Meyers. (Courtesy of Trey Harrison)

None of us had experienced Townes before. I met him in the hotel lobby that June morning in 1993, Zurich, Switzerland. He was the first one down, shaved, dressed, and ready to load out—a professional. He sat in a high-backed chair, staid and quiet, looking like an album cover. The next afternoon, after loading into the venue, I went to retrieve an item from the bus and found Townes standing in the aisle, one hand on his open suitcase and the other holding a quart of cheap vodka bottom side up. The next two weeks blurred into one of the most fun parties I've ever been to.

When off the road, Townes lived in Nashville, two hundred miles from us (and a world apart). Over the two-week tour, bonds formed, and once stateside, he visited our wild bunch, sometimes to record, sometimes for the dance parties. Every visit was one for the books—which is why it must have been so hard to be him. (The most fun I ever had doing laundry was with Townes. We were dancing to "Kung Fu Fighting" in a German bar before eleven A.M. It gave a new meaning to "rinse cycle.")

Days before he died, he'd been recording at Easley-McCain. His road manager doled out vodka shots at a prescribed pace. You could hear the alcohol flow through him—the rush in his slur and in his giggle—then hear it diminish and fade. He'd fallen just before the sessions and was being pushed in a wheelchair. The situation deteriorated, the songs weren't flowing, and producer Steve Shelley (drummer from Sonic Youth) terminated the sessions early. Townes was taken back to Nashville, and a doctor there determined he'd broken his hip and had not tended it for a week. He was a wisp of a man before surgery, but he likely would have survived had he not mixed some over-the-counter medicines with his prescriptions. The Memphis crew attended his funeral.

In Germany, after a few days with Townes and his remote, sage demeanor, his ethereality, I began wondering if, rather than a human being, he was some kind of revenant. I grabbed my camera and snapped a few shots of him, knowing if he was a ghost, his image wouldn't appear on film. That night, I lost my camera.

All the Federales Say

Mojo, March 1997

At Townes Van Zandt's funeral, his longtime friend and fellow songwriter Guy Clark stepped to the microphone and, adjusting a guitar around his neck, said, "I guess I booked this gig thirty-some years ago."

Townes was a man of glorious self-destruction, full of life and talent and scared of both. He'd been drinking cheap vodka for more of his fifty-two years than he hadn't, and when he died on New Year's Day of a heart attack following hip surgery, two days after his final recording session, he was as skinny and frail as Hank Williams exactly forty-four years earlier. Like the *federales* in Townes's song "Pancho and Lefty," made famous by Willie Nelson, Merle Haggard, and Emmylou Harris, among others, death only let Townes "live so long / out of kindness I suppose."

To be around Townes was to laugh and have fun; to hear Townes's songs was to face desperation and dark beauty. He told hilarious stories— about his former shock therapist, about botching record deals, about talking his way out of trouble—and he sang piercing songs. From "Lungs":

> *Breath I'll take and breath I'll give*
> *And pray the day's not poison*
> *Stand among the ones that live*
> *In lonely indecision.*

In the song "Marie," one of his saddest, a rambler settles down with a woman for whom he can't provide; she dies in the cold, pregnant with his child. Other titles: "Waiting Around to Die," "Nothin'," "For the Sake of the Song."

"Living on the road, my friend," is how "Pancho and Lefty" opens, and it became a credo of sorts for Townes. He toured constantly and extensively,

Townes liked to tell jokes. One, fitting, was: An Irishman in the
countryside caught a leprechaun and was granted three
wishes. He said, "I'd like a glass of Guinness that never ends."
Ping, a full pint appeared. *Glug glug*, and when he set it down,
it was full again. "Well," said the leprechaun, impatient, "What
else?" The farmer said, "Wow, I'll have two more of those."
(Courtesy of Ebet Roberts)

throughout America and Europe, laying himself bare with just an acoustic guitar and his voice, plagued by stage fright but comfortable spinning
yarns backstage with strangers. When he hit his full stride, Townes was
going slow enough to make music of the space between the notes.

"He said that every song had to work as a poem on paper first," songwriter Susanna Clark remembers. "That was a Townes rule." (When she'd
tell her friend that he drank too much, Townes would say, "Hey babe,
there's sober people in India.")

The personality with which he invested his songs had widespread
influence. In 1968, Joe Ely was driving outside dry Lubbock, Texas, to get
beer. He saw a hitchhiker with a guitar and knew the guy was lost. Joe
drove Townes to the proper highway, and Townes reached into his duffel
bag and gave Joe a copy of his brand-new debut album. "The bag had no

clothes in it," Ely remembers, "nothing but copies of this album." At rehearsal that night, Ely played it for his bandmates in the Flatlanders, Jimmie Dale Gilmore and Butch Hancock, and Texas music hit a twist in the road.

Others who have recorded his songs include Nanci Griffith, Don Williams, and Steve Earle.

Wealth held no attraction for Townes Van Zandt. He preferred the company of laborers—miners, fisherman, and others who gathered in groups and exchanged stories, lore, and gambling debts. I think he wanted to perceive his own work—songwriting and playing—as a form of manual labor, but it came too natural for him. Sometimes songs wrote themselves, Townes merely the vessel, and profiting from that made him feel guilty when others had to swing a sledgehammer so they could afford Hamburger Helper. Other times, Townes handicapped himself with drink, crippling his skills to even the playing field. At all times, there was more to Townes Van Zandt than we'll ever know, and I'm sure he had his own explanation for the need to kill himself drinking. As Guy Clark's statement implies, being his friend meant accepting that he would die trying.

Townes was a wise and funny man from whom a person could learn a lot about a lot. His self-destruction was a part of him, such that all his happiness was shaded by some sadness, and all the jubilation he created around him was tempered by some pity.

JEFF BUCKLEY

MEMPHIS ALLOWS YOU a great freedom. On the street, you don't encounter stars of today's charts, nor a world of less-heavenly bodies—agents and publicists and managers. There's no mill expecting fresh grist, nor even is there much of a culture-seeking audience; there's better towns for higher culture. You work at your own pace, you develop in public as much as you'd like, then you take it elsewhere to sell—either in a van with a guitar, or through one of the cities of industry, or from your bedroom on the Internet. We are a hole in the wall—some call it a city—for artists, so having the factory two hundred miles away in Nashville seems just about perfect to me.

I think that's why Jeff Buckley came to Memphis—to be free from the factory's heat. He came to experience people who don't care about Manhattan or Los Angeles, don't think of meetings there in the course of their day. In Memphis, the rent is cheaper, the days are slower, the narcissism less tolerated. You can afford to dig deeper, to hew the piece one time more before the forge.

Unlike the others in this book, Jeff Buckley had fame and came here to lose it. Obscurity wasn't his problem. He is, in a way, the anti–James Carr. He came to Memphis for what many residents complain about: the isolation.

'Nuff said. (Courtesy of Trey Harrison)

He wasn't leaving the grid, just resituating himself on it. On the road in the 1990s, he'd befriended the Grifters, Memphis's finest alternative rock band, and he came to see if this town and its indie studio were all these enthusiasts proclaimed. That's when I met him.

I was leaving Hi Records drummer Howard Grimes's house with some photos he'd given me for the Al Green boxed set *Anthology*. I had to show someone and I knew Doug Easley and Davis McCain would appreciate the finds; their studio was on the way home. At Easley-McCain Recording, there was an energetic kid checking out the studio who paced as he talked, moving like Gumby with a wire through him, and he shared the excitement. We didn't exchange names.

Jeff booked studio time and returned—twice. In Easley one night he mentioned moving here and I told him about a house for rent on my Midtown block. It was owned by the couple across the street from me. They were simple country folk in the city. They had performed their wedding vows at home in front of their favorite Sunday morning TV preacher. (When my wife first entered their living room, she exclaimed to the husband at the TV's size. He missed not a beat, answering, "There's only one bigger.") They had a menagerie of pets and raised rats to sell for snake food. They were casually anti-Semitic and rabidly born-again. For me, their life was a reality TV show that ran loudly and without cessation. For Jeff it was a world that had to be explored. He'd walk down with his guitar, compose songs by letting their German shepherd's nose push his hands around the guitar neck, and pick up lyrics from their dialog as he watched them cook dinner.

He also took up a residency on Tuesdays at the punk club Barristers. The gigs weren't announced, but word spread plenty quick. He'd try out material, do fun covers, and run a stream of bebop stage patter like Neal Cassady, as much stand-up comic as songster. During the breaks, he'd shoot pool with challengers. Memphis allowed him a giant step backward, a chance to be a pretty regular guy.

Days before Jeff died, we began discussing a music video. He wanted to model it on *The Party*, starring Peter Sellers. I watched the film and the reasons for his affection were obvious: Sellers was a dapper, daft nerd and a mimic, a stranger in a land of facile, graceful performers who wreaks havoc obliviously and continuously. I looked forward to dressing Jeff in a white three-piece suit and choreographing the stunts. But it was not to be.

From Jeff's Memphis recordings, I'm a sucker for "Everybody Here Wants You." The writing is dense but Jeff's in no hurry, his voice soaring like silk in a pleasant breeze. He's slinking over to Al Green territory, cathedral-like and yet so intimate. And while I know it's a love song to a woman, I can't help thinking that the central line is a recurring thought after his quick success in New York, in Memphis, and in every room he was in: "Everybody here thinks he needs you."

Jeff Buckley, left, and Andria Lisle at Miss Ellen's Soul Food on N. Parkway. Legendary johnnycake. (Courtesy of Lely Constantinople)

Northern Light
Oxford American, August 2000

Thirty-six hours before Jeff Buckley died, I saw him standing on a quiet Memphis street corner. A sheriff's car had pulled over and the beige-suited *federale* stood towering over him. Jeff was my neighbor and friend, so I turned my car around to see if I could extract him from this tangle.

The incident ended before I got there, and Jeff was walking away. Rain began. I pulled up next to Jeff. He didn't like strangers stopping him and he kept his face forward as I drove beside him. He didn't look up until I spoke, and when he heard my voice he stormed into the car, furious that the deputy had stopped to ask who he was. Jeff thought the lawman recognized him from his videos. I tried telling him their paths happened to cross at a spot notorious for drug activity, but he wouldn't hear it.

At the corner, instead of turning toward our street to go home, I turned away. An anger I hadn't seen in him flared. He demanded to be let out and opened his door while we were moving. The rain was hard, heavy, and dark. He did not want to know that I was only going one block out of the way. To calm him I told him I'd take him home directly. Fuck it, if he wanted to act like a rock star, I'd indulge his fame, don my chauffeur's hat, take his assholiness home, and then do my errand.

If he'd not died, the incident would have meant nothing. I see my happening onto him right after a cop as proof—if he was seeking proof—that he could not take a walk and be alone. He had owned Manhattan and walked away for just that—a place he could be alone.

He leapt out of my car, was immediately soaked. "I'll walk," he said. "It's nice out." It was not nice out. Is this what he had to say to find solitude?

ONE DAY A couple weeks earlier, Jeff had rung our doorbell at six sharp. "Look at this," I told my wife, leading Mr. Clean into the kitchen. We'd invited him for a home-cooked meal. He wore a frilly green three-piece thrift-store suit, two-tone black-and-white shoes, and a wide-brimmed hat tilted forward over his face. I assumed a matching green Cadillac with fake fur steering wheel was parked out front. He said, "I like to dress for dinner."

He and I drank red wine outside in the presummer heat. Our four-month-old daughter cooed at him, he cooed back, and they both laughed. After dinner, he wanted to retrieve a notebook he'd left at the downtown club where he had a weekly gig. "Sure they're open," he said, "live bands seven nights a week." We walked to his house where he got the keys to his rental car. Before leaving the house, he put on a Dead Kennedys CD and left it at top volume. In the driveway, I could hear every thudding beat. An Avon lady lived next door to him. I didn't ask questions.

He drove like his verbal riffs: all over the place. The club was, of course, closed. But his outfit was glowing, we were half-lit, and we hit a Beale Street beer hall that had a pool table. He laid two quarters in line for a game and steadily pumped the jukebox.

In Memphis, Jeff could play at anonymity: a dangerous, green-suited pool hustler running Beale. The bartender found his Grifters selection too noisy and pulled the plug. Jeff leapt onto the pool table and demanded not only that the machine be turned back on, but that he be given his money back so he could play the song again. A pretty girl recognized him and between pool shots handed him a menu and asked for an autograph. He was polite.

Usually, we left Jeff to his work up the street. He kept his blinds drawn. One evening I stopped by on my way to the neighborhood bar and he joined me. He talked about his dad that night, also a singer with a clarion voice. Tim Buckley was twenty-eight when he found a packet of powder and, mistaking the heroin for cocaine, laid out a fat line, snorted, and died. Jeff was eight at the time. He lived with his mother, her husband, and his half brothers, and back then his name was Scott J. Moorhead. Then he'd entered his old man's business, and though he didn't know him (he'd only spent a week with his dad), he was feeling the weight of his father's shadow. Dead at such an early age, Tim Buckley would be forever young. "The only way I can rebel against him," Jeff told me, "is to live."

YOU DON'T GO swimming in your boots without some kind of intent somewhere. Jeff was thirty when he drowned in the Mississippi River. I don't imagine that his father's specter ever left him, but I do believe life must have refracted through the ghost differently during Jeff's last couple years. My wife's father died when she was a child, and she speaks of the mixed feelings she had when she passed her father's age. Survivor's guilt ringed with survivor's triumph: "It didn't happen to me" becomes "it couldn't."

People like me who write about musicians have a relationship with celebrity that is either symbiotic or parasitic, depending on the perspective. Jeff and I had met by happenstance. It took an effort by me to suppress the opportunism presented by his fame. We never discussed doing an interview, though I took notes for one. He often covered an Alex Chilton song, "Kanga Roo"; Chilton plays a significant role in my first book, *It Came from Memphis*, but we never discussed that either. He'd never before played his fame card until that day in the rain, and then my own willingness to oblige made me painfully aware of how my friendship with him could shade into fandom, and fandom into servitude.

Fame is a buoy that raises you up and it's a weight that brings you down. Jeff Buckley was beautiful to behold, a blast to be around, a singular talent. He seemed strong enough for fame. His core bubbled with energy, an excitement that sometimes overpowered him. Talking about his dad in the bar, he bent to his drink and gnawed on the glass with his teeth. Though he could wrangle his power, like when he made music, he seemed most at ease letting it pour forth: A rush of comic routines. Impulsive actions. His wardrobe. Swimming in the river.

THE DAY AFTER the rain, I saw a furniture rental truck unloading beds at his house; Jeff's band was arriving.

A British magazine editor called the next morning asking me to confirm that Jeff had died of a drug overdose. "Let him work!" I said. "He wants to be alone." The editor assured me that this news was based in fact, that someone at Microsoft News had—but I cut him off and told him to leave the guy alone. Ten minutes later a friend at Jeff's label called to say reports were that Jeff had drowned, and what did I know about it?

My wife said if I'd been called about another of my neighbors having an accident, I'd have run to their door and knocked, made sure everything was okay. I did walk down to Jeff's house and stood in front of it, dumbly—his house looked like his house—but I wasn't about to disturb him with rumors of himself. An hour later, back home, I glanced out front and an image of his bandmates, their stooped backs, the shade of the magnolia tree, red Converse high-tops on asphalt—seared into my brain. Death. I'd never seen them before, but their dyed hair and disheveled look announced them as Jeff's guests, and their dazed walk and stupefied manner instantly confirmed the worst. It rained for four days after that.

THE FIRST DAYLIGHT hours passed as we waited for the phone to ring—for Jeff to tell us that a current had swept him away and deposited him, tired and delirious, in a forsaken corner of a cotton field and he'd walked for hours between rows to dirt paths to gravel and was finally calling from a gas station near a stupid Tunica casino, could someone please come pick him up right away and bring dry clothes, he was miserable. But that call didn't come. His mother came, his girlfriend, an aunt, a lawyer, and some record company people.

When Jeff Buckley immersed himself in that inlet of the Mississippi River, he swam out on his back, looking at the stars, singing a Led Zeppelin song. A tugboat passed and left a wake. He swallowed unexpected water. The shadow was heavy. The refraction was blinding. His boots were full.

It's said about Robert Johnson, the blues singer, that he lived a compartmentalized life. That to some he was Robert Dusty, to others Robert Spencer, and that his personae were as varied and as independent as the people to whom each was known. Jeff had a life in New York I knew little about, and his family was in California. But his absence broke down those partitions, and we survivors clung to each other in his house, surrounded by his belongings, waiting for our own different versions of the same person.

The tide of gossip rose in Jeff's absence. He staged his death for publicity. Or for solitude. He was on drugs. Suicide. Black magic. Fame worship always conceals a mean-spirited envy, a rooting for the lions over the gladiator. And Memphis is a city that reveres obscurity, is especially hostile toward success.

On the fourth day, before his body floated up, his mother called his friends to his house for a wake. His beautiful photograph was propped on the table, along with a candle and maybe a flower. She wanted to celebrate her son's life and she made a toast, reminding me how little we can each know of even the ones we call friend. She raised her glass, and we raised ours. Her words startled me: "To Scotty."

HIS SINGING WAS magisterial, like a pipe organ, natural like the northern lights. Jeff's voice made me want to build shrines—though now I see Jeff Buckley was the shrine to his voice. His sudden end has seeped into my memories of his passion and vitality, and I can't separate the purity of his tone from the tragedy of his fate.

MY SECOND CHILD is floating off to sleep in my arms. She has learned to crawl, is beginning to understand spatial relations. The puzzle that is everything she sees is beginning to have pieces and the pieces are beginning to fit. Her dreams have become more lifelike, and as she is momentarily disturbed into consciousness, her eyes open. She can't tell the worlds apart, and since the dream feels so much nicer than the coldness of reality, she doesn't fight the return. She drifts off.

BOBBY "BLUE" BLAND

O F ALL MY interviews, this one contains my favorite exchange. Bobby
Bland was all about presentation—in his music and in his person.
Though he came from dusty rural Rosemark, Tennessee, he didn't sing
dirty gutbucket blues; he fronted a sophisticated big band. Raised in clothes
made from sacks, he'd assumed a cosmopolitan flair as soon as he could
afford to, and probably before; since his first recording in 1950, he was
always debonair, usually finished with a nice cap and a pocket square. He
bore no rural accent, his airs entirely urbane. You knew shoes were a rare
blessing in his childhood, but to see him as an adult, you'd think he'd
always had a personal tailor.

As much as I knew all this, I still blew the second interview with him.
The first one, below, was held, per his request, in the Peabody, a distinguished southern hotel. The second was on video for "The Road to Memphis," an episode of Martin Scorsese's series *The Blues*. I thought it would
be great to interview Bobby at a surviving juke joint that his original
manager, Sunbeam Mitchell, had established. He arrived at Earnestine &
Hazel's with a scowl on his face. "We should be doing this at the Peabody,"
he said. Bobby Bland didn't connect with juke joints.

My favorite exchange? About the clothes and socks—it tells so much about
the person. And it was the first cut *Rolling Stone* made. That was hard to let

go of. I told myself that was exactly what was wrong with music magazines: They adhered too closely to music and not enough to the person and context. I hoped that one day I'd be able to present my own edit of the interview.

Love Throat

Rolling Stone, May 28, 1998

Bobby Bland's people seat me in a quiet corner of the Mallards bar in the Peabody, "the South's Grand Hotel." They make sure I'm comfortable. The chairs are plush, the décor is subdued; businesspeople make deals here during the daytime, jazz cats play heavy tunes at night. My back is to the wall, the easier to observe Bobby's arrival: An effective entrance demands the proper setup.

While waiting, I contemplate the country boy from Rosemark, Tennessee, who became the king of the blues ballad, Mr. Suave, the soft man, Bobby "Blue" Bland. Born about twenty miles from Memphis on January 27, 1930, he developed a cool, sophisticated, and smoky blues style. He prefers a bigger band and a classy joint over performing in a juke house, though he can handle both. A Duke Records artist for nearly two decades, his steady hits began in the late 1950s. He developed a trademark vocal sound, a kind of emphatic grunt—he calls it a "squall." It's a sound familiar both from the pulpit and from a bordello.

Since 1985, he has recorded for Malaco Records: nine albums, hits like "Members Only," "Midnight Run," and "She's Puttin' Something in My Food." *Midnight Run* stayed on *Billboard*'s Top Black Albums chart for more than fifty-two weeks, earning a special achievement award. Eric Clapton covered his "Farther Up the Road," the Grateful Dead covered his "Turn on Your Love Light." Whitesnake and Tom Jones have sung his songs. In his autobiography, B. B. King says of his lifelong friend, "He's my favorite singer."

And then from among the patrons, Bobby "Blue" Bland emerges. He is a big man, and he looks sharp in his gray suit, black turtleneck shirt (to protect his vocal cords from the chill), and black Kangol hat. He has long, manicured fingernails and what writer Peter Guralnick has described as "sad, liquid eyes." When he wipes his face with the gray hand towel he carries, his wrist flashes a gold watch with diamonds inset.

ROBERT GORDON: Is it true that you got your start as B. B. King's valet?

BOBBY "BLUE" BLAND: He had been a good friend of mine from day one in Memphis, before his first record came out. I idolized him, and I still do. And I said, B, Why don't you let me help you with your stuff—to drive or whatever. So he'd take me with him to small towns near Memphis if I didn't have anything to do, which was all the time.

RG: How did y'all meet?
BBB: My mother had a restaurant down near Beale Street, the Sterling Grill. And B used to eat there. All the musicians coming through would stop at Mrs. Bland's place. And we were on amateur nights together on Beale Street.

RG: Tell me about these amateur nights.
BBB: I won so often there they had to keep me off for a while. I knew all the new tunes because my mother had a jukebox in the place and I'd get everything first. First place was five dollars. Two–fifty second.

RG: What was the third-place prize?
BBB: I didn't have to find out.

RG: What was the first music you heard?
BBB: Spirituals, actually. It was church all the time for me. Church every day of the week, and Thursday night there'd be a prayer meeting in somebody's home. Sundays was church—all day.

RG: Did your religious background create any conflicts for you about singing the blues?
BBB: No, I talked that over with my mother when I first started getting into blues. She is very religious. I found the flavor of blues was so close to spirituals, and I always used "Oh Lord" in everything that I would record. If you have it in your heart, then the blues and the spirituals serve the same purpose.

RG: How did you get exposed to the blues?
BBB: We lived out in the country until I was about fifteen. This fellow named Mutt Piggee was a friend of my parents, and summer months he'd be drinking on the porch and he'd start to sing and play acoustic guitar. I was about eight years of age. He sang Blind Lemon Jefferson and Big Boy Crudup, Walter Davis, and Big Joe Williams.

There was no black music on the radio in Rosemark, Tennessee. I grew up on country and western: Roy Acuff, Eddy Arnold, Ernest Tubb's "Walking the Floor Over You." Hank Williams had the most understanding stories. He wrote things pertaining to love life and life itself. I loved Red Foley doing the hymns. That's the kind of stories that I come up around.

RG: Did you hear field hollers in the country?
BBB: Yeah, I did it myself. That's to make the time pass, to keep your mind off what you were doing that you didn't want to do. I didn't like to pick cotton or chop cotton, it was just too hot in the field for me. I used to sing on the grocery store porch out in Rosemark, Friday and Saturday. I had my Jew's harp and I had my tin can and I'd have it full before I'd leave. So I gathered that there was profit to be had if I could do it on a bigger scale. And my mother said, 'No, I'm not going to keep you out here, we're going to Memphis.' And that's why I got a chance.

RG: When did you get comfortable with a style of your own?
BBB: I had told B. B., "I can do everything you ever recorded," and he said, "Good, Bob, I love that, but you got to get some identification of your own." The ball just started rolling in 1957 with "Farther Up the Road," "I'll Take Care of You" in 1959, and then "Turn on Your Love Light" [1961] crossed over from the chitlin circuit. It got, if I can say, the white people to listen.

My approach is different from the average blues singer. I tried to do as well as I could with the diction. I studied Nat King Cole from front to back to upgrade my speaking ability and singing qualities. I'm not saying that it's perfect now, but it's a long way from Rosemark.

RG: Your speaking voice has the same exciting timbre as your singing voice.
BBB: Well that comes from your parents and God. You're born with it.

RG: Was there anyone you knew in the country who you thought was suave?
BBB: The first clothes that I got attached to was my uncle's, we called him Dude. He was a sharp dresser. He'd come down from Chicago and I'd see the threads he'd have on. He was wearing those shirts that buttoned diagonally across your chest, and I thought that was so sharp.

RG: Do black shoes go with black socks?

BBB: Sure, only.

RG: Only?

BBB: Only. My colors were gray, black, blue—and brown maybe. And when you wear brown, you wear brown with brown. Some people can wear black with brown, but I wouldn't feel right.

RG: What's the deal with that sound you make? And what do you call it?

BBB: It's been called several things. In England, they described it as "a love throat" and I can live with that. I got the idea from Reverend C. L. Franklin, Aretha's father. I played a sermon that he had, "The Eagle Stirreth Her Nest" over and over and over. They build bigger cages for the eagle as it gets bigger, but when her wings hit the cage, they have to turn her loose, and that's when Reverend Franklin would do the squall. I had to work with that a long time before I got it to perfection.

RG: Earlier you mentioned the chitlin circuit——

BBB: All-black circuit. Racism was out there. Period. From day one and it's always been there. It's a thing you have to learn to live with, because The System has a certain way to project things to you, and it's left up to you to understand that. They made the blues seem as if it was only for black people. But they never listen at how much blues they have in a country and western song.

RG: Have you ever wanted to fight The System?

BBB: That thought may have come across my mind, but why cut off your nose to spite your face? Things have been this way since day one. You've got people out there who like that particular fight. Martin Luther King, Jesse Jackson, they are trying to get things better for everybody, black and white. So I'm going to let people do what they know best. If I can help, do a benefit, sure.

RG: How do your shows now differ from a show you might have done on the chitlin circuit?

BBB: My shows are not any different. I talked to B about it. I said, I'm kind of nervous about a white audience. He said, Did they book you here on what you've done? I said, Yeah. Well then you sing what you know to sing, don't do anything different. You wouldn't be there if they didn't understand you. And that helped me in Japan too. A little Japanese boy came to the back door while we were going into the auditorium and he had an armful of my LPs and he wanted them autographed. I saw this and wondered if he really understood? He said, "I got the brues," he couldn't say *blues*. "I got the brues." That left the door open for me.

RG: What sort of rooms are you playing now?
BBB: I do clubs and auditoriums, and my audience is mixed, which I'm very happy about. It's a good feeling to look out across the house and think about what you came up with and how it is now. It's a big difference. But I've cut down on touring. I had a triple bypass in 1995, so I'm only out like twenty-five, thirty weeks. I was on the road from 1955 constantly, way into the 1970s.

RG: Would you rather play to an audience that's dancing or listening?
BBB: Listening, man! Because I have something to say. Dancing, that's for people spinning records.

RG: What did it mean to you being inducted into the Rock and Roll Hall of Fame?
BBB: I enjoyed it, but I thought it should have been labeled as rhythm and blues, not rock and roll. But I was happy that it happened in my lifetime. These things usually happen after you're gone. "Rock and Roll" Hall of Fame, that's The System again, whatever label they have.

RG: Why do you think the blues survives?
BBB: Because it's true. It's something that everybody goes through one time or another. The blues is just life, disappointments, mishaps. After everything we've been through, the plantation when we couldn't do anything about it, we had to make the day pass. That was The System [he raps his knuckles on the tabletop]. So you just kind of roll with the punches. I learn from mistakes and then I learn about life. That's why I sing about life period. Love and life.

TAV FALCO

Tav looked at me and said, "Our show was great. We cleared the room." A pal of mine was at the smallish San Francisco club where Tav was playing, said that the anticipation prior was palpable. My guess is the audience thought they were seeing a revivalist, a rockabilly band from Memphis, the real thing playing the real thing. They didn't know how right they were, but not like they expected.

Tav Falco's Unapproachable Panther Burns are an art action wrapped in a juke joint bundled in an enigma. Witnessing the Panther Burns is always a surprise—from the personnel to the set list to the range of styles. Besides funked-up versions of R. L. Burnside's one- and two-chord blues drones and keening takes on early rockabilly, tangos are in their DNA and sambas are a recent addition.

Tav came to music in a physical way. "It was the feeling and aesthetic that mattered, more than musicianship or virtuosity," he told me. "I didn't feel hindered by my lack of conventional guitar knowledge. I just went into it full tilt." An admirer of Antonin Artaud's Theatre of Cruelty, he brings a strong sense of drama to his stage. You know how blues players can play out of tune and keep their own sense of time? Tav applied the aesthetic to a band, and it worked even when it didn't work. His early shows were prolonged unhinged explosions, caterwauling spectacles, forces to

The Panther Burns original lineup at the Well, 1979. From left, Alex Chilton, Eric Hill, Rick Ivy, Tav Falco, Ross Johnson. (Courtesy of Ebet Roberts)

yield to. Later, through skills learned over time, the band could lock into a groove and hold a dance floor with a hypnotic Mississippi riff, sending feet, hips, and arms all akimbo. But their hold on the groove was tenuous; the next beat was not assured. A Panther Burns gig was like that bad starter that sometimes cranks the old car—inexplicable and unreliable. It was not the neat and tidy act that San Francisco anticipated.

Gurdon, Arkansas, where Tav says he's from, is actually the biggest town near where he grew up—it's held a population of around 2000 for about a hundred years. It was a railroad stop between Little Rock and Texarkana, and before Tav pursued music, the tracks were his path out of town. "I worked all the branch lines of what they call the dark railroad—where there were no electric signals. Everything was done by lantern and hand signals."

In the 1950s, when his father was away from the family's farm, young Gustavo would play a 78 of Wagner's dramatic "Ride of the Valkyries" at full blast on the old man's navy phonograph. His mother bought him a Bakelite AM radio and the first song that came through it was Wilbert Harrison's "Kansas City." When his family passed through Shreveport,

Louisiana, he'd purchase records by Elvis, Johnny Cash, and the Sun artists. He never lost his appreciation for the music around him, sharing his stage with artists that Memphis had pushed aside. Charlie Feathers, the female rocker Cordell Jackson, Jessie Mae Hemphill—the She Wolf who was the last in her family's line of Mississippi hill country musicians—Otha Turner, and many others; Tav alerted a new generation to their existence.

We collaborated on the music video for "Memphis Beat," and film is how we actually met: In the late 1980s, I had some sixteen-millimeter stock and he had a camera. I earned his respect when his car came at me and I kept filming, taking a hit from an open door and rolling (physically and cinematically)—getting the shot, protecting the camera, and bleeding from my head. It was, in a way, a metaphor for being in his audience.

Panther Burns Forever Lasting
Previously unpublished, 1994

ROBERT GORDON: When did you first come to Memphis?
TAV FALCO: Little Rock to Memphis, zooming across the Arkansas delta on a caboose, 1964. I was a brakeman on the Missouri Pacific Railroad. Coming up to the river atop the trestle, a long wait to get clearance over the Mississippi on the one-track Harahan Bridge into Memphis. Below was this alluvial soil stretching out into the Arkansas quasi-delta there. I came rolling through these little Arkansas towns and music was already in the air. I could feel it.

RG: What did you find when you got here?
TF: For one, there were more black people than I'd ever seen in one concentration. Good-looking black people. Well dressed. Everything really snapping. There was a pleasing intensity in the air.

During the summers, 1965 or so, I was braking on the Missouri Pacific Railroad and going to the University of Arkansas during the school year. In Memphis, a woman named Mae ran this boardinghouse near the yard. Her husband worked for the railroad and she used to live in Gurdon. I had a school friend staying there. I walked up, there's Mae on the front porch in a calico dress, barefooted, in a rocking chair, she was chain-smoking Pall Malls and I swear, man—with one foot she was turning the crank of an ice-cream churn. She said, Yeah, we got a room for ya. My friend who was staying there said, You gotta be careful around Mae, she can read your mind.

In Memphis, I bought a Silvertone solid body electric guitar for five dollars and played that at home until I met Randall Lyon and I traded for a small open-reel tape recorder. And then I wanted to record things.

RG: Randall is such a great character. Tell me about meeting him.

TF: I met an Arkansas poet up in the Ozark Mountains. He was shuffling between the university in Fayetteville and communes around Eureka Springs and certain other Ozark outposts. He was turning me on to Djuna Barnes and Carl Jung and Eastern philosophy, and he had stories of Furry Lewis and Bukka White in Memphis. And this young poet's name was Randall Lyon.

I met Randall in my college dormitory, 1964. He was visiting a literature major and he'd just gotten out of army intelligence, Vietnam. Randall looked like a big baby. A big angel, maybe an evil angel. With real smooth skin and all this baby fat. And had a brilliant way of speaking. He was consumed by poetry and literature and art, talking constantly and laughing. He lived in a garret in Fayetteville. You walked through the curtain and there was Randall in his lair, surrounded by books and candles and weird tapestries. He was part of that bearded, sandaled, intellectual youth culture that Billy Graham was railing against. His ideas were radical and genuine. He brought Buckminster Fuller to Fayetteville. Through Randall I had an idea of what might be—far off in Memphis.

Randall Lyon. "You walked through the curtain and there was Randall in his lair, surrounded by books and candles and weird tapestries. He was part of that bearded, sandaled, intellectual youth culture that Billy Graham was railing against." (Courtesy of Tav Falco)

Randall and I came to the big city armed. And Memphis was explosive. It's always been this cross-cultural town. It's not people from Memphis but people who come here. Teenie Hodges'll tell you this and blues people will too. It's people from other places coming here and doing things.

RG: You realized that at the Memphis Country Blues Festival, right? What year did you first see that?

TF: The Memphis Country Blues Society organized the first Memphis Country Blues Festivals in the Overton Park band shell in 1966, and I was at the first one. I came over from Arkansas and this really turned my head around, hundreds of people coming from all over the country, getting this firsthand, immediate experience and knowledge. I got to be within twenty-four inches of Furry Lewis's hands, saw him reach a crowd of thousands of people, the man with the wooden leg that was cut off on the Illinois Central in 1917 and he then became a Memphis street sweeper, a very lyrical, crowd-pleasing, warm bluesman who had so many girlfriends it was unbelievable. I saw Sleepy John Estes from Brownsville, Tennessee, and Hammie Nixon with him blowing jug. Bukka White was playing the dobro guitar with a jackknife and singing "Parchman Farm Blues." And Nathan Beauregard doing "Highway 61 Blues," ninety-one years old and playing electric guitar solo like I've never heard anybody play. Mississippi Fred McDowell, the most gothic bluesman I've ever heard. And Ronnie Hawkins, he hit the stage with the Jim Dickinson Blues Band.

Furry Lewis and friend. "A very lyrical crowd-pleasing warm blues man who had so many girlfriends it was unbelievable." (Courtesy of Tav Falco)

RG: What of the tape recorder?

TF: The Beat writer John Clellon Holmes came to Fayetteville. He had a whole library of tapes instead of records. And I thought, I'm gonna take this recorder to Memphis and maybe I'll get to do a little work. And then later I moved to Memphis, 1973.

I wasn't railroading anymore. I was living a very bohemian life, a disaffected student. Running barefooted a lot. Overton Square was really happening then. Burkle's Bakery, the Perception bar—I'd hear Furry Lewis there or Gimmer Nicholson. Beatnik Manor was right there, and John McIntire opened the Bitter Lemon, very elegant, very beautiful art nouveau–cum–hungry i San Francisco beatnik woodcut graphic style.

RG: So you made this leap.

TF: I moved here and lived on pimento cheese sandwiches from Leonard Lubin's White Way Pharmacy. I was this strange hophead Arkansas mountain boy driving a 1950 Ford that sounded a little too loud by Memphis standards. I was accepted, but I think Arkansas people in Memphis are always regarded with circumspection.

And then I got a job with William Eggleston.

RG: This was 1974ish. So Bill is just entering the national consciousness. What did you know about him?

TF: People were talking about this elegant southerner living in a quasi-decayed Italianate pseudo-mansion with an Arriflex movie camera in

Photographers Maude Schuyler Clay and William Eggleston. (Courtesy of Tav Falco)

a wicker basket in his darkroom. And he was making a lot of pictures and wore suits tailored on Savile Row in London except when in khakis going through strange neighborhoods in Memphis and Mississippi making Leica pictures.

So finally I rode up to Bill's house on this Norton motorcycle I had and knocked on the door. He hired me right there. We got in his Bentley and bought darkroom supplies and I started to work. I was doing black-and-white printing. His whole approach was literary. It's not the one picture but it's the five hundred pictures that you have to consider, a novel in progress or a novel of pictures. I worked with Bill a couple years. He introduced me to Garry Winogrand and Lee Friedlander. So for me, there's been no separation between literature and theater and visual arts and blues and rock and roll and jazz. And this is my formative experience.

RG: What a great time to be with Bill! This is when he's shooting *Stranded in Canton*. He's got a portable video camera—itself a rarity at the time, to be able to get video and audio on a single unit. And he's adapted it for low-light shooting. What do you recall about that?
TF: He hung out with some very gothic people in Memphis and New Orleans. Eggleston shot Johnny Woods, the Mississippi blues harp player, and Furry Lewis with a very advanced low-light-sensitive, black-and-white, extremely high-resolution camera that he designed and built at MIT. Memphis has always had this overlap between musicians and visual artists that you see in places like New York or San Francisco. *Stranded in Canton* was shown around various galleries in the world. I think you can still get that from Castelli / Sonnabend. And during this time, Bill, with his Memphis entourage, savaged a few art galleries where these were shown.

RG: You performed with his girlfriend Marcia Hare, right?
TF: Around 1973 or '74, after moving to Memphis, Randall Lyon and I and Connie Edwards and Marcia Hare—the go-go dancers for Mud Boy and the Neutrons—formed the Big Dixie Brick Company. We performed on most Mud Boy shows, and we helped create the Dream Carnivals, these ecstatic unleashings of unconscious sub-Freudian urges in a very electric theatrical musical context. A rock and roll Dionysian context. Randall was doing his Guru Biloxi characterization, dressed in a very flowing Blanche DuBois-in-her-terminal-stages-of-dementia type presentation. He would sing "In My Girlish Days" from Memphis Minnie's repertoire. I did the three-legged man wearing one of John McIntire's

fezzes. And we were not above whipping our audience with twigs and other direct hands-on confrontation.

RG: John McIntire seems to have fueled a lot of the seventies scene around here.

TF: He had all the props, the films, the images. And a lot of ideas. He was the real guru of this thing. He could calm and guide you if you were freaking out. It was good to be around McIntire, pick up on his vibe. I've still got a sixteen-millimeter movie camera, a 1941 model, one of two he had. I bought the trashy one. Once you get the image off the film, it looks like a 1929 camera. McIntire sold it for fifty dollars and let me take eight years to pay.

Televista did a series on him when he was building that monumental sculpture downtown, *The Muse*.

RG: Your production company, Televista, captured that great video footage of R. L. Burnside in his Mississippi juke joint. I still think it is among the most riveting documents I've ever seen.

TF: That was 1974. I formed Televista with Randall Lyon. We were inspired by Jean Rouch and Dziga Vertov, the handheld camera filmmakers, and also influenced by William Eggleston's approach, which was quite different from his photographs. There's a powerful emotional gradient that Bill was going for in *Stranded in Canton*. Televista was also into early

R. L. Burnside's chalk house outside Como, Mississippi. (Courtesy of Tav Falco)

telecommunications, setting up video networks with other highly alternative video groups, of which there were only a few: Electronic Arts Intermix in New York, Relay in San Francisco, and Open Space in Canada.

As I began to play guitar, we were making videos with people like R. L. Burnside, and I got very much under the influence of this trance music that he was playing in Como, Mississippi, and this lodge 'tonk that he had out in the country. We made some videos there, all-night things, hours and hours that we edited down in Eggleston's makeshift video-editing facility. And I got very much under the influence of what he was playing, these one- and two-chord trancelike songs that would last fifteen minutes.

Televista made quite a few art actions and videos and had a little archive going. But Televista had no real commercial prospects. It only ever lost money. I did get a small grant from the National Endowment, but money was a subversion for us. We did our best work before we got that grant. We were doing installations with video playback. Randall was making music, along the lines of Stockhausen and atonal La Monte Young things. We were into the orphic vision.

RG: I've always heard that the start of the Panther Burns was at the Tennessee Waltz, when Mud Boy decided if the Band could have a last waltz and retire, so could they. [They didn't.] And they put on that big show at the Orpheum, 1978.

TF: That was the first time I ever sang in public. I asked Dickinson if I could do a song between their sets. There was this rock and roll thing going down so I went out solo. I had my own big black-and-white television monitor and Bill Eggleston's son was shooting video to it. I had my own amplifier that I was running the guitar through. I was independent, freestanding—nobody could fuck with me. I also had an electric chainsaw and an electric Skilsaw. And I started this strange guitar playing—nobody else was playing like that that day, believe me. I began my treatment of the "Bourgeois Blues." It was powerful sounding.

> *Home of the brave*
> *Land of the free*
> *I won't be mistreated*
> *By no bourgeoisie.*

I worked up this frenzy, then I start blowing this police whistle and with the chainsaw I start ripping into this guitar that's still going through the sound system. The sound, man, it was complete sound, extremely chaotic. People were screaming and they're going crazy and I rip through that guitar.

When Alex came over a couple of months later, he recognized me immediately as the guy that was on stage.

RG: Well how did Panther Burns actually become a band with you and Alex Chilton and others?
TF: I lived on the proletarian end of Cox Street, not on the mansion end. My upstairs duplex cost fifty-five dollars a month. The bathroom had no floor, just ceiling rafters. I got a job doing titling in a film lab and worked with Mitchell and Arriflex and Bolex cameras in a graphic context.

My friend Amy Gassner was on the phone at my house and she said this guy wants to bring his guitar and play. He brings an acoustic guitar and I'm playing this funky electric through Lee Baker's Stromberg-Carlson hi-fi amplifier. This guy's got real short hair and kind of freaky looking, and he starts playing "96 Tears" and he sings great. This guy's Alex Chilton. I really didn't know who he was. I was playing this fractured Burnside-style blues and he was playing rock and roll. So there was this rapport between me and Alex.

That night we got to be friends. Alex says, Let's start a band. Televista was out of money. They were trying to repossess our video equipment, so I was getting more underground. So I said, Okay. And we went to one of Sid Selvidge's performances at Jefferson Square and did a couple of numbers. That was the first ever Panther Burns movement action. I think we did "Bourgeois Blues" and "Train Kept A-Rollin'." And at seven one morning they did break down the front door and confiscated all the video equipment. Televista was over and the Panthers Burns had begun.

RG: But you've fallen into a band with Alex Chilton, you find out who he is—that's got to be exciting.
TF: At this point it was a Memphis thing. I've seen bands and bands and bands in Memphis. I thought, That's gonna be groovy, but I didn't imagine we were gonna play out much. We got Ross Johnson on drums and Eric Hill on a very crude synthesizer—see Eric didn't know music, I didn't know music, and Ross didn't. Alex knew musical form and he thought it would be more interesting this way. New York had this No Wave scene. It was the feeling that mattered, the aesthetic more than virtuosity.

The Antenna Club, previously the Well. Home to Memphis's alternative rock scene from 1977 until sometime in the 1990s. (Courtesy of Dan Ball)

RG: Y'all blazed the trail in Memphis for the 1980s counterculture scene, the DIY punk rock that was so unlike the popular southern rock Molly Hatchet scene or the people drinking Singapore Slings in fern bars.

TF: We rented a cotton loft, 96 South Front, for the first Panther Burns show. We were really inspired. That show must have been the rawest, most ripping, and hideous sounding Panther Burns show ever. On our tenth-anniversary single, the B-side is "Red Headed Woman" from our debut, and you can hear just how bizarre and outside it is.

We made a little money that night, more than I'd made in months. The next show at 96 South Front had blues lady Van Zula Hunt and barrel-house piano man Mose Vinson. And Panther Burns. The third show was with Charlie Feathers. Record collectors have supplied me with a lot of ideas, I'm glad they're out there. And we made all our own posters, printed by this émigré from central Europe, he understood us right away. "Oh the anarchists—get special price." Eventually we, along with the Randy Band, took over this little country and western bar called the Well and pretty soon it became the Antenna Club.

RG: I approached you at the Well after a set, over on the side of the stage. Your girlfriend or someone approached and whipped a Heineken bottle right at your head. You ducked, it smashed behind us, and I ducked out.

TF: I escaped the ice picks and the flying Heineken bottles. But it's tough for a band in their hometown to survive, so we had to start traveling. The

Cramps invited us to New Orleans and then to New York. Rough Trade Records was at our first big headline gig in New York and immediately gave us an album deal. For *Behind the Magnolia Curtain* I brought the fife and drum bands that exist only in Tate and Panola counties in Mississippi, Otha Turner playing hand-cut cane fife. That polyrhythmic percussion really distinguished the album. Then New Rose, a label in Paris, brought us to Europe.

We were getting known. The Clash called for Panther Burns to open a couple shows on their last U.S. tour in '84. It's the closest I've ever been to a riot. Nashville was pretty rough, but in Knoxville they set us up in front of the curtain, my little four-piece doing this strange blues. Fistfights were breaking out, the audience cursing us. It was university students' mentality, rednecks for the Clash. I was doing "Tina, the Go Go Queen," truly trying to entertain them, and I stopped the song. I held up my hands and Alex was ghostly white and getting whiter. He threw up his hands and then the audience fucking went crazy, screaming, and I launched into the "Bourgeois Blues." I hit it so hard and so heavy and they understood every fucking word, and I played it a long time and left them howling crazy.

All the people with the Clash immediately flushed over to us, said, *What a show!* At the dinner before, they wouldn't hardly say a word to us.

RG: Alex produced the Cramps in Memphis twice, 1977 and '79. Were you aware of their work?
TF: The Cramps were a big influence on Panther Burns. I did meet them when they came to Memphis for *Songs the Lord Taught Us*, that Alex Chilton produced at Sam Phillips Recording Service. The way they were making their own psychedelic treatment with early rock and roll and rockabilly music forms, Memphis music—this was something I wanted to do with blues.

More than any of the other punk or alternative bands, even more so than Iggy, I see the Cramps as a manifestation of Antonin Artaud's Theatre of Cruelty. The Cramps are the most lyrical. Lux confronts the audience on a more direct, a more personal, unconscious level than any of these other performers. And he's using rock and roll and silly songs as his vehicle. Everybody else is very restrained onstage, but he is a complete contrast. Critics write off the Cramps as a novelty band, and that's absurd.

RG: *Like Flies on Sherbert* seems like it would have opened a door for you.
TF: There's a direct influence from those sessions to the Panther Burns. Alex and Jim Dickinson, they were experimenting: Jim making the synthesizer

sound like a chicken squawking, getting strange sounds out of this real basic machine—this was the sound I wanted with Eric Hill. I think *Like Flies* is one of Alex's most successful records, but it's one the critics understand least.

RG: You've left Memphis, departed the U.S. Where are you living?
TF: I'm living in Vienna right now. After Memphis for thirteen years, I've had that great opportunity to be in a different culture and look back at my environment and at myself. That's important for an artist. If I stayed in Memphis, I don't think I would see enough. I feel more capable of bringing something out of myself than I ever have. I've infused our own Panther Burn ethos into Frank Sinatra songs and a samba and a tango. I think I can do these songs before almost any people now and they will not recoil and say, Oh this is so doggone strange I can't understand you, I can't listen, I've gotta leave.

JERRY LEE LEWIS

THE ODDS WERE long that Jerry Lee would be the last man standing from the Sun Records A-team. But after Johnny Cash died in 2003, no one else was left. Elvis Presley, Carl Perkins, Roy Orbison—the real wild child still reigned.

In 2005, I got word that "the Killer" was recording a new album in Memphis. I was friendly with his longtime associate and sometime manager J. W. Whitten. Jerry Lee is always a story, and when I asked about hanging around, J. W. welcomed me to the closed sessions, saying, "Just don't get in the way." At a Chicago signing for my Muddy Waters biography, *Can't Be Satisfied*, an editor from *Playboy* introduced himself, said he was a fan, and invited me to write for the magazine. He liked the idea of a story on Jerry Lee.

I assumed that I'd sit down with Jerry Lee sometime during the latter half of 2005 when I was attending these intermittent recording sessions. J. W. never said no, but neither did he affirm. Gradually, as I watched Jerry Lee in action over an extended period, I realized the access I was getting was full of more truth than any interview would be. You make your story with what you get, and I got all I could ask for.

Last Killer Standing

Playboy, February 2005

It's a December night and despite the chill, Jerry Lee Lewis enters the Sam Phillips Recording Service in Memphis wearing flip-flops, green-and-blue plaid pajama bottoms, and a loose nylon jacket with a casino's logo on the back. His band, along with the L.A. producer and engineer, have been waiting, and they gather around rock and roll's original wild child, now seventy years old.

"You seen your mama lately?" Jerry Lee asks Kenny Lovelace, his guitar player of thirty-seven years.

"Was in Louisiana last week," Kenny says.

"Tell your mama hello."

Jerry's in a good mood. Every night is different, and it can change from minute to minute, but this night, there's a sharpness to his attitude that indicates all is right in his inscrutable world.

Some of the players are sipping beer, some grape soda. The L.A. producer, Jimmy Rip, tells Jerry that the song they cut at the previous session, a rare Jerry Lee original called "Ol' Glory," now has harmony vocals on it from country star Toby Keith. Jerry Lee's in a storytelling mood, and the mention of one country star brings on a story about another. "You remember when old Waylon Jennings loaned me his fiddle?" Everyone nods and says, Yeah, yeah. "He knew my reputation on the piano and Waylon said, 'I want it back in the same shape you're getting it.'" Jerry Lee giggles a little, then says he told Waylon, "Or what?" There's a beat and then everyone laughs, picturing these two music outlaws in a standoff.

But nothing gets past Jerry Lee. He sees everything that happens and senses everything that doesn't. It's a good story—told well—but it didn't get the guffaws he expected, so he rolls on to another, one that conveys both humor and the sense of menacing hostility that always percolates below Jerry Lee's skin. "You remember that record we cut in London?" Jerry asks Kenny, who played on *The Session* album. "Had all those people there and that drummer showed up, what's his name?" The category's too huge and no one suggests a name. "Played with that English band." It's slimmer now, but not by enough. Jerry Lee stammers, how to define him: "Ahh, ahh, played with the Beatles."

"Ringo," they all say. Oh *that* English band. "Yeah, Ringo. We kept him waiting there, and waiting. Not on purpose, but it just happened, until finally he couldn't get in the room and announced, 'Y'all can shove this record up your butts,' and he walked out of there." This time he gets the laughs. Ringo probably didn't say *y'all*, but Jerry Lee sure did, cackling.

HALF A CENTURY since the sun rose on rock and roll, Elvis and Buddy Holly are dead, Carl Perkins and Johnny Cash are dead. Little Richard is a caricature when he's not a minister, and Chuck Berry's going through the motions. Only Jerry Lee Lewis is still rocking.

The Killer is the unlikeliest survivor, but dying would have been the easy way out. In 1957, he created rock's first great scandal—as an incestuous, cradle-robbing bigamist. He was twenty-two, and his wife Myra, his third wife, was thirteen. She was also his cousin. He tried to assuage the outcry by doubting the marriage's validity, as he had never divorced his first wife. Record sales dried up. Not long past Myra's sweet sixteen, their three-year-old son drowned in their backyard pool. A decade would pass before the public showed renewed warmth to him, and then only when he remade himself as a country singer. Tragedy stayed twinned to his triumphs; his firstborn from a previous marriage was killed in a single-car wreck in 1973.

Lewis is in the midst of divorcing his sixth wife. The onetime Miss Kerrie McCarver, however unhappy, must find relief in being the former and not the late Mrs. Jerry Lee Lewis. After nineteen years of marriage, she's alive to tell the tale. Wife number five, the twenty-five-year-old Shawn Michelle Stevens, was not so lucky; she was found dead of an apparent drug overdose in the Nesbit, Mississippi, bedroom she'd shared with Jerry Lee for less than four months. Only a year prior, wife number four, Jaren Gunn, had also died—a swimming accident while awaiting a divorce decree. There've been fistfights, handguns, shotguns. On a tear in 1976, he accidentally shot his bass player in the chest (not fatally), flipped his car, and waved a handgun outside Graceland when Elvis wouldn't come out and say hello; the next day, Elvis went to visit Jerry Lee, who was out, and wound up signing autographs on Jerry Lee's lawn.

Jerry Lee Lewis drank more whiskey, took more pills, and had more car wrecks than most rock bands combined. He's broken out of hospitals, fled Betty Ford Center treatment, and seen Hollywood make a cartoon of him. Newspapers have had his obituary on file at least since 1986, when he had emergency surgery for a ruptured stomach. Life, it seems, has clung to him, not he to life.

That's unlike his peer, Elvis Presley. Elvis died like a wimp. Elvis was a girl. Wouldn't fuck his beautiful wife? Got so fat he had to wear jumpsuits? Sang suck-ass songs like "The Impossible Dream"? And *that* wore him out at forty-two? "What the shit did Elvis do," Jerry once said, "except take dope I couldn't get ahold of?"

Survivors are the real sufferers.

BUT HERE HE is, in Memphis, still recording and rocking, looking not half-bad and telling the warm-up stories of a rock and roll legend. Within thirty minutes of walking through the front door, Jerry Lee is down to business, running through tonight's song, simultaneously simplifying it and making it more complex—Lewis-izing it. It's a song called "Twilight," by Robbie Robertson, a founding member of the Band, and the lyrics are about yearning for companionship while seeking the freedom of solitude. Jerry Lee really delivers on the refrain: "Don't put me in a frame upon the mantel / 'Fore memories turn dusty old and grey."

Everyone's familiar with the song. Now it's a matter of the band all knowing it the same way, Lewis's way, because he is one of music's great interpreters—a "stylist," he calls it. "There's only ever been four stylists," he's famously stated. "Jerry Lee Lewis, Hank Williams, Al Jolson, and Jimmie Rodgers." You can count the songs Lewis has written on one hand, but none of the hundreds of songs he's recorded can be imitated. "Twilight" is about to metamorphose wildly.

Seated behind the piano, fooling with the progression of the song, he says to himself more than to anyone in particular, "This song's got a lot of chords in it." He begins the process with a sincere respect for the composer's intentions. It's just that Jerry's ideas are better. "We got to play 'em. I don't know 'em."

The bass player pipes up. "I know 'em."

"Show 'em to me."

"Would you take offense?"

"C'mon."

B. B. Cunningham strolls over to the piano. Cartoonist R. Crumb couldn't have drawn B. B. better. He has a long, narrow face, its verticality emphasized by the ponytail that hangs to the middle of his back. His eyebrows can knit like a granny's sewing needles, a worried look that appears when he smiles, which is often. B. B.'s father was a Sun recording artist, and in 1967, B. B.'s band the Hombres had a top-twenty hit with "Let It All Hang Out." He first played with Jerry Lee in 1961, worked with George Clinton and Chuck Berry, and rejoined Jerry in 1997.

At the piano, B. B. runs down the chords. Jerry Lee watches, then does it himself. B. B. makes a correction near the end of the run. Jerry Lee gets it right, then states, flatly, "I don't like it."

"Look," says B. B., "you can do it like this." He runs through the chords with a variation.

"I don't like that either." Then Jerry's talking just to B. B. He says, his voice low, "When I was thirteen years old, my piano teacher showed me a song. He was sitting right next to me like you are. When he got through with it, I said, 'Wouldn't it sound better like this?' And reached in front of him and played my way. And the guy slapped me in the face."

"I bet that got your attention."

"It did more than that," Jerry answered. "Since then I haven't been able to learn anything from anybody. That was my last lesson. Get up and play your bass, B. B." Jerry turns to the studio's control room and says, "Maybe you should put one of those little things on there, ahh, ahh, what do you call them?"

"CDs," says J. W. Whitten, Jerry Lee's road manager, right-hand man, and mind reader.

"Yeah, play the CD." He wants to hear the "Twilight" original again.

As B. B. returns to his position, he mutters, "I never thought I'd do that in my life, show Jerry Lee something on the piano." (Actually, B. B. had done it once before, forty-two years ago, in 1962, at Jerry's home when he was a guitar player in the band. He'd told him that to make a major chord into a minor chord on the piano, he had to change only one finger. Jerry Lee didn't believe him, didn't like the notion at all, and he chased B. B. out of the room and out the front door.)

The song's rhythm evolves as Jerry begins playing. Producer Jimmy Rip, whose roots are in Texas and who evokes a beatnik cowboy, plays guitar. He says to the others, "He's putting a shuffle in it." The band feels their way and the song begins to sway. Jerry Lee's singing, "It never crossed my mind / What's right and what's not," and a yip and yodel creep into his voice. Rip and Kenny Lovelace glance at each other and laugh. On music stands before them, there's a string of chords written out, but Jerry has simplified the song, each slew of chords summarized and expressed in the sweep of a single chord—not just that chord, but the space between that one and ones on either side of it. What's not played is creating feeling, room for Jerry Lee Lewis to make "Twilight" his own.

"We got to come to some sort of collusion here about how we're going to end," says Jerry Lee. "It's hard to end that song, it's so pretty. "

Jimmy Rip answers with understated praise, "I love what you did to it." Then he adds, "It's a thrill to me giving you these songs and hearing what you give back. It's always better."

"If you hear something wrong," Jerry Lee answers, "don't hesitate to tell me so I can kill you."

JERRY LEE LEWIS was born to Elmo and Mamie Lewis on September 29, 1935, in Ferriday, Louisiana, a town that smells worse than shit. Ferriday is on the Mississippi River, across from Natchez, Mississippi, and there's a paper plant there. The waft from a paper plant is all-encompassing. The stench is not something you just smell—you taste it, wear it, turn your face from but can't escape it.

Tragedy first hit Jerry Lee's life when he was three. His older brother, Elmo Jr., already displaying a strong musical talent at seven, was killed by a drunk driver. Around that same time, the Assembly of God church opened in Ferriday, and Elmo Lewis Sr. was drawn there, not just for consolation but also for the raucous music. He collected Jimmie Rodgers records and he liked to play guitar. The Assembly of God is a fundamentalist church that believes in visible manifestations of the Spirit, such as healing, visions, and everyday miracles. Their services capture the spirit of God through rapturous music, often expressed by fits in the aisles, by speaking in tongues, by shaking your nerves and rattling your brains.

Another early rock and roller was raised in a similar church. Elvis Presley got his stage moves from the Pentecostals he'd seen shaking on the pulpit. With their flailing and gyrations, neither Elvis nor Jerry Lee was doing anything he wouldn't do on Sunday in front of his mother.

Like Elvis, whose twin died at birth, Jerry Lee was a surviving son. He was raised to be adulated. His parents risked their house to buy Jerry Lee an upright piano when he was ten. His mother, reveling in the sight of him, would run to his side, lift his arm, and call everyone close: "Look at the hairs!" she'd say to the assembled, and then to the golden-haired golden boy, "Jerry, every hair on your arm is perfect." To which he would respond, "It certainly is."

His style had already been formed. "The first song I learned to play was 'Silent Night,' and I played *that* rock and roll style," he says. His influences at the time included Gene Autry, the singing cowboy whom he'd listened to from the alley behind the local movie theater (his family couldn't afford the dime to enter), his parents' hillbilly records, Hank Williams (since hearing Hank broadcast on *The Louisiana Hayride* in 1948, he'd been a committed fan), and the blues. Jerry Lee could hear the blues in Hank because he also heard it at Haney's Big House in Ferriday, a juke joint for black field hands that Jerry Lee regularly snuck into, usually in company with his cousins Mickey Gilley, who became a country music star, and

Jimmy Swaggart, later a famous television preacher, then an infamous one caught in several tangles with prostitutes.

At fourteen, Jerry Lee made his first public appearance, playing in the parking lot of Ferriday's Ford dealership. "Drinking Wine Spo-Dee O'Dee" was a hit that year, and the audience responded to it that day; a hat was passed and it returned holding thirteen dollars. That was enough to convince Elmo to begin driving his son around the countryside, the piano in the back of a truck, stopping at crossroads, country stores, or anywhere a crowd might gather.

Soon Jerry Lee had his own car. "All the kin people would be out in the field working," says his sister Frankie Jean, younger by nine years. "Mother would be pulling the sack, putting the cotton in it. Daddy would be right behind her, and I would be helping with Linda [baby sister and future performer Linda Gail Lewis]. He had a car, and he'd ride up—I have witnesses—he would ride up and down the gravel road along the river and he would scream, 'Work you peasants, work! For I don't have to work! For I'm wearing the white shirt! I am the great I am!'"

By the time Jerry Lee graduated from high school, he was twice married and a father. He entered his first marriage when he was sixteen, and twenty months later, prior to his divorce, he married Jane Mitchum, pregnant with his first child. With his wife and son cared for by his parents, Jerry Lee went to Waxahachie, Texas, for Bible college with plans to become a minister. He would absorb the fear of God by day, then sneak out to Dallas's bright lights to see movies and ride the Tilt-A-Whirl at night. In assembly one day, his version of "My God Is Real" became a little too ungodly, and though the sounds of his church and his nightclub were often indistinguishable, *this* version was clearly over the line. Jerry Lee was expelled.

He sold vacuum cleaners and sewing machines, he played drums and piano with a local band, he auditioned in Shreveport for a country package tour in 1955. He tried his luck in Nashville, but Nashville was having none of the new sounds; Carl Perkins, another white singer who was mixing country and blues, had already been told by one corporate label rep there, "I like what you're doing, young man, but I don't know *what* you're doing."

That unidentifiable mix was much more suited to Memphis than to Nashville, which the Lewis family realized when they heard Johnny Cash and Carl Perkins in the summer of 1955, both on Memphis's Sun Records, home also to Elvis Presley. To finance the trip to meet Sam Phillips, Elmo Lewis sold eggs—33 dozen—along the 350 miles north.

Working with Sam's assistant Jack Clement, Jerry Lee cut "Crazy Arms," his first Sun single. Though recently a country hit for Ray Price and a pop hit for the Andrews Sisters, "Crazy Arms" got infused with Jerry Lee's personality, a country bounce that swings right to the juke house. His left hand played funky bass on the piano's low keys, his right ran a lilting, wild-style melody. He quickly got good bookings, including a tour with Cash and Perkins.

In mid-March 1957, Sun released Jerry Lee's second record. With Clement, the band had spent a lot of time working up a rollicking number called "It'll Be Me." It was a Clement original—he'd come up with it while sitting on the studio's toilet, pondering reincarnation; the line, "If you see a turd in your toilet bowl, baby / It'll be me and I'll be staring at you" was changed before it was recorded, and became "If you find a lump in your sugar bowl." The song's feel was well-suited to Jerry Lee, but getting the romp just right was proving difficult. "I said, 'Why don't we come back to this later, Jerry? Let's do something else for awhile,'" Clement recalls. "And ole J. W. Brown spoke up, Jerry Lee's bass player, and said, 'Hey, Jerry, do that song we've been doing on the road that everybody likes so much.' I said, 'Well let me go in there and turn on the machine.' I hit play and record, sat down there, and they did 'Whole Lot of Shakin' Going On.' No dry run, no nothin'. *Blap!* One take, there it was! Sprang forth full-blown from its mother's womb. Then we went back to 'It'll Be Me.'"

It was the frenzy of "Whole Lot of Shakin'" that made Lewis a star. In a summer 1957 appearance on Steve Allen's national TV show, Jerry Lee didn't kowtow as Elvis had—standing awkwardly in a tuxedo and singing "Hound Dog" to a basset hound. Whipped up by his own performance, Jerry Lee hurled his piano bench offscreen, Steve Allen threw it back, and "Whole Lot of Shakin'" shot from regional hit to number one country and number two pop (unable to shake Debbie Reynolds's "Tammy" from the top spot). Jerry's next child was named Steve Allen Lewis.

A MONTH AFTER the "Twilight" session when B. B. Cunningham had escaped without getting slapped, Jerry Lee performs at a Christmastime benefit concert in Memphis. Hometown gigs are rare, especially in smaller venues like this club. His touring has picked up since his divorce proceedings began a couple years back. He can command sizable fees for an appearance; he and the band even flew to Switzerland for a single performance. In a Biloxi casino, he set a recent record. Tonight, he's closing the show, and the audience stays late to see him.

Numerous acts have preceded him, and a weariness has set in, but when he's announced, the audience greets him with a standing ovation. His crowds trend toward older, but there's always younger people making sure their lives will include seeing this legendary performer. Entering from the side, he does a fanny-shaking shimmy to great applause. He's wearing a leather waistcoat that he doesn't remove before sitting at the piano. But he's got nothing to hide—he's slender and looking fit. He kicks off with "Roll Over Beethoven" and that bleeds into Hank Williams's "You Win Again." The tempo changes, the feel, the emphasis—but it's still distinctly Jerry Lee. His voice is full of power this night, and he performs both "Great Balls of Fire" and "Whole Lot of Shakin'." He's conjuring the spirit from within, from the place where good meets bad and right meets wrong and the forces push and they pull and the tension is exhilarating so that you find yourself unable to stand still and unable to move—*shake, baby, shake*—and part of you feels like it might explode—*easy now*—until there's a moment of liberation and what's happening on stage is happening in the audience and no one can say who is leading because everyone together is joining everyone else in some kind of new freedom.

For the audience, it's thrills and chills to follow these nonstop twists, but on stage, it's a workout. "I always keep my eyes right on his hands," says Robert Hall, Jerry's drummer since 1996. "There's twenty regular songs he draws on, and sixty or eighty backups that could come in at any time, and a solid forty that I've never even heard. We still get a new one every now and then."

"He pushes you farther than you think you are willing to go," says bassist B. B. Cunningham, who is so comfortable rolling with the punches that he once tuned Chuck Berry's guitar to the A of a hotel telephone's dial tone. "We try to recognize what key he's in, then pick up what he's doing. One night in Vegas he started playing something that even Kenny couldn't follow, and he's been with him for thirty-seven years. Nobody played anything, we just let him play. And all of a sudden he stopped, leaned into the microphone, 'Are you boys going to jump in with me or just take my money?'

"He has no set list, and I think the reason he does that is it gives him the freedom to do what he feels like doing. And it's part of the mystique: What's going to happen tonight?"

IT WAS A hot August day in 1957, before air-conditioning was common, when Sam Phillips gathered Jerry Lee and his band in the breezeless Sun

Studio to record a follow-up to "Whole Lot of Shakin'." Sam's recent Carl Perkins and Johnny Cash singles hadn't hit, and he'd sold Elvis to RCA, so Sam needed "Great Balls of Fire" just right. The song was perfect for Jerry Lee, built around the tension between sexual release and religious exaltation—two of Jerry Lee's favorite pursuits (others include cars, motorcycles, tobacco pipes, and boots).

Sam Phillips was a master of production psychology. (Had he not gone into records, he'd have made a helluva preacher, lawyer, or therapist.) As a warm-up for the song, he and Jerry Lee were discussing theology; Jack Clement hit the record button.

"H-E-L-L!" the Killer exclaims, and he claps his hand on the piano for emphasis. "It says, 'Make merry with the joy of God only.' But when it comes to worldly music, rock 'n' roll, anything like that, you have done brought yourself into the world, and you're in the world, and . . . you're still a sinner . . ."

"All right," responds Sam, maintaining a cool in the heat of Jerry Lee's passion. "Now look, Jerry. Religious conviction doesn't mean anything resembling extremism . . . Jesus Christ came into this world; He tolerated man. He didn't preach from one pulpit, He went around and did good . . . When you think that you can't do good if you're a rock 'n' roll exponent—"

"You can do good, Mr. Phillips, don't get me wrong—"

"When I say do good—"

"You can have a kind heart! You can help people—"

Sam stunned him: "You can save souls!"

"No! No! No! No! How can the Devil save souls? What are you talkin' about? Man, I got the Devil in me; if I didn't I'd be a Christian!"

A few moments later, riled and primed by the record producer, this musician achieved one of the artistic high points of his life. With apocalyptic imagery, lascivious delivery, and unbridled energy, Jerry Lee Lewis cut "Great Balls of Fire" as if announcing the End of Days.

The song was featured in a Hollywood teen-exploitation film called *Jamboree*; it was the movie's only song to feature an electric bass player— Jerry Lee's first cousin J. W. Brown.

Cousin Brown—his mom and Jerry Lee's dad were siblings—was an electrician who opened his Memphis home to Jerry Lee, his second wife, and his young namesake. When the dads were on the road, Brown's preteen daughter, Myra, saw that Jerry Lee Jr.'s mama was cavorting with other men. She already had a crush on her exciting older cousin, and after his divorce, the cousins eloped in December 1957. Myra had turned thirteen. Singing to her, perhaps, his next hits were "Breathless" and the forward-looking "High School Confidential."

While their love was blooming, the relationship between the entertainer and the press was about to wither. Reviewers, critics, and writers had helped launch his career, but with the revelations of his wife's age, their blood relationship, and his past marriages, the press took to assaulting his character. Jerry Lee came to see all journalists as murderous, a stance that he maintains to this day: He has no interest in mixing with the press, no trust that they'll do anything but create bloodthirsty headlines.

"He's a man of a great, contrite heart who's just maybe messed himself up from time to time," Sam Phillips said a quarter of a century ago. "It's a shame he doesn't have anyone to direct his talent—he is one of this century's great, great talents. But he feels a lonesomeness in his talent, *extreme* lonesomeness, for somebody to be strong around him."

Even at his lowest point, he still had the demeanor of an angry god. When touring in the 1960s, playing state fairs and dive bars before his Nashville comeback, he got an engagement in a Miami nightclub following a two-week stint by Conway Twitty, who'd known Jerry Lee since they were both at Sun. Twitty warned the club owner of Jerry Lee's pounding piano style, so the owner bought a beaten upright for the gig. "Jerry showed up the afternoon he was supposed to open," Twitty recalled, "took

Jerry Lee Lewis, 1995. "At a show not long ago, someone passed a request to him on a cocktail napkin; without a glance, he blew his nose on it." (Courtesy of Trey Harrison)

one look at the piano and kicked it off the stage onto the floor. He kicked it all the way out of the building, across the parking lot, and into this lake. Then came back in, blew cigar smoke in this mobster's face, and said, 'Now get me a goddamn piano.'" He got his piano.

THERE'S ANOTHER RECORDING session for the new album. Jimmy Rip has flown to Memphis from Los Angeles, but there's no band this night. They'll record three songs, piano and vocals only, and add guest vocals and backing tracks later: "What's Made Milwaukee Famous (Has Made a Loser Out of Me)" will get a visit from Rod Stewart; Jerry Lee's first ever recording of Hank Williams's "Lost Highway" will be bolstered by Delaney Bramlett's raspy vocal; and "Miss the Mississippi and You," a yodeling classic by Jimmie Rodgers that won't make the album.

He's brought to the studio by his daughter Phoebe. She drove. Used to be, he'd drive her to grade school in his Rolls-Royce—until one day he flipped that car (walking away unscathed) shortly after dropping her off. Now Phoebe's in her early forties and, since her father's divorce proceedings, she has stepped up to help manage his affairs.

Phoebe has long blonde hair and her father's spirit. She speaks with a deep Mississippi twang and smokes a corncob pipe, and she's excited about this new album. "I couldn't believe I was hearing Led Zeppelin's 'Rock and Roll' cranked up full volume blaring out of my dad's bedroom. He was learning the song. And of course he cut it totally different."

Rip is pleased to have Phoebe at the session. Jerry Lee is not allowed to go anywhere alone. He drinks hardly any alcohol these days, and pills, reefer, and all drugs except those prescribed by his physician are out of his life. (At a recent doctor's visit following a teeth transplant, Jerry Lee was pronounced in perfect health. The new teeth have not affected the peculiar wet slur that has always made his speech an effort to understand.) It may be whatever he's taking to keep him from taking anything else, it may be a life of being doted upon, or it's that Jerry Lee feels like he owns every damn place he finds himself—but Jerry Lee needs looking after. In a hotel not long ago, he wound up alone in his room. "Hey!" he shouted, because he needed something, but there was no answer, so he shouted "Hey!" louder, and then again and again, louder and louder, until he left his room in his socks and underwear, wandering the hotel hallway, directionless, shouting, "Hey!"

Jerry's out at the piano noodling around and without pause or introduction, he breaks into "What's Made Milwaukee Famous." The engineer is Roland Janes, who, besides being the house engineer at the Sam Phillips Recording Service, was Jerry Lee's guitar player from the glory days—Roland can read Jerry and he's missed nothing—had the tape rolling in plenty of time.

Jerry moves on to the Hank song. He's reading the lyrics off the piano, but he's singing with fervor. (He was reading the lyrics when he recorded "Great Balls of Fire" at Sun.) "I'm a rolling stone, all alone and lost / For a life of sin, I have paid the cost . . ."

"I tried to find songs that pertain to his life, things that will allow him to be really emotional and expressive and tell the story of what he's gone through," says Rip.

Jerry has switched from rehearsing to recording without telling anyone, and even Roland misses the turn. "Hold it," his old friend says into the talkback, "wasn't rolling."

"Aww now," says Jerry Lee. "You ruffled my feathers. Let me go get my pistol."

A visitor in the control booth gasps and says, "Oh no, not the pistol." After waiting a couple beats, as if he could hear the fear, Jerry adds, "Only a joke. I ain't got a pistol."

"Boys don't start that stupid rambling 'round," he's singing, his back straight, his face stern beneath eyeglasses, beady eyes focused on the page. His profile is sharp, like a hawk's. The piano hides his flip-flops and pajamas. Jerry Lee could be a preacher alongside his cousin Swaggart. "Take my advice . . ."

Jimmy Rip steps out to the studio between takes, says, "One more?"

"One? At least ten more."

"I think one more will be enough."

"Too bad you don't know me," says Jerry Lee, "as well as you think you know me." The honesty is startling, said without pretense. With each take, he's peeled at the song, to simplify and complicate, to reveal more of his terrifying, terrified soul.

"If you let me get this down right, you'll have a million seller on your hands. Twenty or thirty more takes." Jerry's pushing, but the producer resists. Jimmy explains that from the three keeper takes he can build a single solid one on the computer. "Play it back then," Jerry snaps. He's willing to listen to what they've got, to be happy if Jimmy's happy, but he really doesn't feel like he's hit his lick yet. "Don't cover up my mistakes with the band," he protests. "Let me get it right. He writes everything you do in the Book of Life, and He'll hear it. Dim the lights."

Jimmy says, "Lighting is everything."

Jerry corrects him. "Naw, it's a little part of it, but it means a lot." He begins one more take—it opens completely differently from all the others.

"One more," he says again, but no longer means it, having heard what's there and realizing he's done a good job.

After the session, there's small talk in the control room. Jerry's bought his seventeen-year-old son, Lee, a big SUV and he laughs when he complains about the cost of the insurance. Phoebe laughs, then says her dad recently set his Harley-Davidson inside the living room of his ranch, where he can admire it. After several days of looking, he could resist no longer. He opened the sliding glass door so the exhaust wouldn't kill him, mounted the beast, kicked—and unleashed mayhem. The machine roared throughout the house, the dog went crazy barking, and the fumes set off the smoke alarm.

Jerry Lee's Nesbit home is a sprawling ranch built on thirty acres with its own lake. It's got six bedrooms and six bathrooms, and plenty of living space. He's lived there since 1973 and it suits him just fine. Phoebe occupies one of the suites, and their longtime helper Carolyn is often around. She cooks like Jerry's mama—Phoebe's given her the family recipes. He eats only one real meal a day, dinner around eight, but he'll snack. A night owl, he's got a suite in the back where he sleeps, bathes, and watches a big-screen TV—big, like IMAX for the home. His collections are on display there—model cars, tobacco pipes (his many boots are kept in his closet)—and so are his prizes and awards, his Grammy (not bestowed for his hits, but for Best Spoken Word or Non-Musical Recording, 1986, an album entitled *Interviews from the Class of '55 Recording Sessions*), and some of the gifts he's been given. "Little bitty things mean the most to him," says J. W. Whitten, the road manager. "A friend will get him something and he'll cherish it."

Studio talk turns to *Gunsmoke*, an indication that the evening is going great. *Gunsmoke* is Jerry Lee's favorite subject in the world. He loves television, and westerns are his favorite. Of all the westerns, he loves *Gunsmoke*. Of the two kinds of *Gunsmoke*, he prefers the episodes with Chester, the Dennis Weaver character, over the ones with Festus, his replacement. When asked why he likes *Gunsmoke* so much, Jerry Lee answers, "Because it's unique, perfect, and great. I got tapes going back to 1954—Kitty was beautiful. Matt Dillon is my hero." He freely admits that he cried when Harry Dean Stanton's character died in the show.

JERRY LEE IS legendary as a rock and roller, so it's often forgotten that when he came to Sun, he was playing George Jones and Ray Price songs, a Carter Family number, and Jimmie Rodgers. And it was to country he turned in 1967, a decade after his meteor burned up. He signed a deal in Nashville, made classic honky-tonk comfortable in the modern era with "Another Place, Another Time," and began a string of country hits—many in the top three, and more than several that crossed over to pop—that ran all the way through the 1970s and included "What's Made Milwaukee Famous," "She Still Comes Around (To Love What's Left of Me)," "She Even Woke Me Up to Say Goodbye," "Would You Take Another Chance on Me," "Middle Age Crazy," and "Thirty Nine and Holding."

The run ended in the late 1970s, when the individualism Jerry brought to his late-1960s hits was no longer appreciated. By then, the label was shipping syrupy, finished tapes to Memphis onto which Jerry Lee simply added his part, often only a vocal. He'd come to the studio—the same one where he's cutting this new album—so rankled that Sam's son Knox would load blank tape onto which Jerry Lee would pour out his wrath and anger before finally he was weary enough to give Nashville the saccharine they wanted. Those tapes—those documents of rage and sorrow—remain sealed in a dark vault.

He married Kerrie McCarver in the mid-1980s, and initially they ran a nice little Jerry Lee Lewis cottage industry. His fan club was thriving, she opened his home to tours, and she took over management of his career. But storm clouds appeared. Little Richard, with whom Jerry Lee has always gotten along famously, reported to several entourage members, "That fat white girl called me a nigger to my face." After her first European tour, contracts reportedly began having "no-Kerrie" clauses in them; she was not welcome back. "It was a relief for us," says one entourage member.

In 1985, Jerry Lee was fifty and soon to be a daddy. "I want my unborn son to have a drug-free daddy," he said at the Betty Ford Clinic, but two days after checking in, he checked out. "Patients are supposed to clean bathrooms, take out garbage, sweep floors, and pick up after people. Hey, that may be fine for Suzie Homemaker, but it ain't my style." He fled.

The new family moved to Ireland during a protracted battle with the IRS. But over time, the partnerships—the marriage and the business—soured, until Jerry Lee basically quit performing. Kerrie was evicted from the house by a judge's decree, but the divorce, with all its attendant court appearances, lawyers, and gag orders has been ongoing since summer 2003. (The marriage ended in 2005 after 21 years.)

UPON ARRIVING AT Phillips Recording Service, it's immediately evident that this last session for the album—tentatively titled *The Pilgrim*, or possibly *Old Glory* (and ultimately *Last Man Standing*)—is going to be different. There's a tour bus parked out front, and movie lights are glowing. The lobby, usually so quiet the echo of the 1950s can be heard, is a film crew's staging area, with a full spread of snacks and coolers of cold drinks. "When I started doing this record, it was so low-key," says Jimmy Rip. "For this to be the end, it's wild. A studio full of people—I don't know who anyone is."

A couple weeks earlier, Jerry Lee had been in Los Angeles to tape a Willie Nelson & Friends TV special alongside Merle Haggard, Keith Richards, and Toby Keith—all guests (Nelson included) on Jerry Lee's new album. (Other guests include Mick Jagger, Eric Clapton, Jimmy Page, Buddy Guy, and Bruce Springsteen.) Jerry Lee was slated to close the show, in a duet with Kid Rock. If the pairing was unexpected, it was spiritually right, and the music would follow.

Two days before the May taping, Jerry Lee had never heard of Kid Rock. Phoebe looked him up on the Internet and the first picture they saw was Kid Rock standing atop a grand piano. "I like him already," Jerry Lee said.

They were slated to play "Whole Lot of Shakin'," and there was the idea of working up a take of the Stones' "Honky Tonk Woman." Jerry had practiced the song, but under the eyes of five cameras, seventy crew people, and the song's co-writer—Keith Richards—Jerry couldn't get it. The idea was scrapped. But Kid Rock and the Ferriday Kid behaved like reunited father and son. Rock never left the Killer's side, and Jerry was digging him right back.

And thus this last session: That's Kid Rock's bus out front, itineraries having been aligned to record "Honky Tonk Woman." The film crew is from DreamWorks Nashville, the label releasing the new record. The label head is James Stroud, who played drums in Jerry Lee's band in the early 1970s. He's playing on tonight's session. Before the evening's out, he'll have had so much fun that he declares he's making this record the company's number one priority.

The engineer is playing the Stones' version of the song, and the backup singers—who sang on Elvis's "Suspicious Minds"—are working up their "gimme gimme" vocal track—not realizing that Jerry Lee might change the song a bit, a lot—entirely.

Kid Rock is wearing black: jeans, T-shirt, hat. His cigar is brown, which matches his snakeskin boots. His gold cross is bigger than his large plastic cup of whiskey and cola. Waiting for Jerry Lee, he's inviting people onto his bus, where the Detroit Pistons are playing on a TV the size of— the side of a bus. His people are easy to spot—they're burly as bears and they've got electric coils coming out of their ears and going down their backs. They're either looking for assassins or listening to the Pistons game (they're up at the half).

As his car approaches, Jerry Lee's jaw drops. He steps out, says, "I gotta go comb my hair. Looks like we got an audience already." Road manager J. W. Whitten, who's driven him, suggests he use the bus. Kid Rock bows to show his hospitality. "They got one inside," Jerry Lee says. "I been paying for it for twenty-nine years." He's not wearing pajamas tonight but rather crisp black jeans and a black shirt with gold trim that will flash in his video—but he's still got on the flip-flops. His skin looks pastier than usual, and he's sucking on a tobacco pipe. "I like that crease in your pants," Kid Rock says with genuine admiration. "That's old-school. I ain't coming near you, you'll cut me."

As Jerry Lee glides through the track, his "Honky Tonk Woman" sounds appropriate for a honky-tonk. "I'm bad about changing up songs," Jerry Lee says. "But this I want to keep about right. The guy who wrote it is a personal friend of mine, and he gets mad if you change it."

"Let's change it then," Kid Rock says, an eager student in the Jerry Lee school. He suggests starting it as a slow gospel thing.

He is full of ideas—he inserts a break for the drummer, then for the whole band. He modifies Jerry Lee's verse again, telling the multiracial background trio, "Hit on the upbeat," slapping time on his knee. They run the song down. Jerry Lee says, "Well, you might have an idea there." The producer agrees—these pros are ready to recognize positive input. "It's good," Rip says. Kid Rock answers: "It's rock and roll." And Jerry Lee, out of the side of his mouth and a bit under his breath, says into his mic, his voice rising like a question, "That's rock and roll?" It's wry and contentious, just this side of snide, and there's a weighty pause after he says it, everyone in the room reflecting on what's just happened. It's not a put-down, it's just something that the granddaddy of rock and roll is allowed to say, and it's laden with meaning and humor.

After the session, the Killer tells the Kid, "Don't let nobody change your style," and the Kid replies, "I won't."

There's lots of jubilant photo taking, and Kid's standing next to Jerry Lee when he says, "Show me something on the piano." The two share the bench and Jerry Lee pulls out Fats Domino's "Walking to New Orleans." But Kid's really too excited to pay attention, and they wind up doing a duet of Hank Williams's "Lovesick Blues." The talk leads to Hank, then to Louisiana. "Did you ever live near a paper plant?" the Killer asks. "Auto plants," says Kid. "Detroit." "Man, you should live near a paper plant. It stinks." It's been nearly half a century since Jerry Lee lived downwind of Natchez, but there's a lot he ain't forgot.

AT EIGHT P.M. on a summer's night, the band congregates in a Memphis hotel parking lot. A luxury bus will cart us all to Nashville, where Jerry Lee is closing a star-studded night hosted by Marty Stuart at the historic Ryman Auditorium—the mother church of country music. Jerry's due to play at one in the morning. The last one to arrive, he boards and heads directly to his suite in the back, son Lee in tow. He turns on the big-screen TV, settles onto the comfortable sofa, and sits slack-jawed, rapt with a three-quarter smile for the next three or so hours. It doesn't matter that Ronald Reagan's funeral is the only show on; television—sitcoms, a hemorrhoid commercial, Moses coming down from the mountain—makes him oblivious to the world, and happy.

This performance is part of country music's Fan Fair, an annual event at which fans from all over the world can meet their favorite stars. Jerry Lee's never been totally comfortable with fans. At a show not long ago, someone passed a request to him on a cocktail napkin; without a glance, he blew his nose on it. When his bus pulls into the alley behind the Ryman—the alley that Hank Williams used to cross during the Grand Ole Opry to get a drink at Tootsie's Orchid Lounge—fans swarm the vehicle. No one disembarks, but one elderly gentleman is let on. It's Jerry Lee's barber, and they talk about old times while Jerry gets a trim.

Outside, fans wait patiently and expectantly. Nashville is weird—there are no staggering drunks, no rowdy banter, just an orderly combination of grandmas, granddads, and young supple granddaughters. A ponytailed man in his sixties is holding a stack of albums (not CDs) that he's dreaming of getting autographed. Many people have markers and pens at the ready, pick guards pulled off their guitars, autograph books open to a blank page. "Should we just get a picture of the bus?" asks one woman, tired of waiting. "Whose bus is that?" asks another. When she's told, she repeats his name and stares, sounding surprised that he's still living.

At one forty-five, Jerry Lee disembarks and heads to the stage. Passing through the fans, he's anything but fair, greeting the peasants cursorily, making no real contact; he seems repulsed by the idea of touching something of theirs. He's there to perform on the stage, not anywhere else. Strolling directly to the piano—there is great applause—he begins to play "Roll Over Beethoven." He sits three-quarters cocked to the audience. More than half-cocked, fully loaded, bangin' 'em out.

Jerry Lee's hands pound out a fury. Sometimes they seem barely to rise off the piano, and other times he's all asses and elbows, his arms flailing like a roller coaster ride. The piano is an extension of his own being, and he commands it. He pounds and strikes the keys with the seeming

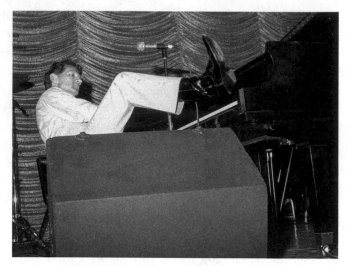

Jerry Lee Lewis, 1982. (Courtesy of Pat Rainer)

randomness of a child, and he makes beautiful music. He's been known to stomp on keys with the heels of his boots, to pound them with his fists, to place his butt squarely on the ivories—and always the piano sounds perfect. He's declared that he can stare at the piano and make it play.

Within seconds of the thirty-minute set's last notes, Jerry Lee is back on the bus, settled on the rear suite's sofa, mouth agape, eyes looking at the TV. A couple hours later, five in the morning, rolling down the highway, I walk back to the bathroom on the bus. It's the last door on the left, just before his suite. He's reclining on the sofa, framed by the doorway, his hair newly trimmed, the TV uncomfortably loud. He's slouched, his feet planted firmly on the floor, ready to kick anyone who dares cross the threshold, who mistakes his door for the bathroom door and tries to piss on him. He looks up as I near and glares—his eyes burning through an unhealthful pallor, but burning. His skin shines like wax, but the meaning in his look is real. He glares like the devil.

Jerry Lee's glare is as intimate and arbitrary as Elvis Presley's gifts of Cadillacs. It's a way to retain control of the moment. When Elvis slurred that he was buying you—a stranger, a friend—a Cadillac, he was purchasing not just the moment, but his control of you. You say no, you piss him off and the relationship is over; you say yes, you've lost your power of independence. So it is with Jerry Lee's glare. Respond to the glower with a challenge—"Yeah, what do you want to do about it?"—and get thrown off the bus; tuck tail and meekly go about your business, you prove yourself a candy ass. In a business of manipulation, the glare, the Caddy, these are masterful moves that make so much middle ground inaccessible. I fumble with the door.

The TV in the back of the bus is so loud—even over the noise of a tour bus barreling seventy miles per hour on the expressway—and the day has stretched so long that someone finally slides the suite door shut. Jerry Lee—rapt at the altar of TV—doesn't notice. Bandmembers climb into bunks, an hour of shut-eye before they can go home and sleep.

The sky is pale purple, becoming the white of day, and the bus is on city streets when there's an angry banging and someone shouts, "Open this door." For a minute, I am seeing the *Twilight Zone* image of the gremlin outside the airplane window who has hung on through the whole flight. The banging continues; it's from the back of the bus—someone's locked in the bathroom?—and as we get oriented from half sleep, we realize it's Jerry Lee. "I want this door open right now!" He's saying it with such force, the door itself must cower before him. *Blam! Blam! Blam!* B. B. Cunningham hustles down the aisle, sees it's a sliding door, feels everywhere trying to find a handle for it, takes a hit as the assault on the door happens right by his head. "Somebody open this door!" There's panic in Jerry Lee's voice, like he's drowning near shore, each pounding blow as strong as a victim's flailing. B. B.'s bent at the waist, trying to get his fingernails wedged between the metal frame and the side of the door to rip it open.

Blam! Blam! Blam! "Somebody open this door right now." There's a syncopation to the banging and the shouting—it's not something you'd dance to, but it sure gets your attention. The bus driver hears the commotion and yells to the back, "It's pneumatic." *Bang! Bang!* "It runs on air," he yells, "push the button." There's a crowd at the door when the message reaches the back: "Push the big black button to the right of the door." Like Batman, like Austin Powers, like Indiana Jones—the door disappears inside the wall and reveals Jerry Lee Lewis, an everyday miracle, stunned but with an aura of fire burning like a voodoo candle, a voodoo bonfire. He is silent, he speaks, he steps out of the room, back in. What he does and says is nothing to how he appears: a ball of fire, of pent-up rage. He's a warm front of vulnerability, a cold front of anger and mistrust, the thundering fury that is Jerry Lee Lewis. Life is hell, and Jerry Lee is still paying.

CAT POWER

Sonic Youth made *Washing Machine* at Easley-McCain Recording, and I hung around a bit. Drummer Steve Shelley liked the studio's vibe and was back within a few months to produce *What Would the Community Think*, the third album by Cat Power, whose given name is Charlyn Marie Marshall, though she likes to be called Chan (pronounced "Shawn"). I took Steve, Chan, and pal Tim Prudhomme for some soul food and during the meal, Chan wandered out the front door and didn't return. The neighborhood was dicey and after a bit, I went out front. She wasn't there. A couple doors down I poked my head into a divey blues joint, let my eyes adjust. She was at the bar talking to someone I knew: James Carr. Memphis had drawn them together.

A decade later she called me, remembering an offhand comment I'd made over sweet potato pie. She was conceiving *The Greatest*, her seventh album, and wanted that silky, sensuous Memphis sound, so could I connect her to the Hi Records players?

The Hi Rhythm Section is the backbone, the core, the soul of the Hi Records sound from the early 1960s to the latter 1970s. That's the era spanning Willie Mitchell's rise as a star recording artist through his ascension to producer and label co-owner, and it includes just about everything Al Green recorded at Hi. There's three blood brothers in the Hi Rhythm

Section—Leroy, Charles, and Teenie Hodges—and two soul brothers—Howard Grimes and Willie's stepson Archie "Hubbie" Turner. That sly funky feel that evokes soft sheets, lava lamps, and close talk? That's the Hi Rhythm Section; they moved soul music from the dance floor to the boudoir.

In the mid-2000s, they weren't getting a lot of work. Some had day jobs, some were scraping by with low-paying bar gigs. I'd heard them recording together and knew they still had the feel. Chan's request was a reminder that the Memphis ghosts still haunted. Work picked up for the band, and when Willie's grandson Boo Mitchell took the studio's reins (Willie died in 2010), the band got a solid shot in the arm. (The studio—its name is Royal Studios but it's often also called Hi—has remained unchanged inside since 1969 when Willie got it sounding like he wanted; gear has been updated, but the facility feels like bell-bottom jeans and sounds like a hit.) The Memphis past is such good business that it fuels much of the present commerce. Mark Ronson's "Uptown Funk," featuring Bruno Mars, is the most popular of the recent successes recorded at Royal, and it has also attracted Keith Richards, Robert Cray, Frazey Ford, and Melissa Etheridge, among many other notables. And the Hi Rhythm Section players are so good, they transcend time. Their sound is thoroughly modern, deeply rooted, always hip.

Chan and Teenie developed a special connection. Teenie (who died in 2014) was a master of the beautiful and spare guitar line, and her vocals allowed space for his small strokes to play large. On stage, his laid-back self would cuddle up with her sensitive and unfiltered self, and seeing the two together was like witnessing old friends share a blanket while watching the Saturday afternoon movie on TV.

Chan "Cat Power" Marshall, left, and Mabon "Teenie" Hodges.
(Courtesy of Rachel Hurley)

Chan gets really personal in this interview. There's not much protection of the private person behind the public one. Despite her years in the biz, these calluses have hardly developed. She hasn't let them, preserving a forthright innocence. (I'm always surprised when she'll toss into the conversation, "Are you mad at me?") She mines feelings and territory most adults have managed to bury, foregrounding her fragility, expressing it intensely, making herself vulnerable. I worried at the time that I shouldn't publish this and I contacted her longtime press agent. "She's very conscious of being on microphone, and she knows what she's saying is for publication," he told me. "She'll tell you if she wants something off the record." Another mutual friend put it like this: "She is not one to hide her past from her fans, and that is why people love her." I've come to think of her words here, then, as akin to her songs: revealing, sometimes untidy, powerful.

This interview was conducted while Chan toured with the group we put together, the Memphis Rhythm Band. She was also picking up work as an actress and being courted by the William Morris Agency, whom she asked not to handle her music work because, she said, "I don't want to be a super-duper star, and that's what they would want to market me as." She'd found a place in the world where she was comfortable, and she was happy.

I lost touch with Chan until she returned to Memphis in 2016 to front Hi Rhythm at a performance marking their induction into the Memphis Music Hall of Fame. While recording *The Greatest* in 2005, she'd taken a shine to my daughters, and the first thing she said when she saw me was, "I'm a mom now!" My heart swelled for her. More than a happy ending, it's a happy beginning.

Kool Kween
Stop Smiling, Issue 28, October 2006

ROBERT GORDON: I know you've recently given up drinking, and I thought it'd be interesting to talk about cigarettes.
CHAN MARSHALL: Cigarettes?

RG: Do you love cigarettes?
CM: *[Laughs]* I need to make a bumper sticker: "I heart cigarettes." There's something antifascist about smoking. I've just been doing it for so long. I started when I was in second grade. My mom would come home from work, before we'd go out with her, and she'd light a cigarette— Kool Kings. We'd sit on her lap and play around for a minute, then she'd go take a shower. She'd always leave her Kool King lit in the ashtray, so that's how I started smoking. I remember first grade and kindergarten, I would beg her, "Please, please don't smoke. You're going to die." Then, when I was in second grade—I'll never forget it—I thought, Fuck, I'm

hungry. All we had was bread, which was kind of old, and the toaster had caught on fire so many times that I was scared of it. I used to put mustard on my bread and we didn't have any mustard. That cigarette was sitting there, so I started smoking it. Do I hate smoking? Yeah, because I'm damaging my lungs and I want to be normal. But for me, normal is smoking.

RG: What do you miss about drinking?

CM: Oh, my Lord. I miss that feeling of warmth. Like when you drink scotch, you down it in a big gulp and there's just something about that association—swallowing the scotch, tasting it in your mouth, that smoky flavor. It almost psychosomatically chills you out. I miss that. I miss being chilled out.

You can tell by all the talking I'm doing that I miss being laid-back. But I don't miss being depressed or so chilled out that I don't want to talk to friends. I don't miss being so depressed that I don't want to see people.

RG: What's been the hardest part about quitting drinking?

CM: The hardest part is remembering things that I've done on tour, on stage, with friends, in hotel rooms, different situations that were just really stupid. That's the hardest part—remembering. Like taking my shirt off at the Chateau Marmont, or hanging out all night with these homeless Muslim guys in Spain. Realizing that I put myself at risk. For instance, I'm not allowed back at that hotel.

RG: What happened there?

CM: All these photographs in the *New York Times* were really disturbing me. The [2004] election was coming up. There were all these mosques and synagogues that were being bombed—just really depressing images, and I kept cutting them out and sticking them all over. I had heavy traffic coming in and out of my hotel room. At the pool, I was just clearly shit-faced, getting people in the pool to sing along and running around topless. I pulled Kirsten Dunst's top down at one point. You know, just drunk— someone who doesn't realize their actions until they get reminded.

If you drink every day, I highly recommend trying not doing it for a while. Being on the road, touring, the many bars . . . you meet so many different strangers. I drank to create a bubble so I wouldn't really have to be there all the time. And alcoholism runs in my family. I thought, Oh, it'll never affect me. I've got a control on it. But there's a good aspect: It helped me understand alcoholics I've known my whole life. It helped me understand their perspective and the crazy things they do that were often hurtful—traumatizing at times. It helped me understand that I can't take that personally, even though it's really hard to accept that sometimes.

RG: You're referring to that story about your dad entertaining at a piano bar?
CM: Yeah. It was my twenty-eighth or twenty-ninth birthday. My boyfriend at the time—the love of my life, Daniel—him and his sister, Margaret, had blindfolded me in Atlanta. They said, "We're going to take you somewhere." I thought they were taking me to a male strip club, which I've never been to. This is actually a funny story. Just because it happened to me makes me hurt, but it can be turned around and told like Larry David. So we're driving further and further, and I thought, Fuck. Are they taking me to where my dad plays piano? Sure enough, we pull up and when they start to open the door to the place, I heard him playing and singing. It was kind of dark, but there was a light on me. I'm sure if my father was asked, he would deny that he said what he said. I went in front of the piano. First, he said what he says to everybody: "Hey, sweetie." My boyfriend and his sister went to the bar and I was there by myself. He finishes whatever song, and he's a funny guy, so he would do little intros to songs. When he was about to play the song, he said, "This next song is about my first wife and those couple of kids. Thank God they're gone." Something like that. That's a fucked-up story. It's really hurtful. It's about my mom, but then he attached "a couple of kids" to it. That would be me and my sister. I immediately felt my eyes crying.

Today, as a woman—I was younger then—I think now I would have been like, "Fuck you." I would have left, and that would have been that—I would've been stronger. But my eyes were watering. Daniel comes up behind me—he didn't hear what he said—but his sister was hysterical. She walks right up, interrupts him, says, "Hi, I'm Margaret. You remember me? Chan's boyfriend's sister." He says, "Oh yeah. Hi, sweetie. How are you?" And she's like, "Chan's here." "She is?" She goes, "Yeah. It's her birthday." "It is?" So then he got on the mic: "This is my daughter, Chan. She's a recording artist in New York City." He wanted everybody to see our interaction, like we're tight, you know? He gave me this hug and I felt so physically repulsed by him that I felt like I was going to vomit. That's when I started crying and just left.

But it could be a comedy. As you get older, you start to understand people's roles. Someone's your father, or you were born at a certain hospital, or you have four fingers instead of five. There are things that you can't control in life. I think it used to really affect me, but now I realize that it's not his fault that he got my mom pregnant. I've become more understanding that he hasn't really been a good father. That's not the choice I would make in a husband or as a mother.

RG: Didn't he buy the piano that you learned on?
CM: I lived with him off and on for a few months at a time. We got shuffled around a lot—to my grandmother, different schools, back again. When he got a piano, I was about fifteen or sixteen. I moved back in with him. I was never allowed to touch it. I'm a gentle person. I've always been a gentle person. I've never been a brat or a bitch, really wild or anything. I would sit down, and I didn't know how to play piano. He confused the sound of me not knowing how to play with me not making music. He would say, "Chan, it's not a toy. Do not play on the piano." It was so insulting, because he knew how much I loved to sing.

RG: How did you learn to play?
CM: I went to a New York recording studio when I was around twenty-six. I played guitar. I sat down at the piano, and I'd been listening to this song by Nina Simone called "Wild Is the Wind." David Bowie did it too. And there's a piano in the studio. While they were setting up mics I started to play on it. They said, "Okay, we're ready to have you play guitar." I said, "Could you press record? I want to record on the piano." That take is on *The Covers Record*. "Wild Is the Wind" was the first time I ever played piano.

RG: You reached in and pulled something out of the song that other people didn't hear.
CM: That's how I always do covers. With "Satisfaction," I had been driving around Atlanta with my cassette tapes in my truck. I had the Stones' *Hot Rocks*, and "Satisfaction" was on there. I'd go in my house and I didn't have a tape deck, so I picked up my guitar and fooled around with the notes. That's how I made up the "Satisfaction" version. It was because I just wanted to hear it, you know? It's not like I was trying to make it different or anything like that.

RG: When did you start playing guitar?
CM: You know Dexter Romweber? He used to have the band the Flat Duo Jets. When I was around sixteen, I went to see the Cramps play. I'd been listening to stuff since I was twelve. My stepdad had all these old records: Buddy Holly, Bob Dylan, Billie Holiday. The Flat Duo Jets

opened and I couldn't believe it—here was this guy playing music similar to the old records my parents had, but I could never talk about them at the different schools I went to because everybody just knew about Madonna or Duran Duran. So I saw that and I was like, Fuck. There are people who actually like old styles of music. Dexter had this old Silvertone guitar, and I immediately fell in love with it. A couple years later, after my dad kicked me out and I got a job at this pizza place, my friends knew that I loved Dexter, so they brought him in. I was so excited. When another friend was selling his Silvertone, which was identical to Dexter's, I bought it for seventy-five dollars. I had no intention of ever playing it. I had it in the corner near my bed like a piece of art or a vase. It was a cool object, and I didn't have much furniture, just this guitar and a futon mattress. Over the next year, on days off, I'd wake up late and fiddle with it. I used to want to be a writer because I love words, and I loved singing, so I'd make up little ditties. Then I started meeting more and more musicians— all dudes, by the way. Atlanta has a big rock community. All these dudes that I was meeting were guitar players. When they found out I had a Silvertone, they thought it was cool and wanted to teach me how to play. One was kind of Iggy-ish, one would be psychedelic, one would be more folksy. So I said, "I don't want to learn from you." I wanted to teach myself. I was afraid I'd have their technique, and I wanted to create my own technique. I was stubborn.

RG: And smart.
CM: Well, thank you. But more stubborn than smart. So we'd get drunk and start jamming. That's how Cat Power became a band. Then it became, "Let's play a show."

RG: Steve Shelley from Sonic Youth was an early ally of yours. How did he find you?
CM: Well, I'd moved to New York and I got this call from Gerard Cosloy, who runs Matador Records, which has been my label these past ten years. I didn't record for him then, but he was friends with my friend. He said, "Do you want to open up for Liz Phair, solo?" I didn't know who she was. I saw her on the cover of the *Village Voice* Pazz & Jop thing, so I thought, She's gotta be good. Gerard liked her. He said, "You'll get two hundred dollars, and you won't even get billing." I'd been working three jobs a day in New York. I was like, "Two hundred dollars and I won't get billed? I've got nothing to lose." So I showed up, played six songs, and got

a standing ovation from the Town Hall. I walked offstage and the stage manager said, "Cat! You wanna go back on? They can't get enough of you." I said, "That's all my time here. That's all they said I could play." They were just freaking out. I had one friend there, and I went and opened the side curtain to get her. All these people—maybe eight journalists— were saying, "Can we get an interview?" Then one of them said, "My professor loves your CD." I said, "I'm not Liz Phair." And they all turned around and walked away. Isn't that hilarious?

RG: That's our press: never interested in the story, only the star.
CM: Steve Shelley heard my sound check and invited me to lunch. He said, "You sounded cool. Where are you from? Do you have any records out?" When we were having lunch, I heard someone say something about Kim and Thurston and I realized, Fuck. That's Steve Shelley of Sonic Youth. I just got up and left the table. I was really, really shy. I was twenty-one. After I played, Steve came up again and said, "I'd love to put out a record with you." I had really bad trust issues. I didn't trust people. But I wasn't a band. I was just a waitress, an artist's assistant, and a maid. I wasn't interested in putting a record out. Six months later, getting to know Steve Shelley a little bit, we ended up playing together, and he said it again. So I gave some songs to this Italian label and did a record for Steve. Gerard said, "You know, Chan, we'd love to do a record with you." I was so flattered because I had all these friends with amazing bands in Atlanta that hadn't seen the light of day.

RG: Did you handle the business yourself?
CM: When I went in the Matador office I said, "I don't want an advance." I didn't know how it worked. I thought I was in control by saying, "I don't want any advance." I had no idea what I was signing. But it's been a good relationship and I can't complain. That's how it got started. Steve took me to Memphis, where I met you. I was younger and I didn't understand mixing records. I thought it was evil. I thought it was recorded and that was it. I didn't know you had to mix. When they started mixing, I was with Stuart Sikes, who engineered it and who produced *The Greatest* with me. I said, "Let's get the fuck out of here. I don't know what they're doing." I was pissed off that they had to mix it.

RG: For *The Greatest*, it seemed like Stuart was running the board and you were running the floor. There was a partnership there.

CM: Oh, definitely a partnership. Of course I have ideas. We don't fight, but sometimes I have to say, "Back the fuck up." But I chose Stuart for a reason. We became friends in Memphis. We kept in touch. We cared about each other, and that's why we worked so well together. There was no power struggle. He has a wealth of knowledge about microphones and amps and vintage equipment.

RG: It was a lot of fun for me to put the Memphis Rhythm Band together for you, getting that mix of Memphis soul and indie rock. I'm amazed you've been able to take the whole group on the road.
CM: They have given me an enormous gift—living the dream. When I was six years old playing "The Gambler" with my grandmother on a tape recorder, or singing some of those songs from *The Color Purple* when I was in junior high in my gym locker with the basketball girls, they'd say, "Oh, you can sing, girl. Where did you learn to sing like that?" I just love singing.

RG: How have your solo shows changed or been informed by your experiences with this large band?
CM: I just feel much more confident. I feel like I have control over my voice, which I never felt I had before. With these guys, I'm figuring out how to relax and not be so hard on myself.

RG: You've become a recording artist almost by chance. Have you got any sense what you would be doing if not this?
CM: I don't know if I'd be alive. If I had stayed in Atlanta, I'm sure I would have gotten on heroin. I'm sure I would've gotten pregnant. I'm sure I would be HIV-positive, like a few of my friends who have been and are. Who the hell knows? Maybe I would have been happy still being a waitress or working at a bank. Maybe I'd have three wonderful kids. You never know. About six years ago, my grandmother said—to her it was a great compliment, and it is to me because I know what she's talking about—she said, "I'm so proud of you. I'm so happy that you didn't turn out to be a prostitute or a drug addict." Because my family isn't educated, doesn't have money. There have never been any fathers. What she meant by that is: "I'm so happy that you got out and are able to make independent choices without being a wife." I know what she meant. I feel the same way.

On the set for the "Lived in Bars" music video. Mabon "Teenie" Hodges, left, and Chan "Cat Power" Marshall. Also, Martha Synk doing the Funky Chicken and Gillian Johnson held by Chan. (Courtesy of Brad Jones)

RG: It seems like there's also a part of you—I'm thinking of the song from *The Greatest*, "Where Is My Love," that—
CM: Longs for stability and a regular life?

RG: A family.
CM: Oh, hell yeah. I think everybody—especially women at my age, thirty-four—really starts thinking about it. A lot of my friends have gotten married. A couple of them are having their second child. A lot of my girlfriends are single. It's not like I'm the only one left. But because I'm not close to my family, there's a question: Where is my family? I think my friends are my family. I hope to make a greater, stronger bond with my mother before too long. It's just that I'm so different. I've gone through so many different changes, it's hard for her to really understand me. They remember me from when I was a kid and think that's how I still am: quiet and passive and very agreeable. I've grown up. I had to be that way for a reason. That reason hasn't changed. But I have and they don't—I love them all and I think I put way too much thought in trying to help something that might just be me wanting to be close.

RG: Do you think they don't want to be close? Or they do but they don't know the *you* that you are now?
CM: From meeting different people and traveling and relationships and seeing their families—most of my friends, their parents, call every day or every other day. Or they have lunch together, or with siblings. They have things in common. I never had that with my siblings or my parents. I never had that communication.

RG: When we were together a few months back, you were real happy dating the boxer.
CM: He dumped me.

RG: Oh no! Let me go beat his ass.

CM: It's really sad. I got attached to somebody, and I hadn't been attached to someone in a long time. We were friends for a couple of months before we started dating. He'd come over every day after work, or he'd call me during work. I'd make him dinner, we'd shoot the shit, hang out and play catch or jog.

RG: Do you like living in Miami?

CM: I love it. I love it because it's like Manhattan after nuclear war. All the things you love about New York are in Miami—the multicultural-ism, the diversity in class and heritage. I get everything I want there—food, different people. New York is like a different country almost, and so is Miami, but it also has a strong sense of community, which New York doesn't have. New York has kind of lost that. Miami is just beginning to create it. It's really awesome. There are a lot of different painters, different bands are starting to grow. Youth culture is thriving here now. No one has cars. They skate, bicycle, and wear flip-flops. It's Florida. It's close to South America. They get a lot of vegetables. People are healthy. There's no pollution. It's on the water. Good living.

RG: How close are you to the beach?

CM: A block.

RG: That must have been a nice thing when you were sobering up.

CM: Absolutely. It's always beautiful. There are flowers all year round; palms are everywhere, coconuts, jasmine. It's amazing.

RG: You mentioned New York. What was Richard Avedon like?

CM: Cool as hell. He does all the portraits of the artists for the *New Yorker*, and he'd been given a record and he listened to it and said, "I want to see her before I shoot her." He wanted to create a relationship before he shot me. So he invited me when he was in the hospital to meet him. I had just woken up. I played a show the night before. I got out of bed and got a bunch of flowers. I looked like shit. That was back when I was drinking. I was half-drunk, probably. He's in the hospital bed and he's like, "Oh, you look fabulous." I was like, "I look like shit." He said, "You look gorgeous. I want you to look just like this." That was no prob-lem, because I had a show the day before he wanted to shoot me. One of the first questions he asked me was, "Do you like Bob Dylan?" I was like, "Oh my God. Are you high?" "Good. Because I sense the struggle in your music." He sent me a book: "To Chan, Yours in the struggle. Love, Dick."

RG: What book?

CM: *The Sixties*. He was talking to me about Malcolm X, Martin Luther King Jr., Bob Dylan, Janis Joplin. He said, "I was doing fashion just to pay for trips to Cambodia and Vietnam. Something about your music shows me that you understand things, and I just want to talk to you." I told him about the show that I was doing for Janis Joplin's birthday in Central Park. He said, "I would love to come. I loved Janis so much. She was a great girl. Such a sweetheart." He came to the show, this eighty-year-old man rocking out to Big Brother and the Holding Company and me.

So then he shot me the next day. He wanted me to come an hour before so we could hang out. He took me upstairs. He has two different studios in New York. This is the one that's around Twenty-First Street. He took me upstairs to his apartment. It was like a museum. It was modest— eight hundred square feet maybe, all open-floor, with a kitchen. He had a portrait of Marilyn. He's like, "I did that when I was forty. I was older than you. You weren't even born." He had all these photos from Africa. He had pictures of his wife and his son and books upon books. It was just a mesh of collectible things from all over the world. He opened up a bottle of champagne, and we sat in the garden and I smoked. He was so accommodating. He was running around doing everything for me—so handsome, such an open-minded person. We talked about Dylan and a lot about the civil rights era. He was just a wealth of knowledge. I wish you could have interviewed him.

Anyway, then we went downstairs and he was like, "I want to show you what I want you to wear." When he opened the little dressing room, it was all Bob Dylan T-shirts. "I just want you to wear this. I'm going to rip it a little." I was like, "No way." He's like, "You look great. Just leave your hair up." He took about six Polaroids, eight-by-ten. I was sick. I'd just gotten back from Mexico. I had some toxin in my blood. On the seventh shot, he had cut my shirt. He said, "Keep pulling it up—just like it's a towel or something." And that's the picture. My stomach was hurting so bad because I wasn't eating and was just manic. My jeans were unbuttoned and unzipped the whole time, but when he told me to take the shirt off to snip it, that picture happened. The first pubic hairs ever to be published in the *New Yorker*. My grandmother shit a brick.

He gave me the sixth Polaroid. I have it. It's eight-by-ten. When the hurricane hit my apartment in Miami, it blew my window out. It blew my kitchen door in. I lost one thing. I lost the photograph of me and my mom and my sister from before she met my stepdad. It really makes me sad. That was a good memory. The only thing I give a shit about was that picture that I lost and the Avedon portrait, which they found.

RG: You're working on a movie now. When I made the "Lived in Bars" video for you, I was so impressed with your acting instincts. I'm thrilled to see that world opening up to you.
CM: I'd like to work with interesting directors. The guy from *Magnolia* [Paul Thomas Anderson] is someone the William Morris Agency wants me to work with. I just want to do a few roles—as an experiment and as an experience. The thing that I keep trying to stress to them is I don't want to play Chan Marshall.

RG: Do you miss the personal interaction of the audience when you're working with the camera?
CM: Having to lip-sync for music videos is strange. You're interacting with the camera as a human, it's really bizarre. You're faking, faking, faking. But doing a film, it's easier because I'm interacting with a person, not looking into the camera, lip-syncing to a song.

I just had a great experience with the audience. I was in Miami, the first gig after I quit drinking. When I told them I was sober, they stood up. It made me really emotional to see that people cared about me, and they never even fucking met me. I'm thankful to those kinds of people. They send me letters saying, "I love you" and "I understand."

RG: What are some specific fan exchanges that have lingered with you, for good or bad?
CM: I've always been the new kid in a different school, and never really had a group of friends. I was the silent kid everywhere I went, because I didn't grow up in one place. When I was twenty-three, I went on my first trip to Europe. My first record for Matador, *What Would the Community Think*, did really well there. So I'm used to playing small shows, and in France it's like a thousand people. The record label there had set up all these interviews. I wasn't used to it. I didn't understand how it worked. I'm an open person, and I didn't realize that with some interviewers, you have to hold back or they'll dig deeper. The experience was confrontational to say the least. So I had one more interview left and I started having a break-down: "I don't understand this attention and these strangers looking at me." I wanted to just kill myself. I took off all my clothes and I shoved

them full of towels, and I put my fake self, with shoes and the socks and everything, on the bed with a sheet over my head to make it look like I was dead. I curled up underneath the thing and was just bawling.

The next interviewer came in, and I wanted them to just leave me alone. It was a girl's voice. I was expecting a male journalist, and I was just bawling underneath the thing. She was about seventeen and she started crying and telling me she didn't want to do the interview. She said, "I just want to tell you that last summer . . ." She had been on drugs and she had been in the hospital for trying to kill herself. She said, "I just want to tell you that when I heard your song it made me want to live." She started bawling. It was a desperate situation. It shifted. I wanted to help her and hold her and give her some comfort, and it snapped me right the fuck out of whatever crazy shit I was feeling. That's one of the most memorable things I've ever experienced. It wasn't that she was upset when I went to hold her. She was crying because she was happy that she had been given the chance to recognize that she's not alone in the world. That made me feel better because I was like, There are other people. It's not a lonely world.

JERRY McGILL

JERRY McGILL IS the legendary outlaw of the Memphis underground, a gun–toting cowboy hero in black, the rebel who does wrong in the name of right. He's the ugly woman who showed up at a Mud Boy and the Neutrons gig and uttered the line, "Known felons in drag," which became the title of their first album. I'd sought information on McGill when writing *It Came from Memphis* and again when making the documentary from Bill Eggleston's 1970s vérité footage, *Stranded in Canton*, but the only evidence of his existence was the occasional collect call from a penitentiary to Roland Janes, the house producer at the Sam Phillips Recording Service and former Sun Records guitarist. Roland didn't mind all that much hearing from Jerry, but he didn't love it either, because it could be a short step from a phone call to your front door. And McGill was, for many people, better a legend than a bodily presence.

For me, finding McGill was a reminder to be careful what you wish for. He remained part of my life until he died, always alerting me in subtle ways that he could find me when he wanted to. There were signs I should have seen, like the fact that when he finally surfaced in 2010, Mary Lindsay Dickinson did *not* want him to know even in which state she and Jim lived. There were many unpleasant days when making *Very Extremely Dangerous*, when the vérité footage of Jerry's ugliness was overwhelming.

Jerry McGill, from William Eggleston's *Stranded in Canton*. (Courtesy of William Eggleston)

For this new movie in which we followed him for about ten weeks—fresh out of prison, newly connected to his old girlfriend, and suddenly diagnosed with lung cancer—we had to make Jerry's character at least somewhat palatable, and we'd enter the edit room saying, Time to chisel off some more hate. But there were also some experiences shooting it that were so full of humanity, my heart could barely take it—more than once he gave advice to little kids, drawing from his mistakes to improve the lives of those he didn't know. The humanity and the venom—an outlaw's realm.

We made this movie knowing only that McGill was a compelling character and trusting that if we stayed with him, we'd find a story. A fictional narrative filmmaker writes the story, then shoots the pieces and edits them together—easy peasy. Documentaries are much more challenging—the footage is all there, what's the narrative? When this film's termination sideswiped us, we found ourselves in the edit room, reviewing the material and asking, What's the story? It is, in a way, the most exciting kind of filmmaking.

I've maintained contact with Jerry's then girlfriend, Joyce. She's a lot more stable since his demise, and she doesn't have his temper. Or his guns.

Very Extremely Dangerous
Liner notes to *Very Extremely Dangerous*, 2014

I made a mistake in my first conversation with Jerry McGill that would (mis)shape our enduring relationship: I gave him my home address. Prior to this first spring 2010 phone call, I'd searched the Florida prison records for information about him, seeking both "Jerry McGill" and "Jerry Cole" (his birth name). Later I'd learn he was serving under the alias Billy Thurman. The first time McGill heard his real name during this prison stay was on his way out. As McGill, just discharged, approached the sunlight, a beefy Florida prison screw pushed open the big office door and called out, "Thurman!" McGill looked up and answered subserviently, as prison had taught him. The screw said, "Who is Jerry McGill?" McGill, smelling freedom, did not miss a beat. "That's my BMI name, that's the name I write songs under." And he was free again.

Jerry McGill first came to my attention through Jim Dickinson, the Memphis record producer, Rolling Stones accompanist, and Big Star producer. Dickinson told me about the 1973 portable video footage that photographer William Eggleston shot, *Stranded in Canton*. Eggleston's movie is stolen—and his life almost taken—by Jerry McGill, behaving at his most out-there (or so one would have thought, until we shot our documentary). The gun in his hand held to another man's temple, McGill turns to Eggleston's camera, steely behind dark shades in a dark room, and says, "I don't care nothing 'bout that." Talking to the camera, about the camera.

After the ensuing four decades, I learned, his sense of bravado had faded not at all.

Jerry McGill was Memphis's homegrown Lash LaRue, our own personal outlaw. McGill traded Lash's black whip for a .44 Magnum, kept the black hat, kited checks, attempted murder, robbed a liquor store and some banks, and stayed on the lam.

Rock and roll led him to his life of crime. He cut the only record he'd ever release at nineteen for Sam Phillips's Sun Records in 1959. He'd play the nightclub stage, then after the spotlight's glare, he'd meet the criminals and make a new kind of record: a sheaf of Memphis arrests and more serious issues with the Feds.

He always loved music, and during most of his thirteen years running from federal agents (the armed robbery charge), McGill was Waylon Jennings's road manager, mostly under the name Curtis Buck. That's how he's acknowledged on Waylon's albums—as rhythm guitarist and sometimes as co-writer (including of "Waymore's Blues," a song basically stolen from Furry Lewis, though Jerry later paid Furry)—and that's the name he was married under on the stage of Nashville's Exit/In while running from the FBI. His main Waylon duties were getting the man to his next gig and collecting the money due. He carried a briefcase full of cash and a very large handgun; and he drove on a driver's license he could not show the law.

Jerry McGill, with aliases. (Courtesy of Robert Gordon)

When last released from prison—his third long stint in two states under two names—his friend Paul Clements showed him a computer and said, "This is the Internet." Jerry said, "Put my name in there," and they did, and found him profiled on a blog, *Boogie Woogie Flu*. Scrolling the comments about himself, McGill saw a message from his 1959-era Memphis girlfriend, Joyce. Fresh from prison, he joined her in Alabama, and days later attended a North Mississippi Allstars gig—Jim Dickinson's sons—letting them know he was looking for their dad. Free, in love, and playing guitar, he was dealt a sudden blow: lung cancer. He declared he'd make good music before he died and booked a day at Sam Phillips Recording Service in Memphis.

My Irish film partner, Paul Duane, had been corresponding with Joyce for a couple years (having found her in the same comment thread on that blog). When Jerry showed up, she called Paul, and he called me. Joyce e-mailed me some stories Jerry had written—they were very well written—and I found myself on the phone with the long-lost Memphis outlaw. I told him how much I liked his writing, and he said, "Give me your address, I'll send you more."

Time stopped in that moment. For twenty years I'd maintained a PO box for just such occasions, but I had let it expire a while back. McGill was seventy now and, I reasoned, he couldn't be the same dangerous man today. Was it really a risk? I gave him my address.

McGill was a professional criminal. He never let me forget that he knew where I lived, knew my routines. (Once, a few years later, he rang while I was driving. "You heading to your weekly workout?" Damn, he was good.) And he was a junkie. During the making of the film, he and Joyce got in a fight, and she kicked him out of the car and drove back to Alabama. Jerry was wandering the Memphis streets, needing a fix, with my home address. I was on my way out of town, so I showed his photo to my wife and two kids, one barely a teenager, and explained that if he showed up at the door, no matter what he said, they could not let him cross the threshold.

Paul and I and cinematographer David Leonard videotaped McGill's final recording session, when he was joined by Memphis greats like Sid Selvidge, Jimmy Crosthwait, and Jim Lancaster, as well as Luther and Cody Dickinson. He was so good on camera—just like he'd been with Eggleston forty years earlier—that we saddled up and rode with him. He was an artist expressing himself in song. He was a budding short-story writer of considerable talent. Free again, he was establishing a home, drawing on the honeymoon feel of his renewed, deep-rooted relationship. And he was a hot-tempered man always armed with both knives and guns (including a very ornate sawed-off shotgun), despite the risk of mandatory prison as a convicted felon. He stole a cell phone off a neighboring table while dining out with us. (We made him return it through the restaurant's mail slot.) In our presence, he threatened his best friend, his girlfriend, and people who'd never be his friend. We held tight until ten weeks later when we jumped off the Jerry McGill marauding maelstrom, fearing for our lives, our sanity, and our movie.

I remember phoning Joyce at one point, after a particularly harrowing outing with Jerry. I told her, "We had no idea that things were going to play out like this." And she said, "I didn't either. I hadn't seen him in forty years. I'm as new to him as y'all are."

McGill's musical tracks were squirreled away by several associates, and as we found them, a larger picture of McGill's talents emerged. The greats wanted to play alongside him. Mud Boy and the Neutrons in the 1970s sessions that Jim Dickinson produced (featuring some of their best-ever performances, with Lee Baker's guitar on "Desperados Waiting for a Train" sounding strung with prison wire). Waylon Jennings and his Waylors joined the Memphis Horns to back him, and guitar great Travis Wammack later leapt to the call. His last session featured the North Mississippi Allstars and his first session Sun's Little Green Men: Roland Janes, Billy Lee Riley, and J. M. Van Eaton. Paul and I found evidence of a Curtis Buck master, but we were unable to track its owner. McGill lost more master tapes than most people ever record.

Things mostly worked out for McGill. Joyce, who knew him before he was Curtis Buck, dug down to the nice guy beneath the thick skin, the one she'd known in the 1950s. After filming was complete, she saw him through his illness—with the understanding that she'd monitor the pain pills—and they lived several happy years together. The two of them were early rock and rollers who'd met in the shade of Sun Records, and they were sharing their sunset years, lying in bed with their heads together, one humming a tune and the other guessing its name.

But that happened mostly when we were done shooting. In *Very Extremely Dangerous*, Memphis's real-life outlaw is battling death, and battling life itself, seeking peace, making war. Joyce demonstrated the power of love, and Jerry's transformation was nothing less than unforeseeable. Both of them were revelatory experiences. Me and Paul, we took a thrill ride with a career criminal living his last days, and while he was someone I may not have wanted in my house, by the end, he was someone I was glad was in my life.

ALEX CHILTON

"The very same people who are good sometimes are the very same people who are bad sometimes."

—Mr. Rogers

WE'RE GOING FULL circle now, back to the 1977 civic blues event where the plug was pulled on Mud Boy and the Neutrons. Alex Chilton wasn't scheduled to play that day, but boy did he. He took the stage and set to thrashing on his guitar, igniting the fuse that would explode a few songs later when he'd introduce Mud Boy and the Neutrons. Alex had been in and out of New York, so he was familiar with the Ramones and the burgeoning punk rock scene. Guitarist Sid Selvidge sat at the piano. Pianist Jim Dickinson picked up the bass guitar. Bodyguard Danny Graflund took a vocal mic. Several months before the Sex Pistols came to Memphis, Alex Chilton pulled back the horizon and let us hear the imminent thunder.

He opened with a guttural version of the song that established the Box Tops, "The Letter." He'd been the golden boy, the coin he generated going to someone else always, never to him. He had earned his cynicism. "I got to get back to my baby once more / anyway. Anyway! Anyway! No way!" Alex knew that what he was singing—no, how he was singing—was not what the blues audience came to hear. He reveled in their revulsion. There's video of him dancing maniacally, luxuriating in the bad boy's dream: a large stage, a captive crowd, a live microphone. On that video, as he begins his Saint Vitus' dance, the audio cord is yanked from the camera. On the screen, the accompanying silence makes his antics all the wilder, especially as the down-front audience catches the fever. The music is so new, no one's sure how to move, so they careen and flay with him.

My introduction to Alex's oeuvre came through *Big Star 3rd*, when it was issued the following year, 1978 (after four years in the can). The most introspective of his work, the songs are relentlessly bleak. I was a teenager roiling in confusion and angst, and *3rd* captivated me with its contrasts and discordance—the music on "Kanga Roo" begins with industrial sounding distortion out of which grows delicate and beautiful acoustic guitar. The album's lyrics were a misanthrope's love poem.

From *3rd* I worked my way forward with his new releases, and also back, through the first two Big Star albums and then further back to the Box Tops. The way stations along his trail were fascinating: Dan Penn, Jim Dickinson, Lesa Aldridge—Alex's muse, Tav Falco, Jerry Lawler . . . Chilton was a traveler and a guide.

With the Panther Burns, Alex was going in yet another direction, one that extended from his 1979 solo album *Like Flies on Sherbert*. When I first heard *Flies*, I was insulted that an artist would subject a listener to such

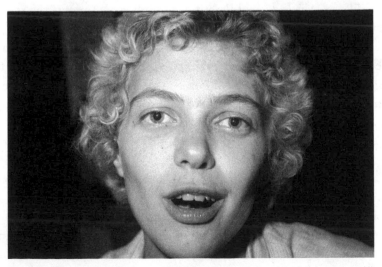

Lesa Aldridge, in the light of dark, 1980. (Courtesy of Pat Rainer)

Alex Chilton, left, and Tav Falco. An early Panther Burns gig at the Well. (Courtesy of Dan Zarnstorff)

abuse—bumping the vocal mic, keeping the distortion in the mix, leaving the songs so raw; within months, however, I'd been exposed to punk and was back at the Pop Tunes record store begging the clerk to look in the back and see if they had any more left. (He returned a long time later, having dug up the store's sole remaining copy.) Alex, the Cramps, Tav, and Dickinson—they all influenced each other, all pushed against the edge and found the battering rams in the sounds of the past. And those past sounds were local—you think Elvis wasn't a punk?

Like Flies on Sherbert is exhilarating, though it documents the start of a tailspin. Three years later, in 1982, Alex took a giant step outside the spotlight, moving to New Orleans to work as a tree trimmer and dishwasher. "The Letter" would come on the restaurant's kitchen radio and no one believed that the guy with his elbows in the dish suds was the vocalist. When he next released a record, six years since *Flies*, he was much more reserved. *Feudalist Tarts*, his return EP (*comeback* doesn't seem the right term) presented a midthirties white soul singer who sounded less wizened than the Box Tops had twenty years earlier; Alex simplified his sound, a bass and drum backing up him and his guitar. The horn arrangements were spare and slightly cubist in a jazzy way. In Big Star and through *Flies*, he'd been engaged with the recording arts, the potential offered by the studio. Through the 1970s, he'd experimented vocally, maturing into a boyish tenor from the coarse deep vocals of his youth—reversing nature, upbraiding the industry that screwed him.

Jim Dickinson, left, and Alex Chilton, during the recording of *Like Flies on Sherbert*, 1978. (Courtesy of Pat Rainer)

After his time-out, Alex was dispassionate, embracing clean, unadorned documentation. At gigs and on recordings, he was professional, but he rarely leaned into the songs. His new model was Chet Baker, Mr. California cool. The sound of Alex's recordings over his final quarter century didn't really change again; his albums contained basically nothing that couldn't be done live. There would be no soundscapes like on *3rd*, no layers like John Fry and Chris Bell created on the first two Big Star albums, nothing churlish and nothing challenging. He presented a new demeanor: He'd seen it all, done most of it, and the catalog was available for purchase if you wanted to know more. Your cover charge tonight, your purchase of the recording—you get the yeoman on the yob. As prominent as anything else on the back cover of his return record was the fact that he'd only put a day into the recording. The wild man had returned to Borneo, and this Alex could be found talking to whoever ran the joint about getting his pay—in cash.

I caught an early tour after *Feudalist Tarts*. He came through Philly, and afterward my pals and I went out hunting for low boots with a buckle like he'd worn. The pair I found were a half size too small but I wore them anyway because he'd defined them as cool. And as before, he was a musical cartographer, his selected covers revealing deep cuts from deep artists: I knew Lowell Fulsom but not "Make a Little Love." Willie Tee, the New Orleans musician and producer was entirely new to me. "Take It Off" by Groundhog: I'm still not sure who that was—or is.

Paul Westerberg, left, and Alex Chilton, at Chilton's 1987 gig at Maxwell's in Hoboken, NJ. (Courtesy of Ted Barron)

When Alex covered Dean Martin's cover of the Eurovision hit "Volare," it couldn't help but be kitschy, except he did it so sincerely and it was so much fun.

I moved back to Memphis in 1988. Alex's presence on the local scene was more intimate than his new national reputation as the high priest of independent rock. Here, too many people had known him as a kid; he was aloof, but he was also one of us. He'd play the Loose End, a club that held considerably fewer than a hundred people, his trio banging out songs like the spinning of a 1969 radio dial. We'd dance like drunk guests at a wedding party, Alex revealing his pleasure with that impish grin he couldn't hide.

Initially, we got along fine. We'd spent an afternoon playing records—he was into Dada-esque musician Fred Lane. He came to my house a couple times, we'd broken bread, had too much wine together. One topic we discussed was Dickinson—Alex was resenting that Jim's version of their times together had become the dominant narrative, subsuming his.

One day at Ardent, Alex asked my birth date. I'd heard he was into astrology. I sort of sneered a half smile when I answered. His eyes went up as he did some mental calculations—the computation, I imagined, clicking like a beaded abacus while one of those grade school models of the solar system—metal rods with plastic orbs—divined the selected individual's narrative. What the ciphering told him, I don't know. But the change in how he treated me was evident.

You know how some people make you feel really comfortable? Alex was the opposite. I remarked to Dickinson how ill at ease I felt around Alex, and I remember the relief I found in his reply: Everyone does.

No Chitterlings Today
Memphis Flyer, March 25, 2010

Alex stuck his finger down his throat and gagged, showing me *that's* how much he hated his hometown of Memphis. We laughed about it. He didn't like me much either, but that didn't mean we couldn't laugh together, and it didn't mean he couldn't enjoy Memphis. We were aboard a flight for a European tour, and the movie showing was *The Firm*, shot in our hometown—he gagged again, the timeless response of a teenage boy listening to his mom. Memphis was a cloak that was hard to shake.

Alex Chilton became a public figure at the age of sixteen when, not long after he'd first seen the inside of a recording studio, a song from that session became a 1967 number one worldwide hit: "The Letter" by the Box Tops. At that impressionable age, he became a product packaged and sold, considerable talent yielding considerable profits for the band's manager but nothing considerable for the artists. Four years later, the monkey walked away from the organ-grinder. Caught so young in the glare of Memphis's bright lights, some part of him was like an image in a camera's flash, frozen there, forever sixteen.

Chilton channeled the future by capturing the underground zeitgeist, three times in the 1970s alone. The audience for the clean pop of the first two Big Star records caught up to the music a decade after it was made; the third Big Star album was nihilistic and beautiful (hello, Elliott Smith and the '90s); the shambolic *Like Flies on Sherbert* deemed hip the wealth and depth of Americana roots while becoming a punk rock classic. The art is canonical, and Chilton a titanic figure. The only thing between him and stardom was good record distribution. Instead of profit, he was assigned prophecy.

His career in song is a testament to his eye for precise detail, his adventuresome ear, his teenaged heart. He could evoke the maelstrom of young adulthood in a way that made listeners feel close to him, sometimes too close for his comfort. The Replacements were prescient in their tribute song. "Children by the million sing for Alex Chilton," they wrote, but if they did it "when he comes 'round," he'd never have stayed. Waves of admiration were an assault, and he was scornful of those who needed to make more of his songs than he did. His lifelong interest in astrology makes sense: What is colder, more beautiful, more distant than the stars?

Astrology is the province of the seeker, not the sought. Fans may have wanted to see themselves in his struggles, but Alex accepted no fellow travelers. Stories of his hostile responses to the passing compliments of strangers are legion. As are his inviting replies to the pretty female fans. He spurned most of those who approached, and if he blessed you with his gaze, he'd not hesitate to turn 180 degrees, snarl, and leave your jaw flapping in midsentence. In the same late-night late-1970s radio appearance when he achingly sang Dolly Parton's "I Will Always Love You"—years, of course, before Whitney Houston—he also broke into a filthy anti-Semitic ballad.

He liked friction, was sometimes a contrarian just for the sake of it. He could be, less notoriously, a sweetheart too. His mind remained curious, making its own way through politics, the humanities, and the sciences as zealously as his music mined R&B, country, classical, you name it. He stole Wilhelm Reich books from the Memphis Public Library because he said no one checked them out, and he gave them to people he thought would appreciate them. When a friend heard him explain his worldview, he chided, "You're right, Alex, the world is wrong." Telling me about this later, Alex added, "And, hell, I believe that. The world is wrong, I am right."

To the end, he did it his way. His song "In the Street" was the theme for the popular TV program *That '70s Show.* He liked to call it *That 70 Dollar Show*—Mr. Chitlins ripped off again—though according to someone involved in that deal, it earned him a considerable chunk, enough to afford health insurance if he'd wanted it. But when he was feeling ill, Alex refused to see a doctor because what did doctors know? He suffered shortness of breath but kept smoking cigarettes; he mowed the lawn in the heat, then, age fifty-nine, he died. The loss magnified by its abruptness, this meteoric musician is stilled but his great recordings live on. The eulogies will too, much to his likely irritation.

He spoke his last words to his wife on the way to the emergency room: "Run the red light."

AFTERWORD:
STUCK INSIDE THE MEMPHIS BLUES AGAIN

"What did I say to make you mad this time, baby?"
—Willie Mabon, "I Don't Know"

IT'S BEEN MORE than forty years since the Furry Lewis fireworks on that liberating Fourth of July. The subject of nearly every piece in this book is dead. The magazine industry is a wasted version of its once radiant self. Daily newspapers are coupon circulars with the occasional news item inserted—written without checking facts, without a copy editor, often without any real reporting. The Internet, glorious and terrifying, projects a false democracy, allowing everyone to be a pundit on the soapbox of their own URL. But dollars continue to control traffic; the still, small voice remains still and small. Corporate narratives dominate, and the critical skills needed to sift through all this information are not taught, not enough. (You can't get that discernment from standardized test bubbles.) The wage for a freelance writer hasn't changed in the thirty-plus years of my practice, nor has the cover charge at the door for seeing a musician play, even as corporate CEO pay, as compared to worker compensation, has risen from nearly 30 to 1 to more than 300 to 1.

The musicians, the writers, the creative people—unemployable in any other form, compelled to grind out their inner spirit for public consumption, for both praise and derision and always for the hope of a nickel. There's the stultifying grind of the incessant demand for the next marketable idea, and the despairing cycle that that routine, that thinking, produces. It's impossible to anticipate the imbalance of time spent shopping ideas to find the funding to produce the work that, if you're lucky, you get to make on a tight budget. You grind out a version of what you've envisioned on the mill of your own overreaching risk: the pulverizing of excitement, good intent, personal time and money so that maybe the next one will pay right. That's not new. That's a continuum as old as the arts.

I am often lauded for having followed my passion in life, especially by people who chose routes with more security. They project a lot of what they think they missed onto my lifestyle: unconstrained, romantic, stimulating. They don't consider what it's like raising a family with no guarantee of work when this article, this book, this film is completed. When someone says, I admire you, I take that to mean, I wouldn't do what you do. The ladder that workers climb has regulated, mandated steps. Mine has rickety rungs and the poles are greased. The successes, unexpected and scarce, often invite antagonism.

Attention all people who wanted to do this but didn't have the guts or the luck. Attention those who now work nine to five at the corporation and live in anguish for having sold your soul. Now hear this: We all sell our souls. I envy your regular job with its regular pay and its regular health insurance and its regular hours. If your spirit is crushed because you're not living your dream, know that the greener grass is hiding the same fire ants, the same dogshit, the same shards of glass.

For example, it's a thrill when a stranger approaches me to say they appreciate my work. But every encounter begins with trepidation, because the stranger sometimes says, You wrote about me and you got it all wrong and you've ruined my life (one person wanted me to phone his mother and apologize). Some people are pissed off if they're in the story, some if they're left out. In Memphis, where everyone is a connoisseur, where everyone has their personal and authoritative narrative and my telling has ruined their opportunity to write their book—every endeavor is laden with potential backlash. Like Willie Mabon sang, "What did I say to make you mad this time, baby?"

Alex Chilton hamming it up, circa 1997, at a Box Tops performance. (Courtesy of Dan Ball)

And it's around this point, bitterness bubbling, when I'm losing myself in hard feelings, that I think about Charlie Feathers and I think about Junior Kimbrough and all these heroic individuals who followed the muse and cut paths of their own, persevering outside society's mainstream, sometimes tasting the transient sweets that popularity tempts with, sometimes replying, No, thank you. Thinking of them, I experience Dickinson's resetting of the context, see the fleeting shimmer of the treasure I've witnessed.

IN THE SUMMER of 2016, I drove about an hour outside of Memphis to the North Mississippi Hill Country Picnic. It's put together by Kenny Brown, who grew up in north Mississippi with bluesman Joe Callicott as his neighbor and mentor, and who recorded and toured with R. L. Burnside

Sharde Thomas, middle, and her grandfather Otha Turner, at Otha's annual picnic, 1996. (Courtesy of Bill Steber)

through much of the 1970s, '80s, and '90s. Approaching the field, I heard Otha Turner's granddaughter Sharde Thomas take the stage. She was his fife protégée, and in the decade and a half since his death, she's continued to lead his Rising Star Fife and Drum Corps. I was still crossing the fields when she started playing a familiar song from his repertoire—and my heart kind of sank. Did I want to be in this hot field listening to live music, especially recycled tunes, when I could be in my air-conditioned home laying on the comfortable sofa reading? Dutifully, I took a spot near the stage.

And quickly something changed. Sharde played the old tunes, but they were different. Another of Otha's disciples was Luther Dickinson, Jim's son, who'd gone from listening to Black Flag to immersing himself in the rural world at his back door. With his brother Cody, he'd formed the North Mississippi Allstars to continue the legacy of their neighborhood, personalizing it as kids who listened to punk rock and southern rock and nonrock would. Luther and Sharde, who is about fifteen years younger, had played together with Otha, had been tutored in not only his music but his wisdom ("Heap see," he'd say, "mighty few know"), and after his death, they'd carried on his style, together and separately. They refracted Otha through different lenses to explore new sounds based on the old sound they'd been given. And as Sharde played that hot afternoon, backed by two other blood relatives of Otha's, performing under the banner that Otha had used for decades—the Rising Star Fife and Drum Corps—a big smile crept over my face. Sharde was playing differently from her granddad.

Luther Dickinson, left, and Jim Dickinson, right. In the background is Chris Chew, bassist for the North Mississippi All Stars. (Courtesy of Yancey Allison)

Her notes didn't pop like his in a staccato manner. Rather, she was drawing elision from the piece of bamboo; she was moving her fingers across
those holes in combination with her breath such that she was evoking her
other major influence: Luther Dickinson's slide guitar.

This was not a museum piece standing before us, this was not an imita-
tion or re-creation. She was taking something old and creating something
new, the continuum extending past Otha, past Luther, past Sharde, reach-
ing out further, seeking still and seeking always, seeking another place to
land, to connect, to play. Otha's music had taken new life in the hands of
his granddaughter. Sharde has pushed his music to where it's not previously been, making it hers. Breath through cane isn't as simple as beating a
stick on a rock, but it must be one of the earliest musics. And the thrill of
hearing something so old become something so new is right there with
the excitement of new life, of recognizing the singularity of who we each
are and the distinct ripples that our own actions create, the possibility of
leaving our handprint on the cave's wall, our own stamp—in music, in
children, in literature or service.

I cannot say I'd do it all again and not change a thing. The constant
insecurity has scraped at my psyche. But I, too, am chastened when I realize the power of the people I have encountered, the obscure figures whose
popular impact is nil but whose jolt to their small audiences is profound.
Seeing Sharde on that stage in the middle of forsaken nowhere, I thought
of the way these many artists have shaped me, the jewels they have shared,
the wisdom they've offered, the kindnesses.

Jim Dickinson's self-penned epitaph is I'M JUST DEAD, I'M NOT GONE.
He's certainly present in this book, published nearly a decade after his death.
Otha is a decade and a half dead, and his influence on Sharde changed me
just the other day. We toil in our lonesome worlds, the darkness all around,
but the past illuminates our future, warms our present. These joyous candles elevate us.

MEMPHIS HAS BECOME a destination for music tourists. People want to soak
up the surroundings that produced the blues and rock and roll, to sing
where soul found its voice. And that's a powerful experience—traveling
the same blues highway from the Mississippi Delta to Beale, standing in
front of the microphone that Elvis and Charlie Feathers used at Sun,
walking through the Stax doors like Otis and Isaac and Carla and Rufus.
Even an abandoned lot can make a responsive heart throb. We can't travel
time, but we can feel history in our marrow when we smell the barbecue
in the air, feel the humidity, touch the bricks and pavement.

Memphis is not about perfection but about the differences, the flaws. It's the kinks that mark beauty and define us, not the lack of them. How remarkable to create something unlike what anyone else can, that even the artist can't repeat. That recorded moment—like Dickinson said—why preserve it if you can recreate it every day? Preserve instead the best ever take, the most unique version, the unrepeatable presentation. Sam Phillips, who tuned the latter half of the twentieth century, and even when recording the unrecordables did not let bum notes or a missed beat or the phone ringing in the background prevent him from releasing a take that had the spirit. The differences he captured became beauty marks. "Perfect imperfection" is how Sam described his goal, and that's pretty much the Memphis approach to art.

To me, Memphis is a verb. It means, To seek and embrace what's different. As far back as the 1960s, the Rolling Stones were encouraging Americans to try it. Stones bassist Bill Wyman told me, "When we brought it to America, it was like a new music to the white kids here. They'd say, 'Where can we get this music?' And it was just down the road there." He laughs. "We had to come across the ocean, you just have to go across the river and it's there."

Beyond the bright lights and the blue screen's glow, beneath the clamorous beckonings for your attention, and not just in Memphis but all over the world, a still, small voice sings. Most discount it if they ever encounter it. It's unfamiliar and not immediately pleasing. Its power is not obvious. But the person who's got it so wrong that it's all right, who opens you up and retools your expectations—sings for thee.

"To Memphis." It's international, can be done anywhere. In urban backyards and on rural screened porches, in the neighborhood dive or in drafty dwellings like Furry Lewis's or James Carr's: Somewhere the church organ swells among the Saturday night cinderblocks. There is drumming in a starlit holler or a child singing to the hallway mirror. In a government housing tower or over on the finer side of town, someone is composing a song or recording a sound or performing a show that might change how we think, how we hear the world and understand our place in it. It's happening most days and certainly every weekend, and it's beyond the hype and the pageantry, outside the spotlight's circle, maybe near the Mississippi Delta or very far from it. What happens in Peoria, Pittsburg, and Petaluma may not become emblematic of a generation, but the expression of something different can still challenge the mind and thrill the heart. That still, small voice, it won't be immediately familiar, and it takes a moment to come in clear, but listen for it, note how near—it's just down the road or right across the river.

ACKNOWLEDGMENTS

I shouldn't have been surprised to learn, only recently, that Knox Phillips was at the heart of having Furry Lewis appear at that 1975 Rolling Stones concert. When the Stones arrived in Memphis the night before the all-day concert, Knox arranged for them to be greeted on the tarmac by Furry and his guitar (with Lee Baker backing him); not the ideal listening conditions, but spiritually perfect. When the night was wrapping up, Knox and the concert promoter discussed having Furry play at the Stones concert the next day. Knox wanted to make arrangements ahead of time so he could enjoy the Fourth of July in his father's pool with family and friends. No need, the promoter determined; with three opening acts there wouldn't be time for Furry.

Cut to the phone ringing at Sam Phillips's house the next day, the holler out the sliding glass door for Knox to get out of the pool. The Stones were delaying their show and they wanted Furry to help fill the time. Departing through the wafting smoke of grilling burgers, Knox left the sounds of laughter and splashing to shepherd Furry through his largest gig ever (thus changing the course of at least one attendee's life).

Knox Phillips, left, and Furry Lewis, center, on the Rolling Stones' stage, July 4, 1975. That's me, way way in the background. (Courtesy of Diane Duncan)

I learned of Knox's role when I saw this photo on his wall. Thank you, Knox!

And thanks to brother Jerry Phillips, the one-time (and all-time) "world's most perfectly formed midget wrestler," rocking hard today, all twisted steel and sex appeal, ready to welcome you with a big hug and make you comfortable wherever you are, whatever you're doing.

Adam Miller, long ago, made being a writer seem possible. Halfway between then and now, when I was envisioning *It Came from Memphis* being something like this collection, he opened my eyes to the larger story to tell and, consequently, opened the door to my so-called career. In a sense, he made both that book and this one possible.

Many of these stories began with a group of high school friends who continue to inspire me. We knew no bounds, had no sense, and we all appreciate how lucky we are to be alive today (with a little more sense). Thanks to the Whole Sick Crew—Mark Crosby, Bruce Gordon, Andy Kaplan, Lonnie Lazar, Melissa Lazarov, Cam McCaa, Ted McLaughlin, Gegnellyboos (the) Quag-Meyer, Tim Monaghan, David Peeples, Lanie Richberger, Jodi Shainberg, Tommy Van Brocklin, and (like Bukowski said) all my friends.

I am grateful to these readers who helped keep the writing tight and right: Alex Abramovich, Paul Duane, Melissa Dunn, Belinda Killough Gordon, Alex Greene, Dennis Herring, Charles Hughes, and Carl Reisman.

Much gratitude to my editor, Callie Garnett—if this were a record, she'd be the producer. Callie kept me on key. Laura Phillips was the gracious managing editor. Others once at Bloomsbury drew me there—Kathy Belden, Rachel Mannheimer, George Gibson. Agent David Dunton, with aplomb, guided a small idea to a larger enterprise (and he used to jam with Adam Miller).

John Fry is a secret hero of the Memphis scene. He founded Ardent Studios in the early 1960s, created a musical home for Jim Dickinson, Alex Chilton, and many others (miss you, John Hampton!) and was a solid supporter of all of the Memphis creative community. Next time you're playing Big Star loud, think of (and thank) the late John Fry.

Many people helped in ways large and small, and with apologies to those I've overlooked, I thank Chet Weise, Peter Guralnick, Mary Lindsay Dickinson, Judy Peiser, Iddo Patt, Susanna Vapnek, Andria Lisle, Scott Barretta, Phoebe Driscoll, Jeff Place, Bob Mehr, the editors who assigned the original pieces, my children, Lila and Esther, and always my parents and their unending support and encouragement.

Nearly all my favorite lines in this book come from Tara McAdams, my first and last reader, my muse and love.

Now, please join me on the dance floor while we spin "(Do The) Funky Chicken" and hail Rufus Thomas, who was a Memphis personality all my life, who took me under his wing (like he did many and varied others). His embrace of life and funk made him the funkiest man alive. His spirit abides.

Rufus Thomas—the world's oldest teenager, the funkiest man alive. Early 1980s. (Courtesy of Patty Padgett)

A NOTE ON THE PHOTOGRAPHERS

Pat Rainer has been so deep in the Memphis scene she's often left no shadow. She's a recordist of all kinds—including audio engineer for Alex Chilton's *Like Flies on Sherbert*. She always kept a camera close (photo and video), creating an archival treasure.

Tav Falco is known for his music, but fans of his albums know his photographic talents. I've featured his portraits, but his candids and landscapes are also powerful.

Axel Küstner was, like me, struck by the blues at fourteen years old—but he was in Germany. He met the artists on the 1970s package tours, and soon began traveling the American South making photographs and recordings. His album series *Living Country Blues USA* is a phenomenal snapshot of southern blues in 1980. He's got tens of thousands of beautiful photographs spanning the 1970s through the early 2000s.

Bill Steber and Yancey Allison have each been shooting the north Mississippi

Pat Rainer at Graceland, the day after Elvis died, 1977. (Courtesy of Pat Rainer)

hill country for decades. Their familiarity with the people, the mundanity, and the poetry of the area has produced intimate, exciting photographs.

Ebet Roberts was shooting around Memphis when the new freedom of the post-hippie 1970s was breaking open; she was poised to capture the punk rock energy. Not long after, Trey Harrison and then Dan Ball were out with cameras; neither was limited to the music scene and both have pursued the conflicted spirit that underlies the city (which is what Ted Barron has done around NYC). Dan Zarnstorff, proprietor of the Loose End, created the right places and kept his camera handy all the time. Huger Foote has made beautiful art prints in the Eggleston school, and has also shot the nightclub nitty gritty. So has David Julian Leonard, whose negative clean-up work made some of these photographs possible (find his *Tender Is the Light*).

The cover photo is among those shot by Bill Steber. It's from Thompson's Grocery, a juke joint in Bobo, Mississippi, that burned in 1996. That's Sam Carr on drums—he recorded for Sam Phillips in 1962 as part of Frank Frost and the Night Hawks (evolving later into the Jelly Roll Kings). The guitarist is Clarksdale's Terry Williams. Dancer Debra Hooks told Bill, "Everybody else acts like they're scared to get up. I'm sorry, I ain't fixing to sit down."

Grateful hat tip to all the photographers who contributed.

DIGGING DEEPER FOR DIFFERENT— FURTHER LISTENING AND READING

Curious how some of these musicians sound? Hear them (sometimes at their most outré) on the soundtrack to this book, also called *Memphis Rent Party*. Order it from your local record store. It features a dozen or so selections from some of this book's artists—hi-fi, lo-fi, glorious, and immediate. The track listing is being finalized, but there's lots of unreleased material on it and it swings hard in moods, rhythms and time. Fat Possum Records is releasing it.

If you like anything about this book or my others, you'll frolic in Peter Guralnick's work. His *Feel Like Going Home* tells the blues story through profiles, from rural Mississippi's Muddy Waters to Jerry Lee Lewis and Sam Phillips. *Lost Highway* swings to the country music side, including a profile of Charlie Feathers but also Rufus Thomas, Bobby "Blue" Bland, and Sam Phillips. (And Cowboy Jack Clement (because you need to know.)) And then comes *Sweet Soul Music*, which braids Ray Charles and Atlantic, James Brown, Memphis's Stax and Hi, Muscle Shoals, and Macon, Georgia. His writing on James Carr and Roosevelt Jamison will make you cry. www.peterguralnick.com

Stanley Booth writes elegantly about Memphis in his collection *Rythm Oil* (including a great Johnny Woods anecdote). Preston Lauterbach has chronicled the Beale Street doorways and byways in *Beale Street Dynasty*, with an imminent volume covering the mid-1950s to late 1960s. There's a transcribed and annotated visit with Furry Lewis in Fred Hay's *Goin' Back to Sweet Memphis*, a collection of 1972 interviews that gives a documentary feel of an afternoon hang at Furry's. Greil Marcus's oft-updated *Mystery Train*—with Harmonica Frank, Robert Johnson, Elvis—remains a provocative American classic. (There are Harmonica Frank releases on Memphis International, Adelphi / Genes, and Mississippi Records; more to explore at all of those labels.) Memphian Ron Hall has a series of books that go deep into the Memphis rock and roll scene of the 1960s and '70s; start with *Playing for a Piece of the Door*, which can be found among other interesting Memphis projects at www.shangrilaprojects.com.

Some blues books of note: For the real-deal feel of an itinerant blues life in the 1930s and '40s, *The World Don't Owe Me Nothing* by David "Honeyboy" Edwards should be your first stop. There are great details in the in-depth interviews in Jim O'Neal and Amy Van Singel's *The Voice of the Blues: Classic Interviews from Living Blues Magazine*. David Whiteis profiles many contemporary chitlin circuit players in *Southern Soul-Blues*. Charles Hughes's *Country Soul* manages a fresh perspective on events long past, such as the influence of country music on disco.

You're bound to make a trip here, and I've written some tips in the *New York Times* that remain relevant: "36 Hours in Memphis," May 6, 2005, www.nytimes.com/2005/05/06/travel/escapes/in-memphis.html. Also "36 Hours in Clarksdale, Miss.," June 16, 2006, www.nytimes.com/2006/06/16/travel/escapes/16hour.html. Your stay will be greatly enhanced if you get the lay of the land from Tad Pierson's tour; the city never looks better than through the window of his 1955 Cadillac: www.facebook.com/AmericanDreamSafari/.

And there's my own stuff—books, the CD series that's a companion to *It Came from Memphis*, the music films. More info at www.therobertgordon.com. Come on in, the water's great.

PREFACE

My favorite Furry Lewis album is *Fourth and Beale*. From 1969, it's two microphones hanging over Furry's bed, and he's comfortable among friends—including Ardent producer Terry Manning. George Mitchell's recording, *Good Morning Judge*, catches Furry in 1962 and '67 playing with a vigor I never knew him to have. (Fat Possum Records bought the entirety of the George Mitchell collection, recordings made from the 1960s to the 1980s across the south. Sleepy John Estes, Dewey Corley, Jessie Mae Hemphill—find George's book, *Blow My Blues Away*.)

For information on the 1968 sanitation worker's strike, read Michael K. Honey's *Going Down Jericho Road* and Joan Turner Beifuss's *At the River I Stand*. The documentary also named *At the River I Stand* remains a long-time favorite. For a more personal and poetic sense of the era's racial tension, devour C. D. Wright's *One With Others*.

SAM PHILLIPS: Sam on Dave

Peter Guralnick's *Sam Phillips: The Man Who Invented Rock 'n' Roll* is a deep and thrilling dive into the world of Sam. It's amazing what fits between the covers—not only encounters with all the great musicians Sam recorded, but also his outsize exploits in radio, zinc mining, and women. The book's companion CD mixes hits and deep cuts—well over two hours of music. The documentary on Sam, also titled *Sam Phillips: The Man Who Invented Rock 'n' Roll*, is out of print but find it if you can. Made by Morgan Neville and Peter Guralnick, it features interviews with many who were close to Sam, including Sputnik Monroe, Jim Dickinson, John Prine—and *lots* of Sam!

Good Rockin' Tonight, by Colin Escott and Martin Hawkins, remains a great overview of the Sun label. John Floyd's oral history, *Sun Records*, has been recently republished and hits hard with the tales from those who were there. Sam's studios—recording artists note—remain active; both Sun and the Sam Phillips Recording Service are available for your recording needs. The latter has been recently refurbished and it maintains Sam's original design.

JIM DICKINSON: On the Edge

There's lots of places to get in deeper with Jim. His autobiography, *I'm Just Dead, I'm Not Gone*, came out in 2017 and feels like a long afternoon's hang with Jim while he recollects the stories that made him who he became. Jim's *Dixie Fried* may be his masterpiece, and it's a great place to start—a big production, but not overblown. There's an expanded edition from Light in the Attic Records (www.lightintheattic.net). Thirty years later, Jim released a follow-up album and then five more (www.selectohits .com and Artemis Records)—each distinct, all good; don't miss Birdman's *Fishing With Charlie*—it's spoken word. Jim occasionally released compilations from his archives in a series he called Delta Experimental Projects. Buy on sight. There's only two Mud Boy albums (a third is a compilation of the two), *Negro Streets at Dawn* and *Known Felons in Drag*. Both are hard to find, both are great. More at www.zebraranch.com.

ERNEST WILLIS: Mississippi Reverie

The Center for Southern Folklore is in downtown Memphis on Main Street and presents live music (www.southernfolklore.com). Their gift shop is stocked with treasures. I made my first film with the Center, *All Day and All Night*—B. B. King, Rufus Thomas, and other musicians rising from Memphis's Beale Street to national prominence. It's available in HD at www.alldayandallnight.com. When managing the center's audio library, I heard my first prison recordings, *Wake Up Dead Man*. Bruce Jackson recorded convicts in Texas prison—some work gangs outside, some individuals in forlorn, echoing rooms. Powerful, and a great intro to the genre.

I've not found a lot of information on Professor W. T. McDaniel, the band teacher whose south side students became soul music artists and north side students jazz players, but there's this: memphismusichalloffame.com/inductee/profwtmcdaniel/.

MOSE VINSON: No Pain Pill

Piano Man, the CD that my liner notes accompany, can be ordered from the Center for Southern Folklore: www.southernfolklore.com/product-page/mose-vinson-piano-man. Mose has a few tracks on the Bear Family label's *The Sun Blues Box*, and a 1990 compilation, *Memphis Piano Blues Today* (Wolf Records), that also features Booker T. Laury, another barrelhouse great (Booker is featured in *All Day and All Night*). Cinematographer David Julian Leonard has posted footage from the Levitt Shell (formerly the Overton Park Shell); see Mose at www.youtube.com/watch?v=-toYnwdc6e0. Search "Levitt Shell archive" and "Memphis" for footage of Calvin Newborn, Phineas Newborn, Alex Chilton, Mud Boy, and many others.

THE FIELDSTONES: Got to Move on Down the Line

There's lots of great High Water tracks. Roam around www.highwater records.com and spend some money. Buy any singles that you find. Some favorite groups:

Fieldstones	Hammie Nixon
Blues Busters	The Pattersonaires
Jessie Mae Hemphill	The Spirit of Memphis Quartet
The Hollywood All Stars	R. L. Burnside
The King Riders (a motorcycle club's house band)	Junior Kimbrough

LEAD BELLY: Nobody in This World

Lead Belly's Last Sessions is available digitally through Smithsonian Folkways at www.folkways.si.edu/shop. The biography, *The Life and Legend of Leadbelly*, by Charles Wolfe and Kip Lornell, is a good place to start. If the photo of Martha and Lead slays you (like it does me), find *Lead Belly: A Life in Pictures*.

The 1935 *March of Time* newsreel with Lead Belly and John Lomax can be found here: www.youtube.com/watch?v=QxykqBmUCwk.

ROBERT JOHNSON: Hellhound on the Money Trail

There's lots of writing on this phantom of the Mississippi Delta. A few recommendations:

Peter Guralnick, *Searching for Robert Johnson*

Tom Graves, *Crossroads*

Elijah Wald, *Escaping the Delta*

Gayle Dean Wardlow, *Chasin' That Devil Music*

Robert Palmer, *Deep Blues* and *Blues & Chaos*

Stanley Booth, "Standing at the Crossroads," in *Rythm Oil*

Greil Marcus, *Mystery Train*

For listening, after the Robert Johnson boxed set, find *The Roots of Robert Johnson* (shanachie.com/genres/yazoo) and float in that pool of lyrics, riffs, and melodies that makes blues authorship perplexing. Some peers of note: Son House (I like the 1965 Columbia recordings), Charley Patton, and Tommy Johnson; the recent *American Epic* versions of their works are remarkably free of the surface noise that has made such old recordings difficult for the inexperienced ear.

A last Steve LaVere note: In the 1990s, he released some 1970s recordings he'd made while managing a touring blues troupe. The two volumes of the *Memphis Blues Caravan* are mostly live tracks featuring the likes of Furry Lewis, Harmonica Frank, Big Sam Clark, Joe Willie Wilkins, and others known in Memphis and surrounding areas. The recordings lack an immediacy, but the range of talent is amazing and the gesture of releasing them was very nice. (Hard to find now, these were once available through the Inside Sounds label, which releases the Daddy Mack Blues Band and others from the area. www.insidesounds.com)

JUNIOR KIMBROUGH: Mississippi Juke House

For me, the recording that best captures the sound of Junior's Chulahoma juke joint is actually by R. L. Burnside, the album *Too Bad Jim*. Produced by Robert Palmer, the journalist and musician (but not the pop singer), *Too*

Bad Jim gets the feel of that rollicking room. Bob also produced Junior Kimbrough's *Sad Days, Lonely Nights*. Start there, and then get real gone in the Fat Possum catalog and the myriad releases from R. L. and Junior. R. L.'s *Bad Luck City* won't disappoint; his *Come On In* is a pretty interesting techno remix, and *A Ass Pocket of Whiskey*, recorded with Jon Spencer's Blues Explosion, gets edgier, and also gets to R. L.'s tale-telling and dozens-dishing. Dig Junior's *All Night Long*, and while tribute records often leave me cold, I found the interpretations on *Sunday Nights*—from Cat Power, Iggy and the Stooges, Jack Oblivian, and others—a great way to rehear Junior's songs.

There's lots of great hill country recordings. And many of those are on the Fat Possum label. I've had remarkable luck with Fat Possum. The records they produce are usually edgy and raw, and they've become a repository of gritty Americana. Hill country artists to look for: Fred McDowell (his *You Gotta Move* on Arhoolie is a favorite; *Amazing Grace* is stirring), Asie Payton, Joe Callicott, Kenny Brown, Lightnin' Malcolm, and Cedric Burnside (that's R. L.'s grandson).

These are some notable Fat Possum blues artists not from the hill country: Cedell Davis, Elmo Williams and Hezekiah Early, Jelly Roll Kings, Paul "Wine" Jones, Robert Belfour, and T-Model Ford.

I came late to Willie King and missed Bettie's, his red-dirt joint near Alabama. Willie plays dancing blues with, oddly and wonderfully, a jam band, groove-heavy feel. Get *Jukin' at Bettie's* or any Willie King you can find.

Shout-out to Spike Priggen and Kevin Salem, then in the band Dumptruck, who left the Aikei Pro in time to meet Junior Kimbrough and introduce me to him. Shout-out to Monsieur Jeffrey Evans, who had just moved to Memphis and came on that fine trip to Junior's with Belinda. And always a shout-out to Belinda Killough Gordon! Her better recollection about fruit beer, in the quote you're about to read, leaves my essay factually incorrect. Since her suggestion, I now remember at that later visit, or I have Photoshopped it into my memory, drinking several Kool-Aids with the patch of sunlight at my shoulder. The fact is lost, the blur remains. Print the blur!

"When we got to the shack, in the middle of summer in the middle of a cotton field," Belinda wrote me, "it was blindingly light outside and extremely dark inside. I remember the vat of pure grain alcohol punch. I remember dancing a lot with other people there. At one point I went out to use the bathroom in the field and then I lay on top of the Caddy's hood and listened. I know we stayed at least twelve hours there. The music just kept churning over and over."

CHARLIE FEATHERS: The Onliest

Over the years, I've come evermore to appreciate the power and beauty of Charlie's voice. *Get With It* collects early material and, though out of print, is worth chasing down. That and everything that Norton Records sells on Charlie at www.nortonrecords.com. And the Elektra/Nonesuch *Charlie Feathers*. And Peter Guralnick's profile in *Lost Highway*.

JAMES CARR: Way Out on a Voyage

One last James Carr story: For several years in the mid-1990s, I wrote the scripts for the annual Handy Awards (now the BMAs—the Blues Music Awards: blues.org). During the Blues Foundation's nadir, the show was in a small theater on Beale Street; that year I was also a stage manager. When the finale began, I stepped outside for fresh air and a moment to unwind. I smiled as I heard James Carr over the PA system. Except, I realized, there was no PA system. On the balcony of

James Carr and Robert Gordon departing for the stage next door. (Courtesy of Trey Harrison)

the empty bar next to the theater was James Carr, singing with no microphone to the empty street below. Roosevelt appeared, said he'd placed James there to serenade the departing blues fans. I brought James from the balcony to the theater's stage; he did not hesitate, he commanded a mic and stepped into the light.

Some favorite tracks: "To Love Somebody," "Forgetting You," "You've Got My Mind Messed Up," and "The Dark End of the Street."

OTHA TURNER'S FIFE AND DRUM PICNIC: Let Us Eat Goat

Otha Turner lived to be ninety-five, dying in late February 2003. One of his daughters, Bernice, who lived next door and was central in his life, died the same day after a long battle with breast cancer. The church in Como, near Gravel Springs, was packed for the double funeral. Afterward, the procession to the gravesites was led by thirteen-year-old Sharde Thomas, playing a fife made by her grandfather.

In addition to Otha's two albums (both on Birdman Records: www .birdmanrecords.com), he's heard on a Sugar Ditch 45 and several compilations. *Mississippi Delta Blues Jam in Memphis* (Arhoolie Records) is a great cross-section of area musicians recorded in 1969; Otha and his neighboring fife star Napoleon Strickland are included. A decade earlier, Otha directed Alan Lomax down the road to Fred McDowell and Fred is here, solo and accompanied by Johnny Woods. (Furry Lewis is also here.) Dive into the Arhoolie Records catalog—their compilations are a great way to hear a variety of artists: www.folkways.si.edu/arhoolie. A few others of note: *I Have to Paint My Face*; the two volumes of *Mississippi Delta Blues: Blow My Blues Away*; and *Country Negro Jam Session*. The Testament Records classic *Traveling through the Jungle: Fife and Drum Band Music of the Deep South* is a great primer. A ten-minute film on Otha, *Gravel Springs Fife and Drum*, made in 1972 by Judy Peiser and Bill Ferris, is here: www.folkstreams.net/film,59.

Here's an interesting crossroads. Luther met Otha at the Center for Southern Folklore's Music and Heritage Festival. That's where Luther and Cody, young teens, first backed their dad on stage—Jim Dickinson and the Hardly Can Playboys. Luther, exploring the crafts area, went to the one man burning an open flame—and began talking to Otha Turner, watching him make a fife. Turns out, they lived near each other and Luther began visiting Otha, hearing his musical ideas, absorbing what Otha had to teach. Luther's interest shifted from national trends to the excitement of his own backyard.

Before Otha died, he'd mentored not only Luther Dickinson and Sharde Thomas but also R. L. Boyce. R. L. played drums in his band and became a great hill country guitarist under Otha's tutelage, now with several records of his own.

MAMA ROSE NEWBORN: Useless Are the Flowers

Good luck finding Calvin Newborn's book, *As Quiet As It's Kept!* His music is more readily available; both discs on the Bandcamp website can be sampled before purchase. His 1978 collaboration with Hank Crawford, *Centerpiece*, is a jazz-blues classic. Stanley Booth has a great piece on Phineas Jr., "Fascinating Changes," in *Rythm Oil*. Look for the 1962 Phineas episode from *Jazz Scene USA*; the performance of "Oleo" is breathtaking.

Jazz great Herman Green—who played a decade in Lionel Hampton's band and had brushes with Miles Davis, John Coltrane, and even caught Louis Armstrong's attention—has a few CDs in his own name. See if you can find *Worthy of Note* or *Best of the Green Machine*. Herman kicks it with FreeWorld, a jam band that blends Memphis and New Orleans with San Francisco. Their playing with Herman is literal old school meets new (free worldmemphis.com).

TOWNES VAN ZANDT: All the Federales Say

My favorite Townes Van Zandt recordings are the ones least produced and least populated; so much of his early work has powdered sugar all over it. Start with *Live at the Old Quarter*—it comes with the jokes and patter, and in 1973 many of these songs were still new. *The Nashville Sessions* is from the same period, but in a studio with a relatively spare band. There's lots of later live recordings—*Roadsongs* is with a good band, light touch. Catch *Heartworn Highways* for a 1975 live hang; the documentary *Be Here to Love Me* is a warm, wistful way in and gives an overview of his life.

JEFF BUCKLEY: Northern Light

Jeff only lived to finish one album—*Grace*. I like the expanded edition with the bonus CD of various songs—traditional, country, MC5, and more. *Live at Sin-é*, which is Jeff performing in the corner of a coffee shop, gets me. Plus, you get some of his between-song raps—it's a lot like the weekly gigs we'd hear at Barrister's in Memphis. The newest release is the oldest recordings; titled *You and I*, it's Jeff solo in a studio, learning his way around good recording equipment and discovering his voice. The album he was making when he died, *Sketches for My Sweetheart the Drunk*, is much more than sketches, though it's built from unfinished material. The documentaries, they make me sad.

BOBBY BLUE BLAND: Love Throat

Bobby Bland made great records all through his career. Even the early, gritty ones have a sophisticated air with the big band behind him. Most any anthology of his Duke recordings will be good; there are two double-CD packages of the Duke stuff and no wasted tracks. Also not to be missed is *Two Steps from the Blues*, his 1961 debut LP. Several of the songs were previously singles, but this collection established him for crossover success. (It's one of songwriter Dan Penn's favorite albums.) Bobby had a great later career with Jackson, Mississippi's Malaco Records. *Bobby Blue Bland: "Live" on Beale Street* gives a good taste of his Malaco work; in addition to the audio, there's a DVD.

TAV FALCO: Panther Burns Forever Lasting

We're close to the bone when discussing Panther Burns, but I'll restrain myself to a manageable list. For starters, I'd recommend the *Sugar Ditch Revisited* EP and *The World We Knew* LP. These are cleanly produced (the first by Jim Dickinson, the latter by Alex Chilton), but you still get that sense of effort that makes the Burns so exciting (that sense of their almost not getting it right). Once you get the hang of it, take a chance with the first EP, *She's the One to Blame*; it's rawer even than the first LP, *Behind the Magnolia Curtain*, which is also recommended. And look for the tenth-anniversary single with two versions of the Sun Records classic "Red Headed Woman." Hear what can happen in ten years. Shopping: www .tavfalco.com.

Tav's book, *Ghosts Behind the Sun*, is an autobiography that goes back to Tav's days as a Confederate soldier in the Civil War (yes, you read that right) and takes us through the highlights of his career, including great profiles of Roland Janes, Charlie Feathers, and others whom Tav has encountered, uncovered, or revivified. Don't be shy about skipping some of the early pages, but when Tav gets to the University of Arkansas, the story really takes off.

This interview with Tav focuses on his visual art: openspace.ca/tav -falco-interview-2003. And you can catch the legendary performance on Marge Thrasher's morning TV show here: dangerousminds.net/comments /tav_falco_and_the_meaning_of_anti-rockabilly_with_special_guest _alex_chilto

Tav was the godfather of the 1970s and '80s local scene, so check out some of the bands he spawned: The Hellcats had an EP and an LP, and when they exploded, several members formed the Alluring Strange (they made one album). The Klitz set the precedent, and some of their lost recordings have recently trickled out: www.spacecaserecords.com/space case-releases. They sometimes play live—slightly more polished than they used to be, but not a lot.

JERRY LEE LEWIS: Last Killer Standing

Alert! The sessions I referenced Jerry Lee doing with Knox Phillips have been released! They are (can I say it?) killer! *Jerry Lee Lewis: The Knox Phillips Sessions* is worth the price just for the smoking version of "Harbor Lights," though the Chuck Berry knockoffs ain't half bad. And "Beautiful Dreamer," sung by his hoarse, coarse, and tired throat is enough to make you daydream about what Jerry was doing the night before, the week before. It sounds like he's not slept in a long long time. I'm putting a track on the *Memphis Rent Party* compilation, but you can check out the whole thing here: www.timelife.com/products/jerry-lee-lewis-the-knox-phillips -sessions-lp

Another of my favorite Jerry Lee records is an LP titled *Ole Tyme Country Music*. It came out during the Shelby Singleton Sun era, and I emphasize the LP because though the track listing on the CD is similar, the takes are different. These songs are Jerry and Roland Janes playing classics together, and it's amazing to hear the way they entwine; when so few people could find a place to fit in Jerry Lee's music, Roland just slid right in. (It reminds me of New Orleans guitarist Snooks Eaglin accompanying pianist Professor Longhair—finding places to fit that are not evident to the naked ear.)

Michael Tisserand's "Jerry Lee's Legacy" in *Offbeat* is not to be missed. Of the Jerry Lee books available, go for *Hellfire*, by Nick Tosches. It's more about the myth than the man, but what a myth!

CAT POWER: Kool Kween

The Greatest remains my favorite Cat Power album, but I can't separate the music from my joyful memories around the making of it. There are several full concert videos of her live shows with the Memphis Rhythm Band on Youtube. Her albums before and after capture her evolution and explorations as an artist. She is a seeker.

JERRY McGILL: Very Extremely Dangerous

The man of mystery, of multiple names, of lost recordings. Meet him in *Stranded in Canton*, the documentary I made from William Eggleston's footage, then live with him in my documentary made with Paul Duane, *Very Extremely Dangerous*. *VED* includes a CD of Jerry's recordings, available at store.fatpossum.com/products/very-extremely-dangerous. If you find more recordings, please let me know via my website: www.therobert gordon.com. The blog where Jerry found Joyce: boogiewoogieflu.blog spot.com/2008/07/jerry-mcgill.html.

ALEX CHILTON: No Chitterlings Today

There's so much Alex out there, it's hard to navigate. You can tell I'm a fan of *Like Flies on Sherbert*, and Omnivore Recordings, a hub of Alex reissues, has a new version that will include yet more additional tracks. Omnivore also boxed up *Complete Third*, which includes demos and alternate mixes. They put out Big Star's *Live in Memphis*, a multicamera concert video of the revived Big Star (of the three formats, the DVD sounds the best). Omnivore also released an expanded version of Sid Selvidge's *The Cold of the Morning*—great stuff. Rhino Records released *Keep an Eye on the Sky*, the 4-CD Big Star retrospective (I won a Grammy Award for the liner notes). For reading, try the biography of Alex, *A Man Called Destruction*, by Holly George-Warren or Rob Jovanovic's *Big Star*; both are well researched and full of facts you're likely to not otherwise know. The book *Big Star: Isolated in the Light* is an amazing collection of photographs and anecdotes.

Bruce Eaton's short book on the making of *Radio City*—it's part of the 33 1/3 series—gets a running start from his personal connection to Alex Chilton; his interviews begin with a trust that most questioners never attain. Big Star's music is widely available again, thanks to Concord Records.

Of Alex's later recordings, I love his contributions to the Chet Baker tribute, *Imagination*. Chet's influence grew during his career, and Alex honors him. (The record was produced by Ron Miller, a one-time Panther Burn.) If I were collecting tracks for a late period compilation, I'd begin with "Don't Stop" from *A Man Called Destruction*—one of my favorite of his pop songs; an expanded version of *Destruction* has been recently released. I also like a lot of *Clichés*—great intimacy on a series of classics. His version of "Nobody's Fool" from *High Priest* is pretty great—Alex interpreting his original producer, Dan Penn. Much of Alex's later career was devoted to his radio favorites from childhood, and *Set*—recorded all in one night and using only first takes—is a full-on sampling of what's on his mind. So is *Electricity by Candlelight*, an acoustic set captured on a cheap recorder when the power at the gig went out. It's like he's entertaining at a bonfire when the second bottle of bourbon is going around.

The Big Star documentary *Nothing Can Hurt Me* is, all things considered, a fine film. The first hurdle it faced was having no archival footage to work with! But they found the right people to tell the stories, and they give pre- and post-histories of the players to create an engaging and revealing story. I'm excited to see the forthcoming documentary built around Chris Stamey's performance of Big Star's *3rd*. It's called *Thank You, Friends*. My compadre David Leonard is working on an Alex documentary; I'm certainly looking forward to seeing that (www.alexchilton.rocks).

AFTERWORD: Stuck Inside the Memphis Blues Again

My information about the ratio of CEO pay to worker compensation comes from the Economic Policy Institute—nonpartisan, nonprofit, and can be found on Table C at www.epi.org/publication/ceo-pay-continues-to-rise/. Note that I've chosen not to use the most extreme examples (over 600 to 1 in present times—the bastards).

The music lives on. Start with the North Mississippi All Stars and the numerous side projects from Luther and Cody Dickinson. The All Stars' *Prayer for Peace* (2017) is a career highlight, even on the heels of another great one, *World Boogie Is Coming*. *Onward and Upward* gathers Jim's family and friends days after his death, a recording raw and ready for heaven.

Luther's side group, the Wandering, gathers Sharde Thomas, Amy LaVere, Shannon McNally, and Valerie June. Their *Go On Now, You Can't Stay Here* redefines Mississippi folk music. Cody has branched into films, producing *Take Me to the River*, which captures the cross-pollinating of Memphis music—by generation, by genre. (Bobby Bland is thrilling with Yo Gotti.) And now he's making a New Orleans version. His debut solo record, *Leeway for the Freeway*, calls on brother Luther and friends like John Medeski, Duane Betts, and Robert Randolph to forge new ground, including takes on a couple of his dad's songs. Each of the ladies in the Wandering has her own stellar records, and Julien Baker's personal songs and delivery make her another Memphis femme to watch.

A trail of breadcrumbs: Light in the Attic Records features lots of over-looked Memphis artists: Bob Frank, Bobby Whitlock, Lou Bond, Johnnie Frierson, Packy Axton, and Wendy Rene. (*Wheedle's Groove* in spirit.) Concord Records, which owns the latter Stax catalog, has reissued the John Gary Williams solo album and unearthed an unreleased one. They're bringing out new talent too, like Southern Avenue. The Hi Records cata-log is widely available through Fat Possum, making your Willie Mitchell explorations easy, and they continue to mine the region, finding the likes of Robert Finley, reissuing the Grifters and the Country Rockers, and get-ting Don Bryant back into the game with *Don't Give Up on Love*, his best

The Country Rockers at the Antenna Club, circa 1995. Left to right: Ron Easley, Gaius "Ringo" Farnham, Sam Baird. (Courtesy of Trey Harrison)

recording ever. (Man, you Fat Possum guys need to buy me some Girl Scout cookies.) Syl Johnson, who did some recording for Hi, is the subject of a boxed set and a documentary on Numero Group. Check out the Bo-Keys, a contemporary Memphis soul band that mixes classic players with their protégés (www.thebokeys.com). Lucero has evolved from an earnest roots rock band to become explorers of Memphis possibilities; many albums and styles to choose from. Stax's David Porter is culturing new talent through his Consortium MMT program and his new Made in Memphis recording studio. Memphis filmmakers have grappled with the Memphis spirit; seek out the work of Craig Brewer, Ira Sachs, Lynne Sachs, Morgan Jon Fox—and check out the Indie Memphis film festival (www.indiememphis.com). Get you some Harlan T. Bobo on Goner Records (also look for Nots and the Limes), some Mark Edgar Stuart on Madjack Records, Duets for Mellotron, and don't forget Big Ass Truck and Lorette Velvette and the Kropotkins, Motel Mirrors (on Archer Records, where Sid Selvidge later recorded and Lily Afshar now records), Magic Kids, Cory Branan ("Love Song #11" rules), Curlew's *Fabulous Drop*, Shelby Bryant and the Clears, Ron Franklin, Keith Sykes, Jay Reatard, Memphis radio at www.wevl.org, LPs at Audiomania, the various Steve Selvidge projects, Jody Stephens's post–Big Star work with Golden Smog and with Those Pretty Wrongs. Riding the crest is Cities Aviv, and Andria Lisle just turned me on to the Memphis label Unapologetic (www.weareunapologetic.com) and I swear the still, small voice is whispering in my ear. And I realized I forgot the Reigning Sound, which means I forgot lots of others (apologies) so I gotta quit.

INDEX

Note: Italic page numbers refer to photographs.

Acuff, Roy, 150
Aikei Pro's Records Shop,
    80–81
Aldridge, Lesa, 25–26, 33–34,
    33, 207, *207*
All Day & All Night (film), 62
Allen, Steve, 173
"All Night Long" (song), 82
Altshuler, Robert, 74, 76
Anderson, Annye, 74–75
Anderson, Paul Thomas, 198
Andrews Sisters, 172
"Another Place, Another Time"
    (song), 180
Antenna Club, 163, *163*
Anthology (album), 141
Apollo Theater, 99
Applewhite, Little, 50–51

Ardent Studios, 25, 135, 210
Armstrong, Ralph, 89
Arnold, Eddy, 150
Arnold, Kokomo, 63
Artaud, Antonin, 153, 164
As Quiet as It's Kept (Newborn),
    124, 129–30
Atlantic Records, 22, 26, 122,
    131
Autry, Gene, 171
Avedon, Richard, 196–98

Baker, Chet, 209
Baker, Lee, 22–23, *24*, 25–26,
    162, 204
Bar-Kays, 101
Barnes, Djuna, 156
Barristers, 142

Basie, Count, 67, 122, 126, 129–30
Beale Street Music Festival (1997), 3–4, 47, 206
Beauregard, Nathan, 157
Behind the Magnolia Curtain (album), 164
Belafonte, Harry, 54
Bell, Chris, 209
Berry, Chuck, 94, 168, 169
Bicycle Music Company, 77
Big Brother and the Holding Company, 197
Big Dixie Brick Company, 32, 159
Big Star, 135, 202, 207–9, 211
Big Star 3rd (album), 25–26, 30, 207, 209, 211
Biography of a Phantom (McCormick), 64, 72, 76
Birth of the Blues, 44
Bitter Lemon, 158
"Black Betty" (song), 54
Black Flag, 216
Blackwood, Dean, 94–95
Bland, Bobby "Blue," 67, 147–52
"Blue Moon of Kentucky" (song), 13, 88
Blue Note, 67
The Blues (TV series), 147
Blues Busters, 47
"Blues Theme for Left Hand Only" (song), 131
Boogie Man, *49*
Boogie Woogie Flu (blog), 203
"The Bourgeois Blues" (song), 55, 161, 162, 164
Bowie, David, 191
The Box Tops, 30, 206–8, 211
Bramlett, Delaney, 177

"Breathless" (song), 176
Brewer, Craig, 75
"Bring Me a Little Water, Silvy" (song), 54
Brown, J. W., 173, 175
Brown, Kenny, *116*, 215
Brown, Lois, 49–51, *49*
Brown Skin Models, 126
Buck, Curtis. *See* McGill, Jerry
Buckley, Jeff, 140–46, *142*
Buckley, Tim, 144, 145
Buford, L. P., 112, 114
Bullet, 32–33
Burnside, Cedric, *116*
Burnside, R. L., 84, *84*, 115, 153, 160–61, 215

Callicott, Joe, 215
Camper Van Beethoven, 8
Canned Heat, 67
Can't Be Satisfied (Gordon), 166
Carnes, Bobby, 49
Carr, James
    and Quinton Claunch, 99–106
    Easley-McCain Recording, 96
    Goldwax recording sessions of, 100–102
    and gospel music, 98–99
    LA Weekly feature on, 63
    and Charlyn Marie "Chan" Marshall, 186
    mental illness of, 96, 101, 106–11
    1979 Japanese tour, 105–6
    photographs of, *100, 104*
    and spirit of Memphis music, 218
    and "The Dark End of the Street," 98, 101, 105
Carr, Leroy, 63

Carter, Jimmy, 44

Carter Family, 179

Casey, Jim, 93

Cash, Johnny

  death of, 168

  moving from rockabilly to
    country music, 88

  as Sun Records artist, 13, 18,
    89, 93, 155, 166, 172

Cassavetes, John, 123

Cat Power. *See* Marshall, Charlyn
  Marie "Chan"

CBS Records, 70, 73–74, 76

Center for Southern Folklore, 36,
  45, 78

Chandler, Chester "Memphis
  Gold," *49*

Charles, Ray, 122

Charlie Feathers (album), 89–90

Chess Records, 80

Chew, Chris, *216*

Chewalla Rib Shack, 84

Chilton, Alex

  and astrology, 210–11, *212*

  and Jeff Buckley, 144–45

  as early punk rocker, 8, 206–7,
    210, 211–12, *215*

  and Easley-McCain Recording,
    101

  and "The Letter," 206–8, 211

  and *Like Flies on Sherbert*,
    22–23, 25–26, 33, 164–65,
    207–8, *209*, 211

  and Jerry McGill, 31–32

  and Dan Penn, 30

  and the Replacements, 29, 211

  and Unapproachable Panther
    Burns, 21, 32–34, *154*, 162,
    164–65, 207, *208*

chitlin circuit, 150–51

Christian, Charlie, 132

Chuck Wagon Gang, 70

"City of New Orleans" (song), 25

Civil Rights Act of 1967, 5

Clapton, Eric, 13, 148, 181

Clark, Elliott, 97, 100, 102–4, 111

Clark, Guy, 137, 139

Clark, Susanna, 138

The Clash, 164

Claunch, Quinton, 27, 97–106,
  110–11

Clay, Maude Schuyler, *158*

Clement, Jack, 173

Clements, Paul, 203

Clinton, George, 169

Cohn, Larry, 69, 73

Cole, Jerry. *See* McGill, Jerry

Cole, Nat "King," 132, 150

The Color Purple (film), 194

Coltrane, John, 122

Columbia Records, 69–71,
  73–76

Como, Perry, 9

Cooder, Ry, 23, 30

"Cool Water" (song), 30

Cosloy, Gerard, 192–93

Cotton, James, 46

"Cotton Crop Blues" (song), 46

The Covers Record (album), 191

Cowboy Junkies, 73

The Cramps, 163–64, 191, 208

Crawford, Hank, 122

Cray, Robert, 187

"Crazy Arms" (song), 172, 173

Cream, 73

"Crossroads" (song), 66

Crosthwait, Jimmy, 22, 204

Crudup, Big Boy, 149

Crumb, R., 74

"Cry Like a Baby" (song), 25

Cunningham, B. B., 169–70, 173, 185
Curtis, King, 100

"Dahoud" (song), 131
Daniels, Chip, *116*
"The Dark End of the Street" (song), 98, 101, 105
Davis, Miles, 128
Davis, Walter, 149
The Dead Kennedys, 144
"Dead Shrimp Blues" (song), 75
DeBerry, Jimmy, 67
Denton, Jeremiah, 52
"Desperados Waiting for a Train" (song), 204
Diamond, Neil, 100
Dickinson, Cody, 113, 203–4, 216
Dickinson, Jim
  author's interview with, 23–34
  and Alex Chilton, 23, 25–26, 29, 30–32, 206–7, *209*, 210–11
  and context of Memphis music, 1, 215
  death of, 217
  and Charlie Feathers, 92
  on Robert Johnson mythology, 65
  on Stephen LaVere, 68
  and Jerry McGill, 200, 202, 204
  as Memphis music scene figure, 20, *27*, 34–35, 36, 202, *216*
  and Mud Boy and the Neutrons, 3, 21–23, *24*, 31–32, 34, 161
  and Phineas Newborn Jr., 127, 134
  as producer of recordings, 27–30, 65

on recording, 218
and Unapproachable Panther Burns, 32–34, 161, 164–65
and Mose Vinson, 45
on white youth's introduction to blues music, 5
Dickinson, Luther, 113, 118, 203–4, 216–17, *216*
Dickinson, Mary Lindsay, 21–22, 25, 200
Dixie Flyers, 30
Dixie Fried (album), 34
Dixieland Folkstyle (album), 29
Domino, Fats, 182
Dream Carnivals, 159
"Dream Lover" (song), 26
Driggs, Frank, 69–70
"Drinking Wine Spo-Dee O'Dee" (song), 172
Duane, Paul, 203–5
Duke Records, 148
Dunbar, Sly, 65
Dunst, Kirsten, 189
Duran Duran, 192
Dusty, Robert. *See* Johnson, Robert
Dylan, Bob, 191, 196–97

Earle, Steve, 139
Earnestine & Hazel's, 147
Easley, Doug, 101, 135, *136*, 141
Easley-McCain Recording, 96, 100–101, 135–36, 141, 186
Edwards, Connie, 159
Edwards, Will, 118
Eggleston, William, 32, 158–61, *158*, 200, 202, 204
Electronic Arts Intermix, 161
Elektra/Nonesuch Records, 87
Ely, Joe, 138–39

Emmet the Singing Ranger Live in the Woods (album), 30
Escott, Colin, 92
Estes, Sleepy John, 65, 67, 157
Etheridge, Melissa, 187
Evans, David, 47, 78
"Everybody Here Wants You" (song), 142
Exile on Main Street (album), 30
Exit/In, 203

Fahey, John, 68, 92
Falco, Tav "Gus"
  and Alex Chilton, 207, *208*
  and William Eggleston, 158–59
  introduction to Memphis, 155–58
  and *Like Flies on Sherbert*, 164–65
  and Randall Lyon, 156–57, 159–61
  on music as art form, 35
  and Unapproachable Panther Burns, 21, 32–34, 153, *154*, 155, 161–65, 207
"Farther Up the Road" (song), 148, 150
Fat Possum Records, 84
Feather, Leonard, 131
Feathers, Bubba, 89
Feathers, Charlie
  death of, 94
  and Tav Falco, 155
  LA Weekly feature on, 63
  photographs of, *90*, *91*
  and Elvis Presley, 86–88, 90–92, 107
  on rockabilly music, 87–89, 94
  as Sun Records artist, 13, 86, 88–89, 93, 95, 217

and Unapproachable Panther Burns, 163
Feathers, Ricky, 93–94
Feathers, Rosemary, 91–95
Feel Like Going Home (Guralnick), 20
Feudalist Tarts (album), 208–9
Fialkov, Jay, 71, 74
field hollers, 55–56, 150
Fieldstones, 47–51, *49*
fife and drum music, 112–13, 115–20, *116*, *117*, 164
Finas Newborn Orchestra, 128
The Firm (film), 211
Fishel, Jim, 71
Flat Duo Jets, 191–92
Flatlanders, 139
Floyd, Harmonica Frank, 13, 67
Folcy, Red, 150
Ford, Frazey, 187
Ford, Fred, 133, 134
"For the Sake of the Song" (song), 137
Franklin, Aretha, 151
Franklin, C. L., 151
Freeman, Charlie, 30
FreeWorld, 124
Friedlander, Lee, 159
Fry, John, 209
Fuller, Buckminster, 156
Fulsom, Lowell, 209

Galbraith, Barry, 131
"The Gambler" (song), 194
Garner, Robert "Honeymoon," 122
Gassner, Amy, 162
Gehrig, Lou, 53
Get With It: Essential Recordings (1954–69) (album), 92, 94

"Get With It" (song), 88

Gillespie, Dizzy, 128

Gilley, Mickey, 171

Gilmore, Jimmie Dale, 139

"Going Home" (song), 122

Goldwax Records, 97–103

"Gone, Gone, Gone" (song), 88

Gordon, Robert
   and Bobby "Blue" Bland,
      147–52
   and Jeff Buckley, 143–46
   and James Carr, 102, 104–11
   on creative freelancing, 213–15
   early interest in blues music, 4–7
   early music writing
      experiences, 7–9, 61
   and Junior Kimbrough's house
      parties, 79–85
   and Furry Lewis, 1–2, 6–8, 10,
      21, 36, 44
   and Jerry McGill, 201–5
   and Mud Boy and the
      Neutrons, 3–4
   and RJ Smith, 62–63

Graflund, Danny, 3, 78, 206

Graham, Billy, 156

Grand Ole Opry, 123, 128, 183

Granz, Norman, 132

Grateful Dead, 148

Graves, Tom, 74

"Great Balls of Fire" (song), 14,
   174, 175, 178

The Greatest (album), 186, 188,
   193–95

Green, Al, 62, 122, 135, 141, 186

Green, Herman, 122, 124

Greenberg, Alan, 65

Green's Lounge, 48–49, *49, 50,* 51

Griffith, Nanci, 139

Grifters, 141, 144

Grimes, Howard, 141, 187

Groundhog, 209–10

Gunn, Jaren, 168

Gunsmoke (TV show), 179

Guralnick, Peter, 20, 62, 71–75,
   92, 148

Guthrie, Arlo, 25

Guy, Buddy, 181

Haggard, Merle, 137, 181

Hall, Robert, 174

Hammond, John, 64, 69–70

Hammond, John, Jr., 73

Hampton, Lionel, 122, 126

Hancock, Butch, 139

Haney's Big House, 171

Hardy, Joe, 25

Hare, Marcia, 159

Harman, Buddy, 29

Harris, Emmylou, 137

Harrison, Trey, 93–94

Harrison, Wilbert, 154

Hawkins, Ronnie, 157

Hawkins, Screamin' Jay, 11

Hemphill, Jessie Mae, 155

Henry Thomas (album), 66

Here is Phineas (album), 131

Hicks, Joe, 49, 51*49*

"High School Confidential"
   (song), 176

High Water (record label), 47, 78

"Highway 61 Blues" (song), 157

Hill, Eric, *154,* 162, 165

Hines, Bessie, 64, 72–73

Hi Records, 141, 186

Hi Rhythm Section, 122, 186–88,
   187

Hite, Bob, 67

Hodges, Charles, 187

Hodges, Leroy, 187

Hodges, Teenie, 51, 62, 157, 187, *187*

"Hold Me in Your Arms" (song), 46

Holiday, Billie, 191

Holiday Inn Records, 93

Holly, Buddy, 168, 191

Holmes, John Clellon, 158

Hombres, 169

"Honky Tonk Woman" (song), 181–82

Hopkins, Lightnin', 66

Horoscope Music Company, 75

Hot Rocks (album), 191

House, Son, 63, 113

Houston, Whitney, 212

Howlin' Wolf, 9, 13, 67–68, 93, 129

Hunt, Van Zula, 163

"I Don't Care (If Tomorrow Never Comes)" (song), 89

"I Forgot to Remember to Forget" (song), 88

"I'll Take Care of You" (song), 150

Imperial (record label), 67

"The Impossible Dream" (song), 168

"In My Girlish Days" (song), 159

Interviews from the Class of '55 Recording Sessions (album), 179

"In the Street" (song), 212

"Into the Groove" (song), 8

Isaak, Chris, 89

"I Slipped a Little" (song), 98

It Came from Memphis (Gordon), 10, 62, 78, 144–45, 200

It Club, 133

"It'll Be Me" (song), 173

"It's Wonderful to Be in Love" (song), 98

Ivy, Rick, *154*

"I Wanna Make Sweet Love" (song), 31

"I Want to Go Home" (song), 59

"I Will Always Love You" (song), 212

J&J Lounge, 47–48

Jackson, Cordell, 155

Jackson, Jesse, 151

Jackson, Michael, 8, 21

Jagger, Mick, 1, 21, 32, 181

Jamboree (film), 175

Jamison, Roosevelt, 99–100, 106, 110

Janes, Roland, 45, 89, 177–78, 200, 204

Jefferson, Blind Lemon, 149

Jennings, Waylon, 31, 167, 202–4

Jim Dickinson Blues Band, 157

"Joe Turner" (song), 113

Johnson, Claud, 77

Johnson, Ken, 75

Johnson, Robert
    as Delta bluesman, 113
    myth of, 63–65, 72, 76
    rights to photographs of, 64–65, 68, 74–76
    and unpaid royalties, 62, 64, 69–71, 73–77
    varied personae of, 146

Johnson, Ross, 33, *154*, 162

Johnson, Tommy, 63

Jolson, Al, 169

Jones, Tom, 148

Jones, Wanda, 129

Joplin, Janis, 197

Jordanaires, 29

Joyner, George, 130, 179
Jung, Carl, 156
Justis, Bill, 29

"Kanga Roo" (song), 26, 207
"Kansas City" (song), 154
Keith, Toby, 167, 181
Kensinger, Campbell, 32
Kesler, Stan, 89
Kid Rock, 181–82
Killough, Belinda, 83–85
Kimbrough, Junior
    droning North Mississippi
        sound, 80, 113
    and Charlie Feathers, 92–94
    juke joint/house parties of,
        78–85
    photographs of, 79, 80, 81, 83
    popularity of, 115
King, Albert, 51
King, B. B., 9, 13, 50, 122, 148–51
King, Don, 15
King, Martin Luther, Jr., 4, 6,
    151, 197
King of Spades publishing, 76–77
King of the Delta Blues Singers
    (album), 69
King Records, 93
Klitz, 34
Known Felons in Drag (album), 31
Krauss, Alison, 47
Kronos Quartet, 73
"Kung Fu Fighting" (song), 136

Lancaster, Jim, 34, 204
Lane, Fred, 210
Last Man Standing recording
    sessions, 166–71, 177–82
Late Night with David Letterman
    (TV show), 11–19

LaVere, Stephen C., 65–77
Law, Don, 64
Lawler, Jerry, 207
Lead Belly's Last Sessions (album),
    52–60
Ledbetter, Huddie "Lead Belly,"
    52–60, 57
Ledbetter, Martha, 53–54, 56, 57,
    58–59
Led Zeppelin, 73, 146, 177
Leonard, David, 204
"The Letter" (song), 206–8, 211
Letterman, David, 12–19
"Let Your Loss Be Your Lesson"
    (song), 47
Lewis, Elmo, Jr., 171
Lewis, Elmo, Sr., 171–72, 175
Lewis, Frankie Jean, 172
Lewis, Furry
    author's relationship with, 1–2,
        6–8, 10, 21, 36, 44
    and William Eggleston, 159
    as Tav Falco influence, 156–59
    and Jerry McGill, 203
    as Mud Boy and the Neutrons
        influence, 23
    performance at the Rolling
        Stones July 4th Memphis
        concert, 1–2, 4, 213
    photographs of, 2, 3, 24, 157
    and spirit of Memphis music, 218
Lewis, Jane Mitchum, 172
Lewis, Jerry Lee
    childhood and youth of, 171–72
    as country music artist, 179–80
    and Charlie Feathers, 91
    and Roland Janes, 177–78
    and Kid Rock, 181–82
    and Last Man Standing recording
        sessions, 166–71, 177–82

and Stephen LaVere, 67
moving from rockabilly to rock
    and roll, 88
performance style of, 174,
    176–77, 183–84, *184*
and Sam Phillips, 14, 172–76
photographs of, *176*, *184*
Ryman Auditorium Fan Fair
    performance, 183–85
scandals and tragedies of, 168,
    171, 175–76, 180
as Sun Records artist, 13, 17–18,
    89, 172–76, 178–79
Lewis, Lee, 179, 183
Lewis, Linda Gail, 172
Lewis, Mamie, 171–72, 175
Lewis, Myra Brown, 168,
    175–76
Lewis, Phoebe, 177, 179, 181
Lewis, Steve Allen, 173
Like Flies on Sherbert (album),
    22–23, 25–26, 33, 164–65,
    207–8, *209*, 211
"Like Someone in Love" (song),
    131
Lisle, Andria, *142*
Little Richard, 168, 180
"Lived in Bars" (video), 198
Living Blues (LaVere), 70
"Liza Jane" (song), 54
Lomax, Alan, 52, 55
Lomax, John, 52, 55
Loose End, 210
Lost Highway (Guralnick), 20
"Lost Highway" (song), 177
Louis, Joe Hill, 67
The Louisiana Hayride (radio
    show), 171
Love in Vain (film), 65
"Love in Vain" (song), 73

Love Is My Only Crime (album),
    135
Lovelace, Kenny, 167, 170
"Lovesick Blues" (song), 182
Lucero, 11
Lunceford, Jimmie, 126
Lunch, Lydia, 101
"Lungs" (song), 137
Lyon, Randall, 32, 68, *132*,
    156–57, *156*, 159–61

Mabon, Willie, 214
McCaa, Cam, 47–48, 51
McCain, Davis, 101, 135, *136*, 141
McCarver, Kerrie, 168, 180
McClain, John T., 133
McCormick, Robert Burton
    "Mack," 64–66, 70–77
McDowell, Mississippi Fred, 157
McGill, Jerry, 31–32, 200–205,
    201, *203*
McIntire, John, 159–60
Madonna, 8
Magnolia (film), 198
"Make a Little Love" (song), 209
Malaco Records, 148
Malcolm X, 197
"Marie" (song), 137
Mars, Bruno, 187
Mars, Chris, 30
Marshall, Charlyn Marie "Chan"
    author's interview with, 188–99
    and Richard Avedon, 196–98
    and *The Greatest*, 186, 188,
        193–95
    and Hi Rhythm Section,
        186–88, *187*
    on interaction with fans, 198–99
    and Miami, Fla., 196
    relationship with father, 190–91

Marshall (*continued*)
  and Steve Shelley, 192–93
  on smoking and drinking,
    188–90
Martin, Dean, 91, 210
Martin, Grady, 29
Matador Records, 192–93
"Members Only" (song), 148
Memphis, Tennessee
  and African-American culture,
    1–2, 4–6, 9, 67, 124
  compared to Nashville, 9,
    21–22, 140
  musical atmosphere in, 1–2,
    9–10, 21–22, 35, 122, 140–
    42, 146, 159, 162–63, 186–87,
    214, 217–18
  race relations in, 1, 4–7
"Memphis Beat" (music video),
  155
Memphis Country Blues Festival,
  67, 157
Memphis Horns, 204
Memphis Music & Heritage
  Festivals, 78
Memphis Music Hall of Fame, 188
Memphis Rhythm Band, 188, 194
"Memphis Soul Stew" (song), 100
Mercury Records, 29
Merman, Ethel, 58
Meteor Records, 88, 93
Meyers, Chris, *136*
Meyers, Eric, *136*
"Middle Age Crazy" (song), 180
Midnight Run (album), 148
"Midnight Run" (song), 148
Milem, Percy, 98
Miller, Bowlegs, 122
Miller, Paul A., 133
Mingus, Charles, 122

Minnie, Memphis, 159
Mississippi River, 36–43
"Miss the Mississippi and You"
  (song), 177
"Mistreatin' Mama" (song),
  58–59
Mitchell, Boo, 187
Mitchell, Sunbeam, 147
Mitchell, Willie, 186–87
Modern Jazz Quartet, 132
Moman, Chips, 100–101
Monk, Thelonius, 129
Monroe, Bill, 92–93, 123
Moody, Clyde, 93
"Moody's Mood for Love" (song),
  128–29
Moore, Bob, 29
Moore, Oscar, 132
Moorhead, Scott J. *See* Buckley, Jeff
Morton, Robert, 14
Mud Boy and the Neutrons
  and Jim Dickinson, 3, 21–23,
    24, 31–32, 34, 161
  and Tav Falco, 159
  farewell performance of, 31–32,
    161
  and Jerry McGill, 200, 204
  at 1997 Beale Street Music
    Festival, 3–4, 47, 206
Muddy Waters Blues Band, 67
Mud Island Blues (album), 48, 51
The Muse (monumental
  sculpture), 160
"My God Is Real" (song), 172
My Morning Jacket, 11
"Mystery Train" (song), 88

Nasser, Jamil, 130
Nelson, Clarence, 50–51
Nelson, Willie, 137, 181

Newborn, Calvin, 13, 121–22, 124–32, *125*, 134

Newborn, Phineas, Jr., 13, 121–23, *123*, 126–34, *132*

Newborn, Phineas, Sr. "Finas," 121–22, 124–33

Newborn, Rosie Murphy "Mama Rose," 121–29, *130*, 132–33

Newborn, Wanda, 129

Newborn Music Shop, 129

Newport Jazz Festival, 122, 130

New Rose, 25, 164

Nightingale, Ollie, 98

"96 Tears" (song), 162

Nixon, Hammie, 157

"No More the Moon Shines on Lorena" (song), 25

North Mississippi Allstars, 113, 203, 204, 216, *216*

North Mississippi Hill Country Picnic (2016), 215–17

"Nothin'" (song), 137

"Old Ship of Zion" (song), 56

"Ol' Glory" (song), 167

Oliver, Paul, 66

Orbison, Roy, 13, 166

Ovations, 98

Owens, Jesse, 39

Pacheco, Gary, 76

Page, Jimmy, 181

"Pancho and Lefty" (song), 135, 137

Panther Burns. *See* Unapproachable Panther Burns

"Parchman Farm Blues" (song), 157

"Pardon Me Mister" (song), 89

Paris, Texas (film), 23

Parker, Charlie, 128

Parker, Junior, 93

Parton, Dolly, 212

The Party (film), 142

Peabody Hotel, 147–48

Peiser, Judy, 36, 44

Penn, Dan, 30, 207

Perkins, Carl
  death of, 168
  moving from rockabilly to rock and roll, 88
  as Sun Records artist, 9, 13, 18, 89, 166, 172

Perkins, Wordie, 50–51

Peterson, Oscar, 132

Phair, Liz, 192–93

The Phantom, 28–29

Phillips, Jerry, 32

Phillips, Knox, 31, 45, 180

Phillips, Sam Cornelius. *See also* Sun Records
  and Charlie Feathers, 88–89, 93
  and Bill Justis, 29
  Late Night with David Letterman appearance, 11–19
  and Jerry Lee Lewis, 14, 172–76
  and Jerry McGill, 202
  and "perfect imperfection," 35, 218
  photographs of, *12*, *16*
  recording philosophy of, 9–10, 13–16, 35, 175
  retirement of, 21
  and Mose Vinson, 46

Phineas Newborn Jr. Quartet, 129–30

Piano Man (album), 45

Piano Red, 32–33, 67

Pickett, Wilson, 100

Piggee, Mutt, 149

Plant, Robert, 47

Plantation Inn, 128

Pleased to Meet Me (album), 22

Post, Mike, 31

Powell, Bud, 130–31

Presley, Elvis Aaron
  and Cadillacs as gifts, 184
  death of, 15, 168–69
  and Charlie Feathers, 86–88,
    90–92, 107
  Peter Guralnick's biographies
    of, 62
  and Jerry Lee Lewis, 168
  and Chips Moman, 100
  moving from rockabilly to rock
    and roll, 88
  Pentecostal influence on, 171
  as punk musician, 208
  as Sun Records recording artist,
    9, 12–13, 17–18, 88, 93, 155,
    166, 172, 175, 217
  and "Suspicious Minds," 181

Presley, Vernon, 90

Price, Ray, 173, 179

Prince, 8, 21

Prudhomme, Tim, 186

Pursell, Bill, 29

"Put Your Loving Arms Around
  Me" (song), 50

Raising Sand (album), 47

Raitt, Bonnie, 73

Ram Jam, 54–55

Ramones, 206

Ramsey, Frederic, Jr., 54–56

Randolph, Boots, 29

Randy Band, 163

Ray, James Earl, 6, 87

RCA Records, 175

Rebel Inn, 87, 91

Redding, Otis, 97–99, 217

Redemption Harmonizers, 99

"Red Headed Woman" (song),
  163

Redmond, Odessa, 5–6, 10

Reich, Wilhelm, 212

Relay (video networking group),
  161

The Replacements, 22, 25–27,
  29–30, 34, 211

Revenant Records, 92–94

Reynolds, Debbie, 173

Richard, Eddie "Hacksaw," 8

Richards, Keith, 64, 181, 187

"Ride of the Valkyries" (Wagner),
  154

Riley, Billy Lee, 13, 204

Rinzler, Ralph, 66

Rip, Jimmy, 167, 170, 177–78, 181

Rising Star Fife and Drum Corp,
  113, 216

*Robert Johnson: The Complete
  Recordings* (album), 62, 64,
  73, 75

Robertson, Robbie, 169

"Rock and Roll" (song), 177

Rock and Roll Hall of Fame, 13,
  152

"Rock Island Line" (song), 56

Rodgers, Jimmie, 169, 171, 177, 179

The Rolling Stones
  and James Carr, 99
  compared to Mud Boy and the
    Neutrons, 3
  and Jim Dickinson, 65, 202
  and *Honky Tonk Woman*, 181
  and Robert Johnson, 73
  and Furry Lewis, 1–2, 4, 213
  and "Satisfaction," 191

"Roll Over Beethoven" (song), 89–90, 174, 183

Romweber, Dexter, 191–92

Ronson, Mark, 187

Rouch, Jean, 160

Rough Trade Records, 164

Ryman Auditorium, 183

Sam and Dave, 99

Sam Phillips Recording Service, 164, 167, 177, 180, 200, 203

Sanders, Dorothy, 51

Sanders, Will Roy, 50–51

"Satisfaction" (song), 191

Savage, Randy "Macho Man", 21

Schneider, Peter, 135

Scorsese, Martin, 147

Searching for Robert Johnson (Guralnick), 71, 73, 75

Sellers, Peter, 142

Selvidge, Sid, 22, *24*, 31, 162, 204

The Session (album), 167

Sex Pistols, 206

Shadows (film), 123

Shaffer, Paul, 13, 16–19

Shakespeare, Robbie, 65

Shakey Jake, 67

Shaw, Robert, 66

"She Even Woke Me Up to Say Goodbye" (song), 180

Shelley, Steve, 136, 186, 192–93

"She's Puttin' Something in My Food" (song), 148

"She Still Comes Around (To Love What's Left of Me)" (song), 180

"Shimmy She Wobble" (song), 118

Shines, Johnny, 73

Sikes, Stuart, 193–94

"Silent Night" (song), 171

Simone, Nina, 191

Singleton, John, 67

Singleton, Shelby, 29, 67

The Sixties (Anderson), 197

"61 Highway" (song), 113

Slim Rhodes Band, *97*

Sly and Robbie, 65

Smith, Elliott, 211

Smith, RJ, 62–63

"Smokestack Lightnin'" (song), 129

Solo Piano (album), 134

Songs the Lord Taught Us (album), 164

Sonic Youth, 8, 21, 136, 186, 192

Southern Comfort (film), 23

Spake, Jim, 11–12

Spector, Phil, 27

Spencer, Robert. *See* Johnson, Robert

Springsteen, Bruce, 181

Stanton, Harry Dean, 179

Staples, Mavis, 11

Starr, Ringo, 167–68

Stax Records, 6, 22, 34, 80, 97–98, 217

Sterling Grill, 149

Stevens, Shawn Michelle, 168

Stewart, Rod, 177

Stranded in Canton (film), 32, 159, 160, 200, *201*, 202

Streets of Fire (film), 23

Stroud, James, 181

Stuart, Marty, 183

Sunnyland Slim, 67

Sun Records
  and Johnny Cash, 13, 18, 89, 93, 155, 166, 172
  and Quinton Claunch, 98

Sun Records (*continued*)
  and B. B. Cunningham, 169
  and Charlie Feathers, 13, 86,
    88–89, 93, 95, 217
  influence on Tav Falco, 155
  and Roland Janes, 45, 200
  and Bill Justis, 29
  and Stephen LaVere, 67
  and Jerry Lee Lewis, 13, 17–18,
    89, 172–76, 178–79
  and Jerry McGill, 31, 202,
    204–5
  and Carl Perkins, 9, 13, 18, 89,
    166, 172
  and Sam Phillips recording
    philosophy, 9–10, 15–16
  and Elvis Presley, 9, 12–13,
    17–18, 88, 93, 155, 166, 172,
    175, 217
  sale of, 13
  and Mose Vinson, 46
"Suspicious Minds" (song), 100,
  181
Swaggart, Jimmy, 172, 178
Sweet Soul Music (Guralnick), 20

"Take It Off" (song), 209
Take Me to the Limit (album), 100
"Tammy" (song), 173
Tatum, Art, 132
Teagarden, Jack, 66
Teal, Alex, 28–29
Tee, Willie, 209
Televista, 160–62
Tennessee Waltz (Mud Boy's
  farewell performance), 31–32
"Tennessee Waltz" (song), 128
That '70s Show (TV show), 212
"That Ain't Right" (song), 50
"That's All Right" (song), 13

"That's How Strong My Love Is"
  (song), 98–99
Theatre of Cruelty, 153, 164
"The Road to Memphis" (episode
  of *The Blues*), 147
"Thirty Nine and Holding" (song),
  180
Thomas, Rufus, 6, 9, 11, 218
Thomas, Sharde, 117–18, *215*,
  216–17
Thompson, Carrie Spencer,
  64–65, 69–75, 77
Thurman, Billy. *See* McGill, Jerry
"Tina, the Go Go Queen" (song),
  164
"Tiny Hineys and Hogs" (song),
  30–31
"Tongue-Tied Jill" (song), 88
Toni (Fieldstones's drummer),
  50–51, *50*
Tootsie's Orchid Lounge, 183
Tosches, Nick, 92
"The Train Kept A-Rollin'"
  (song), 13, 162
Tubb, Ernest, 150
Tucker, Ken, 8
Tuff Green and the Rocketeers, 127
Turner, Archie "Hubbie," 187
Turner, Bernice, 117
Turner, Otha
  and *Behind the Magnolia Curtain*,
    164
  early music experiences of, 118
  as Tav Falco influence, 155
  fife and drum picnic of, 112–18,
    116, *117*, 120, *215*
  and North Mississippi Hill
    Country Picnic, 215–17
  photographs of, *113*, *116*, *119*, *215*
  as teacher of fife, 119–20

"Turn on Your Love Light"
    (song), 148, 150
"Twilight" (song), 169–70, 173
Twitty, Conway, 176–77

"Uh Huh Honey" (song), 89
Unapproachable Panther Burns
    and Alex Chilton, 21, 32–34,
        154, 162, 164–65, 207, *208*
    and Jim Dickinson, 32–34, 161,
        164–65
    and Tav Falco, 21, 32–34, 153,
        154, 155, 161–65, 207
    and Charlie Feathers, 163
"Un Poco Loco" (song), 131
Uttal, Larry, 99

Van Eaton, J. M., 89, 204
Van Zandt, Townes, 135–39
Vaughan, Sarah, 130
Vaughn, Ben, 90
Vertov, Dziga, 160
Very Extremely Dangerous (film),
    200–201, 203–5
Vestine, Henry, 67
Vinson, Mose, 8, 44–46, *45*, 163
"Volare" (song), 210

"Waiting Around to Die" (song), 137
Walden, Phil, 99
"Walking the Floor Over You"
    (song), 150
"Walking to New Orleans" (song),
    182
Wammack, Travis, 204
Warner Bros, 87
Washington, Butterfly, 29
Waters, Ethel, 70
Waters, Muddy, 67, 166
"Waymore's Blues" (song), 203

Weaver, Dennis, 179
"We Can't Seem to Remember to
    Forget" (song), 89
Well (bar), 163, *163*
Wenders, Wim, 23
Westerberg, Paul, 25, 29, *210*
Wexler, Jerry, 26–27
"What'd I Say" (song), 122
"What's Made Milwaukee
    Famous (Has Made a Loser
    Out of Me)" (song), 177–80
What Would the Community Think
    (album), 186
"Where Is My Love" (song), 195
White, Bukka, 67, 156–57
Whitesnake, 148
Whitten, J. W., 166, 170, 179, 182
*Who Is Herman Green? His Music,
    Worthy of Note* (album), 124
"Whole Lot of Shakin' Going
    On" (song), 173–75, 181
"Wild Horses" (song), 20
"Wild Is the Wind" (song), 191
Williams, Big Joe, 149
Williams, Don, 139
Williams, Hank
    compared to Charlie Feathers, 92
    death of, 137
    and Grand Ole Opry, 183
    and Jerry Lee Lewis, 169
    and *The Louisiana Hayride*, 171
    as songwriter, 89, 150, 174, 177,
        178, 182
Williams, R. E., 118
Willie Nelson & Friends (TV
    special), 181
Willis, Ernest, 36–43, *39*, *41*
Winogrand, Garry, 159
Withers, Ernest, 67–68
Woods, Johnny, 23, *24*, 159

World Pacific, 67

World's Greatest Soul Singer
    (album), 107

"Would You Take Another
    Chance on Me" (song), 180

Wright, O. V., 98, 99

Wyman, Bill, 218

Yardbirds, 13

Young, Evelyn, 50–51

Young, Lester, 130

Young, Lonnie, *116*

"You've Got My Mind Messed
    Up" (song), 107

"You Win Again" (song), 174

A NOTE ON THE AUTHOR

Robert Gordon is a writer and filmmaker. His books include *It Came from Memphis, Can't Be Satisfied: The Life and Times of Muddy Waters*, and *Respect Yourself: Stax Records and the Soul Explosion*. He won a Grammy for his liner notes to the Big Star boxed set *Keep an Eye on the Sky*. His film work includes producing and directing the documentaries *Johnny Cash's America* and *William Eggleston's Stranded in Canton*. His *Best of Enemies*, about William F. Buckley and Gore Vidal, was shortlisted for an Oscar and won an Emmy. Gordon lives in Memphis.